THE EVERYTHING

START YOUR OWN BUSINESS BOOK

From the birth of your concept
and your first deal, all you need to
get your business off the ground

Rich Mintzer

Adams Media Corporation
Avon, Massachusetts

EDITORIAL
Publishing Director: Gary M. Krebs
Managing Editor: Kate McBride
Copy Chief: Laura MacLaughlin
Acquisitions Editor: Bethany Brown
Development Editors: Elizabeth Kuball
Michael Paydos

PRODUCTION
Production Director: Susan Beale
Production Manager: Michelle Roy Kelly
Series Designer: Daria Perreault
Layout and Graphics: Arlene Apone,
Paul Beatrice, Brooke Camfield,
Colleen Cunningham, Daria Perreault,
Frank Rivera

An Everything® Series Book.
Everything® is a registered trademark of Adams Media Corporation.

Published by Adams Media Corporation
57 Littlefield Street, Avon, MA 02322 U.S.A.
www.adamsmedia.com

ISBN: 1-58062-650-5
Printed in the United States of America.

J I H G F E D C B A

Library of Congress Cataloging-in-Publication Data
available upon request from publisher

This publication is designed to provide accurate and authoritative information with regard to the subject matter covered. It is sold with the understanding that the publisher is not engaged in rendering legal, accounting, or other professional advice. If legal advice or other expert assistance is required, the services of a competent professional person should be sought.
—From a *Declaration of Principles* jointly adopted by a Committee of the American Bar Association and a Committee of Publishers and Associations

Illustrations by Barry Littmann.

This book is available at quantity discounts for bulk purchases.
For information, call 1-800-872-5627.

Visit the entire Everything® series at everything.com

Contents

INTRODUCTION

Transforming Your Idea into a Plan

It all starts with an idea—one moment it dawns on you that, like so many other people, you could run your own business. You want to step out on your own, and take control of your financial future. You're confident that you have what it takes to buck the odds and succeed. But you also know that launching a business comes with risks that you're willing to take on.

Where Ideas Come From

Ideas come from people of all ages, all cultural backgrounds, and all income levels. So what separates those ideas that emerge into business plans (and eventually businesses) from those ideas that die on the vine? Personality, determination, and tenacity.

For many people, a business is the culmination of a dream or ambition based on a specific skill or interest. You may know the type of business that you've always wanted to open, but because of lack of finances, resources, time, or self-confidence, you've never been able to put that plan into action.

An entirely different group of people are also looking to start businesses. These are the many students of business and industry who've learned the leadership, decision-making, and organizational skills, but only need to find the right business to go into. Rather than a specific passion or skill in an area of interest, *business* is their interest and they need to find a business that they can open and run.

Either approach can lead to great success. If you have a passion for cooking and want to open a bakery where you can display your culinary talents, you won't need to seek out a type of business to open. Instead, you can begin by putting together your bakery business plan. If, however, you're tired of working for someone else, have honed your business skills, and want to start a business, but you're not sure which type of business would be best suited for you, then you need to start researching various business alternatives. Either way, this book is for you.

So Much to Know

Starting and running a business requires a great deal of knowledge. Setting realistic goals for yourself and your business, and setting them for a week or a month at a time, is critical. Build step by step, and focus on the process of getting the business off the ground (instead of thinking only about the end results). After all, you can't own the finest family restaurant in Denver if you don't order tables and menus and hire the chef. After you've launched your business, continue to set reachable goals, make new plans often, and don't let the business become mundane (or your motivation will slip away). Even if business is going well, you can't just coast. Longevity may mean reinventing yourself from time to time with a new look or a new image.

Become familiar with who your customers are, what they like, what they want, and what they don't want. Reading the trade magazines (every industry has them), networking with others in the business community, joining organizations, and communicating with your clientele are ways to stay in touch with those people who will make or break your business—your customers. Good customer relations is a key factor to any successful business.

To start and run a successful business you'll need a lot of information, but the basics are simple. Maintain a good attitude, keep up with the times, stay focused and motivated, plan step by step, get to know your customers, and keep a watchful eye on all monetary transactions.

What's Ahead

In this book, you'll find information on each area of starting and running a business. Because there are a myriad of possible businesses, the book takes a general approach that you can apply to your individual business needs. You'll find a combination of personal details that need to be addressed, such as balancing time with family or simply deciding on a business that you'll feel good about running. Also, you'll get specifics, such as setting up a business plan or the different business structures from which you can choose. You may find yourself looking back at different chapters as you build your own business, first on paper, and than for real. The most important function of this book, and of all resources that you use when starting and running a business, is that you get your questions answered. And this book is a great place to start.

Acknowledgments

First, I'd like to acknowledge the many entrepreneurs who were helpful in putting this book together, including:

Lisa Morbete, Morbete Group Public Relations Agency in Los Angeles, CA; Andy Sernovitz, CEO of Gas Pedal Ventures in New York City (*www.gaspedal.com*); Bob Stone, owner Danesi Optical; Raymond D. Leahy Opticians in Long Island, NY; Roger Abyiss, CEO and founder of Sites.com, based in Toronto, Canada (*www.sites.com*); Fran and Larry Heit, owners of Reeds and Cricket clothing stores in St. Helena, CA; Trudi Bresner, owner of T. Bresner Associates in New York City (*www.tbresner.com*); Karen Anderson, owner of KA Enterprises in Ontario, Canada (*www.primary-ed.com*); Jennifer Dirks, founder and owner of The Writers' Group in Seattle, WA (*www.thewritersgroup.cc*); Michael Russello of Scotsdale Pension Systems, Inc., in Scotsdale, AZ; Tony Maniscalco, owner of Rose's Pizza and Restaurant in Hanover, PA; Robert Blackwood, co-owner of the Loss Prevention Group; Sid Kerber, founder and owner of the Catalog Consultancy in FL (*www.catalogconsultant.com*).

I'd also like to thank Felix Fornino, Lynne Crowley, Avery Marder of Trade Mark Graphics in Brooklyn, and Mary Gardner, president and founder of the Coaches Certification Institute in New York City and creator of the Intensive Executive Workout.

And finally thanks to Carol, Eric, and Rebecca for their love and support as daddy finished book #24.

CHAPTER 1

Do You Have What It Takes?

Millions of people start their own businesses every year, so why not you? Skeptics will scare you with the statistics on how many new businesses fail every year and how long it takes before your business could possibly show a profit. But if everyone listened to skeptics, Dave Thomas wouldn't have owned Wendy's, Lucille Roberts would never have made her mark in the fitness world, and Michael Dell wouldn't own a $10-million mountaintop estate. Read on to find out if you have what it takes.

The Pros of Starting Your Own Business

While nonprofit organizations serve the needs of others, most commercial businesses are built on someone's desire to chase the American Dream. If you aren't looking to reach a goal by opening up a business, then why go through all the trouble?

In the following sections, you'll find the pros and cons of starting your own business.

You Are Your Own Boss

No longer are you working for someone else. You have only yourself (and your investors, the bank, the IRS, and regulatory agencies) to answer to. You get to make the big decisions for a change. You may also be the boss of other people, which will let you display your leadership abilities.

The Sky's the Limit

Hoorah for capitalism! You can become the next Bill Gates, or at least enjoy financial independence. Working for yourself affords you the opportunity to make more money (usually) than working for somebody else. The risks are greater, but the potential rewards are greater as well.

You Can Prove Yourself

You have the opportunity to use your skills, abilities, and creativity to do things your way. You can fully utilize your attributes, ones that may have been stifled in the workplace in the past.

You'll Have a Hand in All Aspects of the Business

Unlike working for a company or someone else's business where you're only responsible for your area of expertise, you'll be involved in other areas of the business—from funding and finance to many of the smaller daily details.

You'll Take Pride in Promoting and Marketing Your Own Company

While many sales and marketing people take great pride in the work they do and the company they work for, there is a special feeling you get when touting your own business. "Welcome to Fred's Catering . . . I'm Fred" sounds better to the ear than saying "Welcome to Fred's catering . . . Fred will be with you in a minute."

You Can Choose Where to Locate Your Business

Tired of commuting an hour every day in slow moving traffic to get to the office? Now you can set up the office closer to home or open up a store just ten minutes away. You might even work *from* home. Your business, your location.

From the color of the sign and company logo to the sales strategy and marketing plan, it's your call, your ballgame, and your business. There's something both exciting and invigorating, yet scary about going into business for yourself. Like a roller coaster ride, starting a business has the proverbial ups and downs. For all the parts of your business plan that work, there will be a few parts of the plan that won't work at first and will need revising. Good ideas will compete with bad ones, and all the positives of going into business will have a flip side, reasons for not going into business.

You'll see many business ads for "instant businesses," particularly through e-mail ads. Resist them. Business takes planning and hard work. Don't get suckered into buying some pre-packaged "pyramid scheme" to success that won't work. Remember, if success came in a bottle, every business would make a killing.

The Cons of Starting Your Own Business

Wherever there are pros, there are cons. In the previous section, you saw some of the positive aspects of starting your own business. This section is the flip side of the equation, some of the negatives.

No Guaranteed Salary or Paycheck

There is a financial risk involved in starting a business. Not only may you not make money for some period of time, but unless you have investors (and even with investors) you may very likely have to put your own money into the business. This may mean tightening your belt until the business gets airborne. It may be a while before you get to pay yourself. Depending on the type of business, it often takes three to five years before a business shows a profit, and sometimes even longer.

It's All on Your Shoulders

While it's good to be the king during times of prosperity, you will also occupy the throne during times of poverty. In other words, along with making the easy and the fun decisions like where to hold the grand-opening party, you'll have some tough decisions to make, like which of two valued employees you have to let go because you can't afford to keep them both on the payroll.

You Can't Please Everyone

When you work for someone else, you may be able to excel in the art of making your boss happy, or even thrilled, over the job you do. As the boss, however, you'll need to make decisions that are best for the business, which may impinge on other relationships. (Kissing up will not work . . .) You will find occasions where you won't be able to make everyone happy if it isn't in the best interests of the business.

The 168-Hour Week

There are 168 hours in a seven-day week. And you may find yourself sacrificing other aspects of your life to work a good portion of those hours. Starting a business can take you away from a lot of other aspects of your life. There are numerous responsibilities and plenty of administrative details that won't be the fun part of being a business owner, but will all need to get done. If finances allow, you can hire people to handle much of this work. However, it's not that simple. You will need to train people, review the work of others, and maintain some control over all areas of the business. No matter how much you delegate, you still need to keep a watchful eye over all business transactions.

Growing Pains

Some businesses grow smoothly while (most) others experience growing pains—times when they see a dropoff in progress when the market, industry, or economy slows down. You will need to be ready to ride out the storm each time business hits a dip in the road.

Get a separate business bank account. Before you go to open a business account at your bank, you may need to file either incorporation or doing-business-as (DBA) paperwork, or obtain a business license if your state requires it. Some banks will allow you to open a business account with your social security number. Check with your bank before you go.

Evaluating Yourself

While it is true that starting and running a business is difficult, it's done all the time—and done very successfully—by many individuals and partners who have built up empires large and small. It's done by Wall Streeters and by laypeople who simply want to be their own bosses. Business takes on many forms and thanks to the capitalist system, a business can flourish if it's run well.

Before you even consider starting your own business, you need to determine whether you're the right person for the job. Would *you* hire you? The position in question is one of being your own boss and running the show, which includes bookkeeping, organizational skills, possibly maintaining an inventory, supervising other employees, marketing, offering customer service, and establishing investor relations. Most importantly, the job hinges on your ability to make many key decisions, some on short notice, and to utilize your people skills, since nearly every business involves interaction with others. You may not be skilled in all of these key areas, but if you aren't, you'll have to find other people who can assist you by providing strengths in areas where you aren't as well versed.

Here's a list of traits and characteristics you may need to run a business successfully:

- The ability to make important decisions.
- The ability to stay motivated, even when the business starts off slowly, as most businesses do.
- A knack for organization.
- Good communication skills.
- Stick-to-itiveness, or the drive that keeps you working long hours to get the job done.
- Good physical stamina to survive the long hours and little sleep that may be part of the job.
- The ability to get along well with many different types of personalities.
- A manner of harnessing or managing anger and frustration.
- Confidence in your skills, knowledge, and abilities to run a specific type of business, and confidence in your ability to find the answers to questions you don't yet know.
- The ability to be firm or flexible, so you can make adjustments or changes in your plans.
- The ability to do research and weigh options before jumping into a situation or making a hasty decision.
- The ability to balance a business and a personal life successfully.

The last item on this list is the toughest one for many people, who find that their business eats into their family time, social life, and leisure time. There are 168 hours in a seven-day week. You need to know from the outset that you can't work all of them, or even half of them, and remain sane. While a business takes many hours and extreme dedication, if you sacrifice everything else in your life, you will eventually have regrets and even jeopardize your own well-being as well as the business. A business is not worth building if you can't stick around to see it prosper. It's important to be able to enjoy the fruits of your labor.

Be honest with yourself and determine how many of these skills and talents you possess. How many do you see yourself learning? How many indicate the need for a business partner to fill the void? How much of the description is simply not you? If it's more than 40 percent, then you may not be ready right now to go into your own business. It's better to make that determination early on—after all, if you conclude that you aren't ready to start a business, all you've invested thus far is the price of this book.

Advice can be a blessing and a curse. Take that which you need and discard that which doesn't apply. Too much advice can only lead to confusion. Everyone will have his own opinion on how to run things. Listen politely but selectively.

Knowing What to Handle Yourself— and What to Hand Off

Running a business means wearing a variety of hats. It requires you to fill various roles and handle aspects of business other than your primary skill. It's important that you evaluate your abilities in several areas to best assess your own strengths and weaknesses. Many companies that are founded still lack one of the fundamental aspects of business because the founder did not possess the skills necessary in a particular area.

You need to assess your abilities in not just your area of strength, but in all of the areas necessary to run a successful business. Just because you're a brilliant baker doesn't mean you know how to market a bakery and make customers appear. Likewise, you may be brilliant at setting up the business from an organizational standpoint, but have a very hard time dealing with the customers. It's not uncommon that one person has the business know-how and another person is brought in to handle customer relations. Commonly, you will find one person who excels in the nuts and bolts of business management and another who is the people person. Both are necessary for most business endeavors. They can be partners, or one can hire the other to work for them.

As the manager of an adult seminar center said while fumbling his way through a meeting with the lecturers and teachers of the center, "I should have had my wife do this. I'm the behind-the-scenes guy and she's the people person." Just as you will likely need a lawyer to read over contracts and your lease, you may need marketing and promotional help or someone to assist you in setting up a bookkeeping system. As you're thinking about what you can do yourself, and what you should hand off to someone else, think of the following common tasks in running a business:

- Setting up a business plan, a course of action, and scheduling.
- Meeting with investors, presenting your ideas to others.
- Money management, bookkeeping, and record keeping.
- Hiring, assessing potential employees, and dealing with a staff.
- Marketing, promoting, and researching demographics.
- Handling forms, paperwork, IDs, permits, and so on.
- Establishing a working system for the business.
- Setting up a technical and communications system.
- Selling, retailing, and dealing with customers.
- Vendor relations, ordering, and purchasing.

Just as you assess your own strengths and weaknesses, don't forget to do the same for your business as it grows. You'll see some strengths and weaknesses even before you open the doors. Others will become evident once you're officially open for business.

Before You Start

Plenty of business owners, for better or worse, don't sit down and evaluate their goals before starting out. Some of the most successful entrepreneurs will tell you that if they had thought it through carefully, they probably would have lost the nerve to open up a business in the first place. Other business owners say that they wish they had thought it all through more carefully and been able to foresee some of the pitfalls they had to deal with once the business was off and running. To get a basic feel for the road that lies ahead, it's important to ask yourself three questions, listed in the following sections.

What Are Your Goals?

Yes, you want to make money, but how much and how fast? Do you see yourself running a mom-and-pop store, or do you hope to own a national chain in several years? Is this a business you hope your children will run for years after you retire, or do you hope to build a successful business over the next ten years, sell it, and move to Florida with plenty of cash? Are you looking at altruistic goals? After all, people don't open recycling centers or even thrift shops without a sense of responsibility to the environment. There are many goals beyond that of the obvious (making money). You may also ask yourself how much money is enough? How will you know when you can call it a successful business if you have nothing by which to gage success?

How Well Do You Understand Business?

You don't need to be an astute reader of *The Wall Street Journal* to open a business. Eight-year-olds who can barely read the famed financial paper can set up a lemonade stand and rake in some cash on a hot day. However, it's important that you understand business as it will pertain to *you.* Do you have a good idea of all that is involved in running a business? This includes bookkeeping, taxes, paying employees and vendors, signing contracts, making deals, marketing, and operating in accordance with state, local, and county rules, laws, and regulations. You don't have to know all of this before you start out, but you will have to learn a great deal as you go and be ready to research and find out about what you don't know.

FACTS

Experience and aptitude count. Want proof? According to analysis by Dun & Bradstreet, poor management is the leading cause of business failure. They estimate that a lack of managerial experience and aptitude accounts for almost 90 percent of failed businesses.

How Will Running a Business Impact Your Life?

Can you emotionally and financially handle the uncertainty that a business faces until it shows a profit? Can your family handle it? Can you maintain a life outside of the business? How motivated are you? How well do you deal with adversity? If running a business is going to turn your hair gray before you reach forty and give you an ulcer, then perhaps the comfort and security of working for someone else isn't so bad after all.

Emotionally and physically, you need to assess how well you can balance the many demands of a business and the rest of your life. You need to be able to have a life away from your business, otherwise you'll lose all perspective. If you neglect other areas of your life such as family and health, in the end the business will also suffer as a result.

Avoiding Common Mistakes

Often, the best way to get a feel for what to do is by being aware of what *not* to do. Instead of making mistakes and learning the hard way, you can learn from the mistakes of others. In the following sections, you'll find some of the pitfalls and common mistakes to be aware of when starting out on route to your own business.

Being Married to Your Ideas

Don't become so wrapped up in your ideas that you can't see potential pitfalls or even alterations that need to be made. It's unlikely that your initial idea will fly as is. You'll probably need to make some modifications and even compromises for the sake of the business.

Not Determining Your Target Audience

Too often, people starting a business, when asked whom their business will appeal to, say "everybody." Unfortunately, while you would like everyone to be a customer, demographics, various lifestyles, cultural differences, and other factors will make it virtually impossible to attract *everyone.* Most businesses cater to a particular segment of the population.

If you're lucky, there will be some crossover audience, but for the most part, you'll need to set your sites on a specific target audience of potential customers, whether it's baby boomers, seniors, investors, athletes, or kids.

Business is not just selling, marketing, manufacturing, bookkeeping, or people pleasing. It's all of the above. Make sure you stand back and look to see that all key areas are covered, even those that are not your area of expertise.

Acting Impulsively

Not doing the proper research. You need to know all about the business you're going into. Learn *all* the details. Spend time checking out locations, competitors, banks, places to find resources, and so on. Know what permits and licenses you need to obtain. Impulsivity does not usually work in business.

Not Having a Marketing Plan

There are plenty of ways to spread the word that your business is out there. However, all of these methods take planning. You may have the best product to sell or service to offer in the world, but if you don't market it, no one will know you have something to offer.

Ignoring the Competition

How will you know if your prices are competitive if you don't know what your competitors are up to? You need to do research even before you open your doors for business. Find out who's selling the same products or offering similar goods or services. Get a feel for what the competition is doing, how successful they are, and what you can do to carve a niche in the market.

Underestimating Your Timeframe to Profitability

Having a sound business plan, being aware of the competition, meeting the needs of your customers, and doing solid marketing can make your business successful sooner than later. However, it takes time to build a reputation and gain steady customers. During that time, you will exhaust a great deal of funding. Don't ignore the numbers. If they tell you that it should take three years to show a profit, then don't start spending the money you don't yet have in the first six months. Too many businesses (especially Web-based ones) have made the mistake of spending paper profits. At first, this system worked as everyone went along with high hopes and dreams of the new technology. And then reality set in as banks and venture capitalists said to Webmasters, "Show me the *real* money," when looking at profit and loss statements.

Trying to Be a One-Person Show

Yes, it's your business. No, that doesn't mean you know everything about every aspect of business. The most successful businesspeople know exactly when to ask for help and seek out competent professionals to assist them. Don't try to do everything yourself.

QUESTIONS?

Which organizations offer advice for small businesses?
The Association of Small Business Development provides information, education, and support for those interested in starting a small business. Contact them at 703-764-9854 or on the Web at *www.asbdc-us.org.* The Small Business Association (SBA) is also extremely valuable. Call 800-827-5722 or visit them online at *www.sba.gov.*

Cutting the Wrong Corners

While you don't want to spend money foolishly, the places to save and spend money need to be carefully determined. Spending a fortune to create a product, but saving money by not having an advertising or marketing campaign is a colossal waste of your efforts. Don't just decide you're spending too much money so cut the sales force. Find appropriate places to save money.

Focusing Too Much on Technology and Too Little on People

While technology can do wonders, it will not substitute for good customer relations and good employee relations. Don't let yourself become so overwhelmed by technology, or anything else for that matter, that you neglect to train, motivate, and appreciate your staff. And always practice good customer relations. Remember, technology cannot forge strong relationships.

As hard as it is, you have to learn how to say no if the request means straying too far from what you can realistically do within the scope of your business. Going the extra mile for a customer is a nice gesture, but going an extra ten miles out of your way will likely throw you off course.

Biting Off More Than You Can Chew

Many businesses are built in phases and this is for a reason. If you plan to stock your bricks-and-mortar location while building the Web site and starting up a mail order division, plus a book to coincide with the grand opening and maybe a catalog, you may very possibly be trying to do too much at once. Even major companies roll out new products and open new divisions one at a time. This allows them to focus heavily on each step of the process. Start small, then let the business grow. From a financial standpoint, as well as time and resources, this works best.

Getting Help from Advisors and Mentors

It's very hard to build a business in a vacuum. The feedback, suggestions and opinions of others can be extremely valuable in getting a business off the ground. In fact, companies pay large sums of money for studies and focus groups that answer a lot of their key business questions before they present goods or services to the public.

Advisors need not be business success stories. They can be friends or even relatives who simply promise to provide objective opinions. You might even put together an advisory board to bounce ideas off of as they arise. A mentor, however, may be someone who has already opened a business and knows how to get from the idea phase to turning a profit.

Whomever you choose, be ready to ask them many questions. Keep thinking of new angles to approaching your business and bounce them off other people. Ask others to play the devil's advocate. They used to say that you could pan thousands of pieces of rock before coming up with just one piece of gold, but in the end it was worth the search. The same holds true with ideas. The more you put out there, the more likely you'll be to find the ones that are best for your business.

FACTS

When you're starting your own business, it's easy to feel like you're in it alone. But keep in mind that there are more than 22 million small businesses currently operating in the United States, which accounts for 99 percent of all businesses in the country and employs 53 percent of the workforce.

CHAPTER 2

What Type of Business Is Right for You?

Whether you start a business from the ground floor, step into the family business, or buy an established corporation, chances are you're heading into an area that you have an interest in, are knowledgeable about, and see as a potential for making big profits. Your personal interests and skills, coupled with market research, will help you determine which business to go into and how to set up the operations of that business.

Knowing What Comprises a Good Business Idea

Ideas are a dime a dozen. But it only takes one marvelous idea (and plenty of hard work and planning) to get the next Microsoft off the ground. Even though people probably laughed at the initial ideas to create and market the Chia Pet, Rubik's Cube, or the hula hoop, all of these ideas made substantial sums of money. So don't discount or discard ideas that may, at first, sound absurd.

First and foremost, a good business idea should be one that you believe will bring you a profit. Beyond that, a good idea for business should meet some of, or all of the following criteria:

- It should fill a void or meet a consumer need.
- It should offer a faster, better, easier, or less expensive service or higher-quality product than is currently on the market.
- It should be cost-effective to run.
- It should be realistic—within the scope of something that you can do.
- It should be something that has a defined target audience.
- It should be something that is not over-saturated in the current market.
- It should be legal.

To determine the merits and shortcomings of your business idea, you'll need to do research, punch numbers, and examine all the practical and not so practical aspects of making your idea a reality. You'll need to nurture this idea and help it grow into a full-fledged plan. Then you'll need to put together the elaborate puzzle that takes your idea from the drawing board and turns it into reality.

FACTS

It is now estimated that nearly 25 million Americans are considered entrepreneurs, owning either a full-time or part-time business. And every year that number continues to rise as more and more people want to reap the rewards of owning their own business.

Deciding on the Right Business

There are several significant factors that will be part of your decision-making process as you set about to find the right business for you:

- What would you enjoy doing everyday, that could be profitable?
- Will people pay for this service or the products you want to sell?
- How much financial backing do you think you can get?
- What resources can you gather to run a business?
- How much time and effort can you put into a business without sacrificing other aspects of your life?

Starting up a business means factoring in your interests, a buying market, your financial backing, and your time and dedication. For just a moment, put aside all the research that you'll need to do to determine whether your business venture appears worthwhile. Think about a perfect world in which your business is sure to be a success. Ask yourself the following questions:

- What is it that you really enjoy doing?
- What would give you a sense of satisfaction?
- What type of business could you take pride in?
- What type of business could you immerse yourself in for fifty, sixty, or seventy hours a week?
- Do you want to run a full-time business or a sideline, part-time business?
- Do you see yourself in an office? A storefront location? Working from home?

Design the perfect business scenario for yourself. No, you probably won't end up with that exact picture, but at least you'll have an idea of what it is you're looking to achieve. If, after five years, you find yourself in a situation that's close to what you pictured, then you've done very well indeed. After all, since we aren't living in a perfect world, you can't expect the scenario to play out as you envisioned.

People who've become successful in business often forget to look back at their initial dream and realize how close they are. They focus on the 30 percent they *haven't* accomplished and neglect to stop and look at the 70 percent that they *have* achieved. If your dream is owning a chain of very successful bakeries in the state and you end up with one successful bakery in your neighborhood, you should take pride in the fact that you've achieved some aspect of your dream. You're not working as a gardener or bookkeeper, doing something that has nothing to do with your love of baking. Nor are you working for someone else. To approach your business dream, start thinking small and realize that most successful big businesses grew step by step.

For some people, the right business is centered around a practical skill such as sewing, carpentry, or cooking, while for others it is knowledge or expertise in a technical area. Surround yourself with people, articles, books, magazines, and anything else you can find to support your area of interest. Take classes to hone your skills and enhance your knowledge. Join an organization or association. The idea is to get yourself immersed in this area of interest and determine whether it is an avocation or something you really want to pour your heart, soul, and money into. Meanwhile, you also need to be looking to see if the marketplace supports your desires. Unfortunately you may love to do something that is either too narrow in scope to make money at or so popular that other people with the same interests and skills have gained a foothold on the market.

QUESTIONS?

What characteristics and abilities are necessary to run a business? You need to be motivated, have an I-will-not-quit mentality, be willing to take risks, have confidence in your abilities (which includes decision making), and be able to communicate effectively with others. Nowadays, technical ability helps too.

Thinking Like a Businessperson

If you're going to be an entrepreneur, you'll need to think like one. So, before you determine which business is best for you, take a moment to make sure you've mastered Business Think. It's not all that difficult.

First you need to see yourself as a people person. You need to feel comfortable with numerous relationships, including those with suppliers, customers, investors, and the bank. You also need to see yourself in a leadership role, being able to successfully motivate and manage employees. You need to be able to establish and maintain many relationships in a professional business manner and communicate effectively with a variety of personalities. Honing your people skills for business means thinking in such a manner whereby you present yourself professionally, offer the short version of what your business is all about and listen and learn from others. You need to guide and conduct yourself without letting your emotions take control. You also need to hone your networking skills. Collect business cards and practice matching names to faces so that you remember who's who.

Next you need to be both driven and confident in your ability to stay focused and not lose sight of, or give up on, your goal. Your business will be a 24/7 proposition. Even during non-business hours you need to focus on aspects of the business and constantly be thinking of ways to improve on your current position in the market. You have to make a number of key decisions, some during the business day and others after hours. You need to be able to act and react when necessary. For example, you may be on vacation in Tahiti and suddenly see a newspaper headline that the new Talking Hyena Dolls are accidentally saying an obscene four-letter word. Well, like it or not, you're going to have to call the main headquarters of your nine toy stores and make sure someone is getting the foul-mouthed dolls off the shelves. In other words, you're never completely away from a business, if you're in charge.

And finally, you need to think like a successful entrepreneur, which means looking for new opportunities and figuring out how you can utilize them to your advantage. Your mindset includes a business radar, which has you looking at products and services in a whole new way. Now you look for what is being done well, what can be improved upon, and what is lacking or missing. You become much more critical of other goods and services. You may find yourself thinking as a consumer advocate. A shrewd business thinker can assess the positives and negatives of products, services, and of other businesses and evaluate the strategies of the competition's every move.

Measuring Your Progress

Once you're confident in your leadership abilities, have the drive and determination to see your business ideas through to fruition, and learn to look at the business world as a strategist sees new opportunities, you will have mastered Business Think. Here's a checklist of questions to ask yourself to measure your progress:

- Can you establish and maintain relationships in a professional manner?
- Can you deal with conflicts or disagreements that may occur without losing your temper or becoming unprofessional?
- Can you remember to keep track of names and numbers?
- Can you establish ways in which to regularly keep in touch with people?
- Can you present your business to others in an enticing, not longwinded, manner that holds their attention?
- Can you take in what other people have to say, offer suggestions, and take feedback and criticism constructively?
- Are you able to effectively present a positive image of your business and get your employees or staff to do the same?
- Can you gain the respect of your employees or staff?
- Can you make other people want to work with you and for you?
- Can you make customers or clients feel special?
- What people skills do you need to hone?
- How much of your time can you devote to your business?
- Can you open your eyes and ears to find new ideas for your business from other areas of your life?
- Can you motivate yourself to stay focused even when things go wrong?
- Can you motivate others and rally employees, family, neighbors, and friends around your business venture?
- With the possible help of black coffee, can you put in 15-hour days?
- Can you handle the risks that come with starting your own business and remain focused on the long-term goal of turning a profit?
- Can you find people in your life who can be valuable resources?
- How well can you spot potential opportunities to enhance your business?
- Can you analyze and evaluate other businesses that you encounter?
- How well can you formulate new business strategies and research them?

- How good are you at staying abreast of new developments in your chosen industry?
- Can you focus on, and stay ahead of the current business trends?
- Can you keep excellent records?
- How good are you at judging the value of a product or service?
- Can you see where profits will come from and how to cut unnecessary expenditures?
- Can you gauge how much you can sell your products or service for?
- Are you good at maintaining a budget?
- Can you find ways to maximize profits through modifications of the business?
- Can you adequately gage the value of specific goods or services?

These are just some of the questions that you can ponder while teaching yourself Business Think. Each of these areas will become part of your mindset as you explore business possibilities. The areas in which you're stronger will be those that may point you toward one type of business instead of another. For example, a people person will be more likely to open a retail business or service business that deals with the public, than someone who is a skilled craftsperson and is not interested in dealing directly with the public.

Realizing Strengths and Weaknesses

It's also very important to realize your strengths and weaknesses so that you can hire people accordingly to handle various areas. Someone who is a craftsperson might want to run an Internet retail business selling his crafts over the Web. He may not be versed in the technical aspects of the Internet, however, and should bring in someone who is able to set up and maintain the site.

One of the leading causes for the failure of Web sites is the relationship between the business owners and the technical team. Make sure your technical team understands the goals and needs of your Web site. Point to existing sites as examples of what you want, and maintain constant communication.

Looking at Your Business Options

Whether you're starting up a home-based business, opening an office or a store, launching a Web site, or laying the foundation for a factory, odds are that your business will have you doing one of three things: selling a product, providing a service, or manufacturing something. Within each of these areas is a broad range of possibilities.

Retail Sales

Whether you're selling insurance policies or T-shirts, the principle is the same: You're trying to get people to buy your product. The sales approach, venue, and products are quite different, but the idea is to make your customers see why your product is right for them.

Retailing is a special entity unto itself. It means selling to the public, which most often includes drawing customers to your store or sales location. You then need to present your merchandise in an appealing manner. You need to have strategically placed displays, a well-stocked inventory, and a store layout designed so that customers will easily find what they're looking for and discover new items you hope they'll find appealing.

A traditional retail business comes with numerous specific responsibilities beyond the business plan, need for capital, and other aspects of business in general. You need to:

- Find the best possible location.
- Determine which items are more popular than others and, hence, more marketable.
- Locate suppliers, wholesalers, or distributors.
- Buy display cases, equipment, and all the necessary accoutrements.
- Hire employees whom you can trust.
- Stock the store and maintain the stock.
- Establish pricing and store policies.
- Purchase insurance.
- Set up an alarm system and possibly include cameras and a security guard.

- Offer amenities such as free parking or gift-wrapping.
- Market, promote, and advertise
- Keep tabs on your competition.

And that's just the beginning. While you may know a wealth of information about antiques and want to open an antique shop, there's much more than knowledge of the product that goes into a retail business. Besides all that it takes to open the store, you'll have to market your store and establish your presence in the community. There's also customer relations. It's important that you find ways to make the customer feel special. Some stores today go to great lengths to enhance the shopping experience. The more you offer, the less likely your customers will be drawn to the competition.

People going into business usually hire someone to help with record keeping and money matters. Hiring someone to handle your record keeping is fine. But don't walk away from the responsibility of knowing what is being recorded. Pay attention to what your bookkeeper is doing.

Once your retail business is off and running, you'll need to focus on maintaining the inventory and adding new products. This provides you with an opportunity to get creative with new displays, promotions, and ideas to attract customers.

Many people thrive on the busy, round-the-clock effort it takes to open and build a successful retail business. They work very hard to get such a business off the ground and take great pride when it becomes successful. It requires a great amount of time and effort, plus a good location, organizational skills, and retail know-how (which often comes from being in business a while). It also takes a keen awareness of the industry. Ask someone in the clothing business a question about two different fabrics. If she's been in business for several years, chances are she'll be able to talk for five minutes on the virtues of each fabric and why it's chosen over the others.

Online Business

Rivaling traditional retailers today are online retail businesses. For the most part, e-tail (as it's affectionately called) has not made a significant dent in the retail world . . . yet. In fact, many people still research products on the Internet and then walk into a bricks-and-mortar retail location to see and purchase the products. Certain products, such as books, CDs, and toys have shown tremendous results over the Internet. For someone who wants to maintain a low overhead, selling a niche market item via the Internet can also be advantageous for a small business. Specialized services such as gift items or custom-made products such as golf clubs have also enjoyed success. The Web has also proved a marvelous way to promote and increase sales for established bricks-and-mortar businesses that do additional sales over the Internet but don't base their entire business on e-tail sales.

One of the biggest concerns of many customers shopping over the Internet is not knowing from whom they're buying and not feeling confident that their privacy is respected and maintained. Other than dealing with established online companies, many people are reluctant to give their credit card number to an unknown and possibly unsecured source. While many sources show more breaches of security with traditional credit card methods used in retail stores, consumers are still wary of cyberspace. Fraud and privacy issues as evidenced by the ever-increasing rash of unwanted spam mailings that occur whenever they sign up or put their personal information on certain Web sites. If you're going into e-tail, be sure to make yourself as accessible as possible with a toll-free number, good customer service policies, a business address, and so on. People have become quite concerned about the anonymity of many e-tail-only businesses.

Another problem of starting a Web-based business is, unlike hanging a sign out front—as you would do for walk-in business with a retail location—you need to find a way to draw people to your site. For many entrepreneurs, Web marketing has not been an easy venture. The glut of sites that emerged in the late 1990s and the subsequent, and highly reported, demise of many of those sites, has not been as favorable for new e-tail businesses in the new millennium. It has become increasingly difficult for Web startups to find venture capital. While this trend may change in the near future, at present most people looking to start up an Internet business are thinking small or looking to start up an adjunct business (to a bricks-and-mortar business) but not to use the Web site as their primary business source.

There are plenty of Web-based success stories, and if you find a niche, a way to market yourself, and enough venture capital to survive, you can still get a Web-based e-tail business off the ground. To your advantage is that you can very likely get by without many (or possibly any) other employees. Other than possibly needing someone to help set up and run the site from a technical standpoint, it's quite possible that you can handle the orders yourself with a fulfillment house. You also don't need an inventory, an alarm system, a night watchman, or a shovel for clearing the snow off the sidewalk so that customers can get to your shop.

A few of the things you will need for online retail sales include:

- A Web hosting service that specializes in e-commerce.
- An uncluttered, well-designed page layout.
- Easy navigation for browsing, getting detailed information, and purchasing items.
- Clear, concise product descriptions with photos.
- An easy point-of-purchase method that moves customers through the process quickly and doesn't intimidate or overwhelm them with the need for personal information.
- Good customer service.
- Clear graphics that load quickly.
- A page clearly explaining return policies, shipping charges, and so on.

To succeed with an e-tail business, you need to think like an online consumer. It helps to either be one yourself or, at the very least, talk to regular online consumers. Get to know what people look for from an e-commerce site. Browse numerous sites to get a feel for how they look and how they operate. (Visit *www.gomez.com* or *www.sites.com* for Web site reviews.) Evaluate which sites are easy to navigate and purchase what you want and which ones are not. The point of ordering is the most important juncture of the process. If customers are clicking repeatedly to get through the process, they will simply click off of the site. You need a fast, dependable, foolproof server. You need to be able to handle various payment methods, not unlike a bricks-and-mortar location. Because the Web is global, you may improve your sales potential by being able to handle foreign currencies as well. Finally, you need to have very reliable methods of shipping; otherwise your reputation will diminish quickly. Web sites have gone out of business by taking more order than they could handle or ship.

Remember, you're providing customers with the ability to shop from the comfort of their own homes or offices. Ask yourself: How can you capitalize on that? How can you gain their trust and confidence? How can you make the shopping experience easy and time efficient?

FACTS

One of the largest target audiences online is the college student. About 90 percent of U.S. college students have access to the Internet—most through their schools. College students spend an estimated $700 million online annually. Now that's buying power!

Catalogs

The catalog business, online and offline, has become very big, with faster shipping possibilities than ever before. A successful catalog business is based on a strong mailing list to potential customers and excellent fulfillment of orders in a timely fashion.

While catalogs provide an attractive way for customers to purchase items from the comfort of their own homes, they can be a very difficult business to start up. Sid Kerber, founder of the Catalog Consultancy *(www.catalogconsultancy.com),* a consulting business that helps both existing and startup catalogs as well as direct marketing and mail-order businesses, warns that you need a lot of capital and an extensive database of names before you should even consider starting a catalog business.

"The days of starting a catalog business at the kitchen table are long gone," says Kerber. People who can be successful with catalogs already have established lists, such as retailers. They can expand from a successful business, but they need an inventory of merchandise and goods plus established vendor relationships. On top of that, there are numerous costs, including layout, design, graphics, printing, advertising and marketing, mailing and postage, and fulfillment. Kerber adds, "Without most of these areas already in place from an existing business, the start up costs can be quite prohibitive."

In addition, Kerber points out that someone starting up a catalog business needs to know both retailing and merchandising: "The way items are displayed and placed on the pages of a catalog is very important. Just like a retail business, a catalog is driven by merchandise," explains Kerber. "For example, you can be a computer whiz, but if you don't know how to present the computer products on the page you won't be successful. Retailers and merchants need to translate the skills it takes to set up a successful store to setting up a catalog. They need a merchandising instinct."

If you know you already have access to a significant databank, plus retail and merchandise experiences, and you're considering a catalog business, you may look for a niche item. Products that aren't readily available in retail stores are the best bet. You should also consider a product that will be marketable all over the country, since you want as wide a distribution as possible.

One of the biggest problems in making and distributing a traditional catalog (as opposed to online) is that once you send it out, the catalog cannot be changed. If a product is not performing as it should be or is suddenly discontinued from the manufacturer, you have no way of letting people know. In a store you can sell off products in a sudden sale or remove them from the shelves altogether. A sudden turn of events might make something the hottest trend overnight. You can move the products up front or put them in the store window. Likewise, on a Web site, you can delete a product or put it front and center on your home page. You don't have this kind of flexibility with a catalog, however. Many experts recommend that you start online or in a retail business before branching out to a catalog. If nothing else, test out the products online and build up your database.

FACTS

In case you think you're the only one with numerous catalogs appearing in your mailbox, rest assured you're not alone. Believe it or not, there are now roughly 10,000 different catalogs circulating in and out of mailboxes all over the United States.

Selling to Other Businesses

Rather than selling to the public, you might elect to sell to other businesses. You may be selling wholesale to a company that will resell the product to the general public, or you may be selling business-to-business (B2B) products, such as telephone systems for offices or stage lights for theaters. There are numerous B2B businesses you can start up, some of which sell products and others of which sell services. Integrators combine the two and sell a product (generally technology related) and then sell the services that relate to that product. As an integrator you can install, customize, and maintain the products that you offer to meet the needs of your clients. Selling products, combined with servicing, is a way of expanding your business and increasing your potential profit margin.

While a store has the benefit of walk-in business, and a good location can make all the difference in the world, B2B sales is very much built around contacts, networking, and creating a list of potential customers. It is also based on maintaining satisfied customers. Relationships and repeat business is key. The more specific the product, the more you will need to rely on steady clients.

Often a startup sales business begins when someone in a sales position for a larger corporation decides to go solo. He can then take their Rolodex of names and numbers with him and already have some client base. You'll use several means by which to find potential clients including:

- Referrals and word of mouth
- Direct targeted mailings
- Advertisements in trade journals
- Trade shows and conferences
- Networking

You may attend meetings of the local Chamber of Commerce, link to Web sites of colleagues, or mail a CD-ROM to prospective customers. In whatever manner you do it, you need to find new clients and stay in touch with your current clients to make sure they're satisfied. Let your regular customers know about new products and special deals or offers that only they can get in on.

A knack for selling successfully includes having the right look (polished and professional) and the knowledge to present yourself and your products and/or services in a confident self-assured (not cocky) manner. Presentation is very important, so you'll need to hone your sales skills. You'll also need to convince potential clients why they should establish a working relationship with your company. You'll need to make sure they clearly see the benefits of your products or services.

Top salespeople learn that fine line between selling and overselling. They are able to hear what their customers needs are and immediately direct them to the right product or service. Boilerplate, one-size-fits-all selling is almost nonexistent in a day and age of detailed technology and customized services. There are numerous sales courses offered at universities and through business schools. Finding a successful salesperson as a mentor is also advantageous because he will know the tricks of the trade in the area of sales you're looking to enter.

Manufacturing the Products You Sell

Opening a manufacturing business definitely requires significant capital. This is simply because you cannot manufacture anything without the parts and equipment necessary. Whether you're weaving rugs or building carburetors, you need to purchase your initial tools and materials.

The advent of the Internet and catalogs allow someone in manufacturing to produce a small quantity of the product and then make more as orders come in. However, to really make profits in manufacturing, you'll want to sell to large retailers, which means having a product made in quantity and delivered quickly. The larger the companies that you have contracts with, the faster you'll need to increase production. This will also mean mass-production without losing quality.

Like all other aspects of running your own business, manufacturing takes ingenuity. If you can create a product that isn't on the market and it is cost-effective for you to create and then sell, you're on your way. The old supply-and-demand theory is never clearer than when you take a year to design your latest creation, only to find there is absolutely no demand for glow in the dark toilet seats. Therefore, unless you're simply enjoying a hobby with hopes of selling a few of your hand-carved duck decoys to local hunting shops, don't dive headfirst into manufacturing anything until you have proof that people will want what you make.

Also, manufacturing means studying up on the details that make up the product. People who think about starting a manufacturing business should have both a thorough knowledge and a strong interest in that which they are about to manufacture. If you know nothing about sofa beds, chances are you're not going to start a successful sofa-bed manufacturing company.

Often manufacturing businesses start small. They may consist of two people making clocks in the basement on weekends and selling them to local stores or at flea markets. If you enjoy making something, and you can make it inexpensively and without taking a great amount of time, you can start a small manufacturing business. Such businesses grow as the item catches on. There are numerous stories of individuals who sold an item to a local store and eventually the product went national.

Creating the product is only half the battle. There's marketing, sales, and delivery involved, as well as keeping track of costs and overhead. One positive aspect of manufacturing is that there is often less competition because fewer people have the same skills and resources to make the product that you're making.

If you're thinking about starting up a manufacturing business, you should consider the following:

- Whether you have the initial funding.
- How to create something that there is a need for in the marketplace.
- How well you can evaluate the strengths and weaknesses of your products.
- How well you can think of ways to improve upon your products.
- How much you can manufacture.
- What resources and equipment you'll need and how much it'll cost.
- How to get work from major corporations, many of which outsource much of their manufacturing needs.

Consider expanding on that which you manufacture, not only to add more products, but to do repairs and design tools or parts that will help others more efficiently use the products. For example, if you're manufacturing eyeglass frames, you might also manufacture, or at least sell, the tools used to repair them. In addition, if you can provide training in eyeglass care, you can make additional income. Manufacturing today often starts with making the product and branches out to maintaining it, fixing it, and learning new ways to use it. Then the product line expands into your new lemon-scented version, low-fat version, and so on.

While some people use their own skills to actually manufacture products, many manufacturing businesses are a matter of designing and creating the right products and having others do the actual hands on manufacturing to meet your specifications. Whether you're making jewelry yourself or have a small factory manufacturing handbags or sweaters by machine, you need to test market your goods. You may ask friends and neighbors what they think or bring in focus groups—but either way, you'll want good, honest appraisals on the positives and negatives of that which you're manufacturing. If the public doesn't find it practical, useful, helpful, or attractive, you may be sitting on a lot of goods with no place to sell them. It's also very important that you keep up with the sales trends, particularly if you're entering the fashion or technical arenas, where change is a daily occurrence.

How you introduce your line of products is also significant to your success. Golf-equipment manufacturing companies try constantly to come up with new innovative clubs made from various metals designed to hit the ball harder and straighter, balls that will travel farther, and the perfect golf shoe. They boast about the strengths of their products and the inner workings of the club or ball and compete heavily for their share of the market. It's very important that they meet the demand for new products at the major golf trade shows that take place twice a year. They then market their wares at other golf trade shows and at tournaments around the country.

As in all business, marketing is key to your success. Good salespeople are also very important. If you're running a small manufacturing business in which you're the person behind the handmade goods, you may do your own marketing and sales. You will need to reach out to the people in your industry who sell and market the products that you create. As the business grows, you'll seek out help in these key areas so that you can concentrate on creating the best golf clubs, making the best chocolate cream pie, or designing and manufacturing the world's smallest thumbnail clock radio.

Selling Services

From dog walkers to financial consultants, people all over the world are selling their abilities to provide their expertise and to perform tasks. Clowning at parties, window washing, computer repair, catering, childcare, hairstyling, public relations, graphic design, business consulting, and countless other services are ones that you may be able to perform.

To enter the service field you need to ask yourself the following:

- What are my special skills and abilities?
- What field have I studied or been trained in?
- What certificates or licenses do I have or need to obtain before performing a specific service?
- Can I take my skills and use it to run a business?
- Is there a market for this service?

Having the ability is only part of the plan. The best accountant east of the Mississippi River is not going to succeed in business without clients. Not unlike sales, to start a service business requires contacts, contacts, and more contacts. It means finding ways to spread the word and let people know that you're ready to perform your service for a fee. You'll need to investigate the going rate for your service, based on what others with your background and knowledge are getting. You'll also be guided by the geographic part of the country where you're planning to provide the service.

The more you specialize, the less competition you'll have. However, the more you specialize, the smaller the potential market. A public relations firm for medical and pharmaceutical companies for example, will not be in competition with PR firms for entertainment. However, you will have to market yourself that much more carefully to your defined target audience. Finding a niche or specialty can make you highly sought out if you're good at what you do and can spread the word that only you can do it.

Sometimes the market is in need for (or has room for more) businesses providing your service. For example, an entertainment PR firm might still be able to find a market in Los Angeles even though there is stiff competition, because the entertainment industry is so large in that area. However, they may need to focus on a niche, such as child actors, and provide services or contacts that the competition cannot provide. This can make a new company valuable.

Billable hours are the key to making profits in the service industry. Overhead can be low, but time is money, and you will need to keep precise records of how many hours you put into a project. Many skilled individuals fail in business for themselves because they don't keep careful track of their hours and spend way too much time on a project without being fairly compensated. Flat fees can spell trouble unless you do the math ahead of time and calculate how much you're actually getting hourly.

A good service provider knows how to walk the fine line to make the business a success. He charges a competitive but fair rate and offers first-rate service with extras, while not compromising professionalism or wasting valuable time.

You can also set up and run a service-oriented business without providing the service yourself. You may decide to open a catering business because you know several excellent cooks and own a van. You would approach the business as the coordinator and manager, making sure that all the pieces fit together. Building a service business means finding the right mix of talent who possess the necessary skills, the ability to work well with clients, and the ability to follow direction—both yours and the clients'.

The key to a service oriented business is providing services that gain you a strong reputation. Service providers can build their business through satisfied customers telling other potential customers how wonderful they are. Word-of-mouth promotion can save you a bundle on paid advertising and make or break a service business.

If you're thinking of opening up a service type of business, consider that you will:

- Need proper licensing for many businesses.
- Need promotion and marketing.
- Have to handle the bookkeeping and record keeping—or hire someone to do it for you.
- Need to provide good follow-up with clients or customers.
- Be able to gain an advantage if you specialize, but lose that advantage if your specialty becomes too narrow to meet the needs of the market.

The research and marketing discussed in Chapter 3 is just as important to success in the service industry as in the retail sales industry. After all, you're selling a service and you need to have buyers. Depending on the service, your target audience can be local, national, or global.

More and more services are requiring that you have a license to perform that service. Make sure you are licensed by the local, state, or national authorities. Do not fall for licensing scams, like "$10 Licenses on the Internet . . . Just Click Here."

Making Your Decision

Most businesses fall into one the categories covered in this chapter—retail sales, e-tail sales, manufacturing, or providing a service. There is generally some overlap, as a manufacturer needs to sell his goods and a retail store needs to provide services to its customer base.

Your reasons for wanting to start your own business, coupled with your personality and your likes and dislikes, probably points you in one direction over the other. It's important that you feel both knowledgeable and confident in the area you choose.

While there are many aspects that are common to all businesses, such as making a business plan, getting the financing you need, marketing, finding a competitive advantage, and looking for profits, the specifics to each type of business can be tailored to fit your lifestyle. For example, many people have family obligations and want to run a business from their home. This will obviously preclude them from opening up a store, since they probably don't want people traipsing through their living room everyday. And it will probably hinder their chances of starting a helicopter manufacturing business—unless they have a very, *very* large garage. However, an e-tail business, a jewelry manufacturing business, or providing a service could easily be run from home. You just need to be practical in your planning.

Your choice of business should suit you as an individual. It will be sized according to your goals, available space, funding, and available resources, including how many friends and family members are going to help out. It should reflect who you are and what you enjoy doing.

Wherever your interests and abilities lie, you'll have to channel them according to what the market needs. Therefore, you'll need to do your share of researching the market before you make your final decision. If you're looking to open a daycare center, for example, you'll need to determine if the area you're looking at has enough young families with children who would require daycare to make it worth your while. Likewise, if you're looking starting a Web site in an industry where your research shows that three Web sites dominate the online traffic and e-commerce, then you may have to rethink your plans.

CHAPTER 3

Researching the Market

The key to operating a successful business is to combine your interest and knowledge of a business with the needs of other people in a particular market. After you've determined what kind of business you'd like to open, the next step is making sure there's a market for that business.

Analyzing the Market

So, where can you do the research you need? A competitive market analysis by an expert would be terrific, but you may not want to spend that kind of money to start a small business. You could check with some market-research firms and get quotes. Your goal is to get them to do an analysis of your target area, which may be your community, an entire county, or a national market. Naturally the larger the report, the more money you'll need to spend.

ESSENTIALS

Simmons Market Research *(www.smrb.com)* is a multimedia research company that helps product manufacturers, sellers, and media vehicles gain a competitive edge. It has a database of over 8,000 products. You can also check *www.hoovers.com* for information on numerous businesses plus lists of top businesses in a variety of industries.

You can, however, do your own market research. Some places to find vital information include:

- Your local library or any good business library, where there are numerous research volumes that will provide you with up-to-date data on companies, demographics, and market research.
- Newsstands where you can pick up *Forbes, The Wall Street Journal,* and numerous other business periodicals.
- Trade publications, including newsletters for the industry of your choice, so you can get to know exactly what is going on in the industry before you jump in.
- The Chamber of Commerce or City Hall records office or bureau, which can provide you with data on competitive businesses.
- Annual reports from other companies, which help you get an idea of what your own expenditures, income, and overall cash flow might look like.

- The Internet, where you can get your hands on numerous facts and figures.
- Individual company Web sites, where you can find out what's going on with similar businesses.
- The Small Business Administration (SBA) at *www.sba.gov*.
- Other business owners, who can tell you what it's like on the inside.
- Associations that have members in the same industry you're considering.

Knowing What to Look For

Through all this research you should be looking for substantial information that supports your idea and your business plan. If you find the right supporting information, then you proceed forward. However, if all signs point to "No go," you may just save yourself from a potential disaster. In essence, you're doing a feasibility study to see if your plan is feasible based on the current market and economic climate, and on the prospects for the future.

Examining Your Potential Market

You want to get an idea of the size of your potential market. Will you be catering to a specific market by selling a specialized service like home health care for seniors or will you be reaching a mass audience with a product like chewing gum?

Industry Information

It's important to gage the overall industry and where it's headed. Opening a business in an industry that's headed for a fall is fraught with disaster. Conversely, you may find the hottest growing industry. Can you tailor your skills and passion to fit into an up-and-coming industry?

Overall Competition

How many competitors are there? What companies are capturing the lion's share of the market? Is the field over-saturated? Can you carve a niche market from a larger one? What can you do to differentiate yourself from the competition?

FACTS

According to Hoovers.com, three of the top five food/restaurant business concepts in the nation at the turn of the twenty-first century were fast food burger businesses—McDonald's, Burger King, and Wendy's—combining for over $55 billion worth of business. Still want to open a burger franchise? You'd better have a very inventive idea.

The Success of Your Competitors

What type of sales figures are your competitors looking at? If they're doing poorly, could you do better? If they're doing well, will you be able to compete?

Industry Trends

Besides looking at the dollar figures and competition within a certain industry, you should look at trends, both in business and in lifestyle. For example, if more people than ever own dogs in your neighborhood, then there may be a need for pet care or pet accessories. If there is also an increase in people traveling, then you might look to see if there is a need for an innovative kennel, perhaps featuring doggie vacations in your area. You could start your own doggie resort or a fancy kennel with some nice amenities that would appeal to dog owners for their pets.

You may find that there have been a great number of layoffs from major companies. This does not mean you can't start up a new business. There may be a greater need for outsourcing, because these companies still have tasks that need to get done. You might open a placement service for freelancers and contractors. You could also open up a resume-writing service or even start career coaching for people who are going on interviews. Perhaps the companies need to use your manufacturing skills because they can't afford to keep in-house people full time to manufacture goods.

The point is that if you look at the trends taking place around you, locally and nationally, you can start to think about what is needed in any specific market. Trends that illustrate needs in specific areas are places where you can look to fill a void. Then determine if the need is great enough that a business would profit by filling the void.

Also look at the overall economic climate to determine if the time is right for your business. A town experiencing layoffs and going through hard times will not be the place for selling luxury items or extravagant services. Timing is also very important when opening a business. These are among the many statistical questions that you're looking to answer from your research.

You can also use your own awareness as a consumer to find voids in the marketplace. If you always find yourself unhappy about having to drive five miles to find a stationery store, than perhaps others are experiencing the same needs for greeting cards and paper products in your area. Conduct your own survey. Hand out 100 short questionnaires asking people where they buy greeting cards, stationery, and other such products and if a store opened in their community would they shop there. If 60 percent say they would, then you know there's a need for such a store. However, if 60 percent said they order cards and stationery goods online then you're not going to fill a void.

You'll also see products and services that you feel you could improve upon. You need to be careful, however, to determine whether the product *needs* to be improved upon. One gentleman commented, upon seeing a garage door opener that would open the door from 100 feet away, that he could devise such a product that could open a garage door from 500 to 1,000 feet away. The question he was asked was simply, "Why would anyone need to open a garage door from 1,000 feet way?" Making something more powerful or potent is only marketable if it's worthwhile. Battery-powered dice, for example, did not catch on.

Here are some key questions to ask yourself when you're looking at your industry trends:

- What is your target market group?
- What does your research indicate that this group needs?
- How much will people pay for these goods or services?
- Will it be enough money to make for a successful business venture?
- What trend or trends will be prevalent in the near future?
- What impact will these trends have on your target market group?
- What is your competition and what are they offering or not offering?
- Based on current needs, upcoming trends, and the competition, what can you do to gain a competitive edge in the market place?

ESSENTIALS

It's essential that you keep up with the latest developments in your industry of choice. Look at new technological developments, changes in styles and taste, plus key indicators. When you're armed with this knowledge, you'll be prepared for what lies ahead.

Staying Current

Staying current is an important aspect of business that may mean being ready to change your direction or strategy. One popular entertainment trade magazine, in the very early 1980s did not see the need to incorporate the computer and high-tech industries into their publication. Needless to say, as computers and technology worked their way deeper into the entertainment business, including computer games and high-tech imagery generated for films and television, this magazine found itself missing out on large chunks of computer-driven advertising. By the time they realized that computers were the wave of the future, even in the entertainment business, it was too late and the magazine folded.

From the time you come up with your initial business idea until you actually open the doors or launch the Web site for business, things will change. Business moves quickly, as do trends, styles, fashion, and technology. There are numerous stories whereby someone had a great idea but by the time they hit the market with their plan, someone else had beaten them to it. It's important to stay on top of what is being manufactured, as well as what's in the planning stages, in your industry.

You need to be aware of the present and put your focus toward the future. It's to your advantage to be able to foresee demographic shifts and changes in the economic climate that lie ahead. If you can continue to structure and restructure your business in accordance with what's going on in the world (not just the business world) around you, you'll be able to stay on the cutting edge—or at least be keeping pace with the competition.

Several years back companies needed to move their data to computers to keep pace. More recently companies needed to add a modern communications system or add price scanners in retail outlets to keep up competitively. The next phase may be smart card technology, which may replace credit cards. They are already gaining in popularity on a global level and in closed environments like military bases and universities. These examples are broad based. Each industry has specific new technologies, styles, or manners of handling business that are becoming the norm.

But trends are more than that which is new to the industry. They also represent that which is changing in society. Are there more single-parent families that may need your services? Are more seniors buying certain holistic medicines and vitamin products? Are more teens able to travel abroad than ever before? Look at rising numbers in demographic groupings.

Scouting Out the Competition

To be competitive in the marketplace, you need to know exactly what the competition is doing. Therefore, if you're going to have the best pizza in town, you'd better see what the most popular pizzerias are offering and figure out what you can offer to draw customers to your establishment.

One pizzeria owner realized that the neighborhood had an increase of families and that many of the trendy new pizzeria restaurants were quite yuppie in their attempt to woo the business clientele. He noticed parents with restless kids waiting to be served, and he decided to do something a little different. Well aware of how much kids love good pizza he decided to go after the family market with a special selection of children's pizzas, sized accordingly for smaller appetites and including a soda and Italian ices (which are incredibly inexpensive) at a lower overall cost than the combination would be at the competition. He then enhanced the child-friendly appearance, put crayons and entertaining placemats on the tables, and drew the families with kids. The pizzeria found a share of an existing marketplace without taking away from its regular walk-in business of all ages.

Gaining a competitive advantage can mean changing the style, image, packaging, or service; adding new selections; changing the pricing structure; or trying a whole new look. Whatever the competition isn't doing that will draw customers is what you need to do. Change for the sake of change, however, doesn't work, so research what you think is a viable plan of action. When Coke switched to New Coke, Pepsi did not respond with New Pepsi. They waited to see what the effect was on Coke's business. It wasn't very good and New Coke disappeared. You may need to wait to see if your competition's bright idea is a hit or a dud.

ESSENTIALS

Reference-book publishers hire fact checkers to make sure the information in the book is accurate. If you're gathering information on demographics or on the competition, make sure it's accurate. Changing your prices or policies based on a well-spread rumor about your competition can bury you. Double-check your research.

Filling a Void

Filling the right void in an industry can also make you an industry giant. Federal Express saw a need for prompt overnight delivery that either wasn't being addressed or marketed in a strong manner by another company. They stepped in, promoted overnight shipping, and have become industry giants. Naturally, you have to make good on your claims, but finding new ways to do something, make something, or sell something will put you in an advantageous position.

Once you find a competitive advantage or fill a void, you need to make sure to promote that fact. Federal Express made it clear from the start that overnight shipping to anyplace in the world was their specialty.

Filling a void and finding a niche are two different manners in which to approach your business and gain a competitive edge. The former is finding something that isn't readily done and stepping in and doing it. The latter means taking something that *is* being done and doing it better. For example if a company came along that specialized in overnight animal transport, they would be moving into an area that is already being covered by delivery companies. However, they would be specializing in one small aspect of that business.

You might be able to corner an industry by becoming a specialist. Just make sure there is a large enough potential market for your specialty. Just Kites, for example, is one of a few small kite shops in Manhattan. Sure, other stores may sell kites, but this is the definitive place to go for kites, because they have expertise in that one area and a wider selection—kites are the cornerstone of their business. While such a store might not succeed in a small town where only 3 percent of the population cares about kites, 3 percent of New York City is still a potential audience of nearly a quarter of a million people. Add to that the fact that they are within walking distance of Central Park and local playgrounds, and they have a successful business.

Before you go into business, assess the competition carefully. While it's always advantageous to beat the competition's prices, you may not be able to do so and still turn a profit. You should certainly try to at least match the competitive prices. Meanwhile, see if you can offer more in the area of services. Can you offer any of the following:

- Free, or at least more accessible, parking
- Warranties or service plans
- Free repairs
- Gift-wrapping
- Free shipping
- Overnight delivery
- Personalized attention
- Twenty-four-hour service
- A secure payment system online

As your business grows, determine what you can do to improve service and customer relations. Keep track of what the competition is doing so that you can plan your own strategy. It's no coincidence that every time one fast food place has a movie tie-in promotion, their competition ties in with another hot movie. You need not go so far as to attack the competition—leave that for politics—but always be ready to think of your next move. Remember, it's like a chess match. Company A makes a move, and Company B needs to make a counter move, and so on.

FACTS

Customer service can be the difference between beating the competition and lagging behind. Provide service that makes people want to come back and do business with you again. Not surprisingly, surveys show that customer service is the leading concern among customers.

Naming Your Business

Finding a name for your business isn't always as easy as it sounds. Often, you need to do a bit of research to see what name will work best. What's in a name? Potential business! While it may not sound like all that much, choosing a name for your business is very significant. The right name can make the difference between success and mediocrity. It can make you stand out from the crowd or blend in. It's important that your name be:

- Short
- Easy to remember
- Easy to spell
- Easy to pronounce
- Original
- Defining

The first five on the list are self explanatory, but the last one—defining—means that you want the name to indicate what your business is all about. Aunt Peggy's Bakery or Mrs. Field's Cookies not only tell you who makes them, but more importantly, what is in the package. The store, Just Kites not only tells you what they sell but what they don't (namely, anything else). Fred's Corner Store tells you nothing, except that the store is on the corner.

You can include a lot of information in a name, even a concise one. Ace Overnight Shipping tells you that you're dealing with a shipping company and one that provides overnight service. If possible, it's advantageous to include a feature of your products or service in the name that gives potential customers a heads-up on what you offer. Federal Express clearly tells you that they work quickly.

Of course, there are many companies that have simply utilized a common name such as Wendy's or Uncle Ben's. If you can heavily promote a name that's easy to remember, (and it need not be a first name—case in point: McDonald's), then you can also grab attention. People relate to the personal feeling that a name with a name exudes.

More often than not, the name is something that sounds right to you. You'll probably write down numerous possibilities before coming up with the one you like best. Perhaps your own name will be included, such as Arthur Murray's Dance Studios or Jack LaLaine Fitness Centers. Sometimes initials catch on, like J.C. Penney or P.C. Richard. For a legal practice, it's customary to be more formal and use last names of the partners, such as Steinman & Harris, Attorneys at Law, which sounds more professional than "Mark and Ted, Attorneys at Law," or "The Little Shop of Law." Keep in mind who your target audience is made up of. Fun, trendy names may attract a young audience while more formal names may be better suited for the financial industry. The product or service provided will also dictate the formality of the name.

Sometimes the town or location draws attention and puts you one step ahead of your competitors. Yorktown Deli sounds like the official deli of the town, which it isn't. However, when looking for a deli in Yorktown, you may think of it first. You might also use the name associated with the town or city in which you're doing business. New York City, the Big Apple, is home to the Big Apple Circus and you will likely find a Big Apple Cleaners or Big Apple Diner. New York is also known as the

Empire State. So you'll find New York businesses with the word *Empire,* just as you'll find Washington D.C. businesses with *Capitol* in the name or businesses near the Grand Canyon with the word *Canyon* in them.

Many business owners think large. Shoetown, Record World, and CD Universe are all the result of thinking big. The reality is that Auto World may be a larger store than Auto Universe, but either way, they both sound like they have a major inventory and can service the needs of any car owner.

Bounce names off of other people and see what their knee-jerk reaction is. If the name is throwing them off, then it may be misleading. The name Monsterdaata.com for example may confuse people who focus on whether or not the word is misspelled (or why it is spelled in such a manner), rather than on the services of the Web site. Also, if the name has people thinking of another, similar business, it might be too close to another company's name.

There is also a propensity to combine names and words in this day and age of brevity. ExecuNet is one such example. You might think of appealing alliterations, catchy phrases, or even play off of another popular phrase, such as the Chinese Takeout restaurant Wok-N-Roll or the bar/restaurant Who's On First?. Be clever, succinct, and fit the name to the tone of the business. Lucky Number Casino for example, works a lot better than The Lucky Number Mortuary.

There are numerous ways to derive a name, so take your time, research the market, and in the end find one that makes you feel good. Like a comfortable shoe, the name should fit just right.

Have your attorney do a name search or go on the Internet and search to make sure your name is as original as you believe it is. If a trademark, corporate name, or domain name search reveals a similar name, don't give up! Try using a unique spelling or a variation on the name, or add an additional defining word.

CHAPTER 4

Structuring Your Business

Going into business does not necessarily mean you need to go it alone. Some people are soloists while others prefer to harmonize. Only you, and your accountant, can decide which method suits you best when determining the legal structure of your business.

Partnerships

Once they were Sears and Roebuck, now they're just Sears. Whatever happened to Roebuck? Comics ponder this question, while business partners often wonder which one of them will be Sears and which will be Roebuck. Will you be the next Ben and Jerry? Will you be together for many years? You'll find business partners that have been in stride for twenty-five years and others who split up shortly after the sign on the front door is put into place. It's all in how you approach the business and whether or not you have common goals. If one person sees the business as a friendly, local, mom-and-pop operation, and the other is thinking about new locations, franchises. and four catalogs a year, the pairing may not be right.

It's imperative that everything be set up carefully and spelled out on paper, even among the closest of friends—*especially* among close friends, who may need that written agreement as a legal document at some point in their business future. Most significantly, people who team up to go into business need to be on the same page. They also need to:

- Recognize each other's strengths and weaknesses.
- Accept that one partner may put in more hours while the other may be highly visible and get name recognition.
- Divide up tasks fairly based on their respective strengths.
- Have an open line of communications.

General Partnerships

The choice of a partnership also has legal implications. In a general partnership, partners are equally responsible for the business, both sharing all profits and liabilities. Partners determine in advance who is responsible for which aspects of the business and contractual agreements are carefully drawn up with good legal council.

A general partnership can be advantageous because it allows you to pool resources and often makes it easier to gather funding. There is a greater compendium of knowledge and skills. If partners share the same common goals and visions for the company, they can often compliment one another by doing different functions. Any liabilities incurred, however, are shared among all the partners.

On the other hand, sharing liabilities can be a disadvantage if one partner is clearly at fault or causes the business to go into debt. Each partner is responsible for the actions of the others and for the overall business in a general partnership. So if your partner sends the company into debt and takes off for Rio, you are still held responsible. Less drastic, but more frequent, is the simple matter of different aspirations for the business. One partner may want to embrace technology while the other may want to do things the old-fashioned, tried-and-true way. This can present operational problems.

From a tax standpoint, partnerships are not taxed as a business. Instead the partners are taxed individually. Each partner pays personal income tax. An IRS form (Form 1065) shows the pass through of income/loss to each partner. You will also be able to deduct business losses when filing your income tax.

You need to file with the state for any type of incorporating. In a partnership, you just need an agreement between the partners (and a business license, if your community requires one), but you don't have to file with the state. For a sole proprietorship, no agreements or filings are required—only business licenses that are required where you live.

Limited Partnerships

Limited partnerships can be advantageous as well. A limited partner, unlike a general partner, takes on limited risk and is only liable for his investment and not for the entire business. If, however, the limited partner is a manager, he can be liable for debt. Even in a limited partnership, a general partner is necessary to take on the overall company liabilities. Also limited partners can be replaced, or leave the business without having to dissolve the partnership, which makes legal entanglements less detailed.

Sole Proprietorships

If you choose to go it alone, you are in essence a sole proprietor. This is the easiest form of business to start because you don't need to draft partnership agreements or register to incorporate. You may need to obtain proper licensing in your state, county, town, or city to conduct your type of business, however.

Being a sole proprietor means that you are the boss, the head honcho, the top dog, the big cheese whose name will appear on greeting cards and other congratulatory notes when you announce that you are officially open for business. Save all the cards and letters wishing you well. You'll need to look at them for moral support when the road gets rocky—and it will. Few businesses get off to a smooth start and see profits in the first, second, or even third year. As a sole proprietor, you'll be the one lonely soul most patiently awaiting the profit-and-loss statements. You'll be the one with the tough decisions to make, and no matter how much you delegate responsibilities, the overall accountability of the business will fall on your shoulders, for better or worse.

On the plus side, if and when the business takes off, you'll be the one reaping the rewards. You will have total ownership and control of the business. Of course, if the business fails, you'll be responsible for answering to the investors and the bank.

Being a sole proprietor means you don't need approval to make changes and implement ways of running the business. In fact, others need *your* approval. You don't have to worry about a partner being in agreement with your decisions. Even taxation is a simple process as you pay taxes based on your income.

One of the problems of being a sole proprietor, however, is that you are responsible as an individual—so if your business goes into debt, even if you shut the doors and take down the sign, you can still be held liable. You can take out product insurance, insure your equipment, or take out other forms of insurance to try to cover yourself, but it may not be enough to cover yourself completely.

It can also be difficult from a psychological standpoint to go it alone in business. Just as you have no one to answer to, you have no one to do half the work, raise half the money, and solve half the problems as you do when you have a partner. If you're confident in your abilities and can handle a wide range of responsibilities, calling in the right people at the right times for help, then this might be the best way for you to go.

FACTS

Even though you can set up your business in several different ways, the sole proprietorship is still the most common type of business structure in the United States. More than 70 percent of all businesses in the country are sole proprietorships.

Corporations

A corporation is a business unto itself. In a corporation, you don't operate alone, as a sole proprietor, and you don't just team up with a few partners. Instead, a corporation is a legally formed business entity with laws, rules, and guidelines to adhere to. The process of incorporating is done in accordance with state laws and can be completed by filing the proper paperwork and paying certain fees. You'll need an attorney to assist you in the process and to review the state requirements. Once filed, you will be incorporated in that state. Subsequently you will need to incorporate in other states in which you plan to conduct business. You can generally contact the Secretary of State for guidelines in the state where you are planning to incorporate. You will pay a fee to the state for incorporating and pay annual franchise taxes. It is also advised that you get a corporate seal in case documents require it.

Once you begin the process of incorporating (and select a name), you will also need to search to find out if there is another business with the same name that has been incorporated in the state. You may need to change the name slightly. Conversely, you may find several variations on the name you like and incorporate under a few names to keep other companies from having similar names.

The most significant advantage of incorporating is that it allows your business and personal responsibilities to be handled separately. Therefore, you are protected to a much greater degree. Your corporation can be held responsible without *you* being held personally liable. This is very significant in the event of a lawsuit, because you can protect your personal assets. You can also leave a corporation without having to dissolve the business, since you and the corporation are separate entities.

As corporations grow, they may take on stockholders who are not involved in the day-to-day activities of the corporation, but have a vote in the policies set forth by the corporation and share in the profits. It can also be easier to obtain funding as a corporation than a sole proprietor or partnership.

Once you incorporate, you pay yourself a salary from the corporation. You also pay corporate taxes as well as your own income taxes based on how much salary you receive. Unlike a sole proprietor, whose profits land on top of his taxable income, a corporation pays tax separately.

SSENTIALS

One disadvantage of incorporating is the additional corporate taxes that need to be paid. Also, business losses are not deductible by the corporation. For someone who is looking to protect personal assets and attract investors, incorporating can be advantageous. Otherwise it may not be to your benefit. It's worth discussing with your accountant.

It should also be noted that there are different types of corporations. A "C" corporation is most common (and it's what's described earlier). There is also an "S" corporation, which provides some aspects of personal liability protection. However, the profit and loss from the "S" corporation are not federally taxed but are passed through to your own personal income and taxed accordingly.

Often, someone running a small business does not incorporate until the company is seeing significant profits because:

• There are franchise fees and attorney fees to pay.
• You are responsible for filing both corporate and personal tax returns—and this can be time-consuming and costly if you are paying an accountant.

On the other hand, you may choose to incorporate if you:

- Want to keep your business and personal assets as separate as possible to guard against lawsuits or paying higher personal income taxes.
- Are suddenly seeing significant profits as a sole proprietor (you're more likely to be audited if your personal income jumps dramatically because of your new business venture).

You can also form a Limited Liability Corporation (LLC). This is a form of incorporating that provides some of the benefits of limited personal liability. Taxes are passed through to you and profits are paid as part of your personal income tax. An LLC can, when you reach that point, have unlimited stockholders, like a "C" Corporation (an "S" Corporation, on the other hand, is limited). An LLC can be more complex to set up and includes more paperwork.

You should weigh the pros and cons of incorporating, discuss the pros and cons with an accountant, and hire an attorney to guide you through the process. There is no set rule dictating who does and does not need to incorporate. It's a personal decision based on the size, structure, and type of business as well as your personal assets, tax status, and potential for liability.

When deciding to incorporate, you will need to select a state in which to incorporate. Generally it is the state in which you will have physical facilities. You can, however, select another state and qualify to do business as a foreign corporation in your own state. Corporate laws, costs of incorporating, and the state's tax structure will usually be deciding factors. As it turns out, any state in which you qualify to do business, whether you are incorporated or a "foreign corporation" doing business there, makes you subject to that state's tax laws.

In most states, the office to contact for information on registering your corporation will be that of the Secretary of State, found in the state capital. In the District of Columbia, it's the office of Business and Economic Development; in Delaware, Florida, Maine, New Jersey, New York, and Pennsylvania, you should try the State Department; in Maryland, you'll need the Maryland Business Assistance Center in Baltimore; in Massachusetts, you'll need to contact the Secretary of The Commonwealth in Boston; in Oregon you'll go to the Corporation Division in Salem; in Virginia, there's a State Corporation Commission in Richmond. In other words, each state dictates exactly where you will need to go to incorporate. If you're not sure, contact the State Department.

FACTS

Half of the *Fortune* 500 companies in the United States are incorporated in Delaware. There's no corporate tax for companies incorporating in Delaware but doing business elsewhere, a separate court system is headed by judges appointed with corporate law familiarity, and it has one of the lowest costs in the nation to incorporate.

Buying a Business

Whether you're going solo or teaming with a partner, you not only have the option of starting from the ground floor, but you can also buy an existing business. When you buy an existing business, it may not be new at all, but it's still new to you and you will have to maintain the prior success or improve upon it. It's, therefore, very important that you do your research, and find out how well the business is doing and what their reputation is in the industry or community. You need to:

- Find out if there are any outstanding judgments for which you may be liable.
- Review the books carefully with your accountant.
- Review the profit-and-loss statements.
- Determine why the business is being sold.
- Determine what you can do to improve upon the current status of the business.

For example, if it's a radio station you want purchase, you want to know about the sponsors, listenership, licensing situation, and whether they've been sited by the FCC for any wrongdoing. You'll want to see the bottom line sales numbers and determine whether the station is profitable and, if not, whether you can turn it around. Many people make the mistake of looking very carefully at the past track record of a business but do not look at what the future holds. Not unlike investing in a mutual fund or buying a stock, you will use the past success or failures as a guide to what the future holds. You need to remember that the hot company of 2000 wasn't necessarily the hot company of 2001.

If you're buying a business, be sure to have everything properly checked out and inspected so you're aware of any hidden liabilities. The business may come complete with tax payments that are due, an inventory of faulty merchandise, bad wiring, a poor foundation, a technical system that doesn't work, bad plumbing, and so on.

It's important that you investigate the structure of the business, whether it is the foundation of the store or the technical team behind the Web site. You want to know if there are any leaks in the ceiling or viruses in the hard drive. If there is merchandise involved, make sure you determine the condition and freshness of the merchandise. An electronics store selling faulty stereo equipment or a clothing store stocked with last year's fashions is not the best purchase. If you're buying an inventory, or even a mailing list, make sure it is current! (If the heading on the mailing list says "Listings in all 48 states," you know the list is a bit dated.)

If you're opening a storefront or manufacturing business, you are not only buying a business, but a location and the neighborhood that comes with it. It's just like buying a house. You want to be sure to check out the neighborhood carefully.

Finally, you should gather some information on the background of the previous owner and find out why he's selling. Often the current owners have simply taken the business as far as they can—for better or worse. They are either ready to cut their losses, enjoy their retirement money, or move on to a new venture. For the buyer, there are several positive aspects of buying a business including name recognition, existing customers, and an established presence in the industry, the community, or both. As a new owner, you can also start off, in many instances, with established vendor relationships, an inventory, or a staff of knowledgeable employees who are familiar with the way the business has been run.

Of course, for this head start, or foot in the door, you will pay a hefty price. Reviewing the dollar figures carefully will tell you whether you're paying too high a price. What you can do to improve the business will also factor into your buying decision. Determine how long it will take to get returns on the investment you are making.

When you've done thorough research and have determined that you can make a go of the business, you will need to analyze all that is right about your new empire and all that needs to be improved. Make necessary changes, not sweeping changes. Remember, you should have regular clients or customers to start with and you do not want to scare them away. If you understand what it is that they like about the business, then you will maintain those areas. If you can see the shortcomings, then you will make the right improvements.

Although your enthusiasm may tempt you to make major changes immediately after purchasing a new business, it's to your advantage to make gradual changes to maintain your steady customers. It's important that you see how each new idea is received before making more changes.

Buying a Franchise

A franchise is a business that has a contractual relationship with a larger organization (the franchiser) that has already established a well-known product line or service. The franchise is allowed to operate under the franchiser's name and often receives other corporate guidance in exchange for a fee. Many of the most successful business chains, including numerous fast food restaurants, are examples of franchise businesses.

A car dealer is also a franchisee, selling the cars distributed through a franchiser, the carmaker. Therefore, if you open a licensed Toyota dealership, you are selling the cars franchised to you by Toyota. Automobile sales is one common example of setting up a product and trade-name franchise in which you're selling the name-brand product to the consumer. You pay a fee to the carmaker for selling the car, and you earn a commission based on how many you sell.

While some of the most common household names are well-run franchises, others can be quite misleading. Be careful to check out any franchise operation you aren't familiar with, because they may be selling off worthless franchises with no intention of helping you get anywhere.

To your advantage, a franchised product is generally well known through advertising and marketing done by the franchiser. Franchise dealers can also advertise, often with agreements from the franchiser who may foot part of the cost in a cooperative advertising arrangement. For that matter, many franchisers actually maintain ownership of some of their stores or restaurants while franchising out others.

A business-format franchise, in which you buy into a business with all the parts ready to roll, can be costly. However, you would be running a business with the backing of a major company. Also, by starting out with an established brand, popular name, and reputation you will draw customers much faster than you could with a brand-new establishment. Like an instant business, where you just add water, you will be able to get all the equipment, fixtures, and products directly from the company. It's advantageous to have a working system already in place that includes product distribution, signage, and so on. Since a franchise business like Dunkin' Donuts is already known to the public, you can buy raw materials in larger quantities and enjoy a bulk discount. This helps raise your profit margin. In addition, Dunkin' Donuts, McDonalds, or Burger King will do plenty of advertising and promotion, so you won't have to. And finally, they often provide training, a bookkeeping system, and in many cases, financing options.

On the other hand, most franchise businesses have very firm guidelines about how they are to be structured and run, so you don't have much flexibility to do things your way in your business. You are the owner of your franchise, but you have to play by the company rules. This is advantageous in that the company and its rules can help you, but it's limiting if you have ideas that you think might work better. It's a tradeoff: You get a name business with customers at the ready, but you don't have a great deal of control when it comes to the decision-making process. In addition, franchises may ask for initial investments of upwards of $300,000 and often more. On top of that, you may be required to pay a percentage of what you sell and be at the mercy of the franchiser if they decide to shut down your location.

QUESTIONS?

Do I need to hire an attorney?
Yes, read a franchise agreement very carefully with your attorney's help. Keep in mind, that while a franchiser may require you to sign a ten-year deal, it can often end that franchise agreement abruptly if you're not meeting the franchise's expectations. You want to know what's expected of you going in.

For more franchise information, you should check with the International Franchise Association (IFA) at 800-543-1038 or *www.franchise.org.*

CHAPTER 5

Writing a Business Plan

Buildings have blueprints, teachers have lesson plans, ball clubs have game plans, and projects have network diagrams. Like so many other endeavors, businesses need a plan of action. Whether it's a simple two-page outline for your own dog-walking business or a comprehensive forty-page plan for an international children's clothing manufacturing company, you should have a business plan.

Business Plans 101

More than just a package to draw interest from investors, a business plan sets the foundation from which you will build your business. You will use it as an outline to guide you and to help you make sure each area is covered and each goal is met. The plan will help you make sure you stay on track and not lose your focus. According to Andy Sernovitz, teacher of entrepreneurship and founder and CEO of Gas Pedal Ventures, a company that specializes in helping companies start out and grow to become more profitable, "Most businesses that fail do so because they lose the original focus." Andy stresses the importance of covering all key areas and notes that marketing is one of the most frequently neglected areas of concern.

A good business plan will not only keep you on track, but like a good outline for a screenplay or novel, it will allow you to put your thoughts and ideas on paper, and manipulate them until they are just right. You will then expand upon them as the business takes shape. When it's completed, the business plan will, like a good mystery, answer all the pertinent questions and tie up all the loose ends, which in your case will be the details that are part and parcel to running a successful business.

While business plans will differ depending on the structure and the type of business, many of the principles remain the same. Commonly found in a business plan are:

- The overall vision of the business.
- The goals and objectives.
- An overview of the industry.
- The company and executive summary.
- Market information and analysis.
- Comprehensive description of the product and/or services.
- Marketing plans and strategies.
- Overview of the competition.
- Financial plan and information, including projected income figures.
- Overview of key personnel.

The degree of details and the manner in which the plan is written will vary from industry to industry or business to business. Plans will include other information depending on what is necessary to tell the overall story of how the business will be formed and evolve into a profitable entity. Furthermore, the business plan will demonstrate how your business will move forward once you have opened your doors or launched. Projected one-, three-, five-, and ten-year sales figures will help you illustrate the anticipated results of your plan.

Many business owners don't write their business plan from beginning to end, but start with areas in which they feel most comfortable. In other words, they may write the marketing section first. The executive summary, which comes near the beginning, is often written at the end.

Getting Ready

Writing a business plan may sound like a daunting task at first. However, if you take it step by step, you won't be intimidated by the thought of creating this important document. It's important to realize before you begin, that you will have to revise the plan as you go to incorporate new ideas. As you show portions of the plan to other people for feedback, you will be able to assess what's missing or unclear. Then you'll return to the plan and make revisions. So don't sweat over every word you put on paper—numerous changes will be made down the road.

Since thousands, if not millions of business plans have preceded yours, you don't need to reinvent the wheel. You should look at sample business plans (see Appendix A) and get a general idea of how other plans have been put together. Look at plans for businesses closest to yours so that you can get a general idea of what you're looking to accomplish in your business plan. These plans may be more detailed than what you will need for many smaller businesses, but they will give you an idea of the different types of information that can be included. Remember, the best plan is not the one with the most jargon, most pages, or most use of the words *network, leverage,* or *equity.* The best business plan is one that clearly paints the picture of your business and demonstrates how and why it will be successful.

Neatness also counts. While it probably won't make or break a business deal, it is certainly to your advantage to have a professional-looking business plan, complete with cover page and binding. You should also make sure you have proofread and edited the document. Graphs, charts, and even illustrations or photos can enhance a presentation if you're looking for backers. Don't use them, however, just to fill up extra space.

Remember, a business plan doesn't have to be a certain number of pages long or include a certain number of graphs and charts (keep in mind, however, that people will not be as quick to read a seventy-page plan as they will be to read a twenty-five-page one). If you don't need to get investors, and the plan is for yourself and your partners, you may be less formal. Either way, don't cut corners. Include all the pertinent information. You'll be glad you did when you refer back to the plan.

Remember, far too many businesses fail each year because they were missing a key element or two (or several) that would have been there if they had taken the time to put together a sound business plan. Just like you shouldn't set forth on your vacation without any directions detailing where you will be going, you shouldn't start a business without some type of business plan.

If you say you'll be profitable soon, specify when and how you will get there. If you say you'll be receiving outside shipments of materials, explain from whom and when they will arrive. Don't be vague or ambiguous. Fill in the answers and substantiate your statements with facts.

A Step-by-Step Guide

Writing a business plan can be an intimidating task. But it doesn't have to be if you take it one step at a time. In the following sections, you'll find all the information you need to write a plan that tells the world what your business is about and why it will succeed.

FACTS

One of the best places to look for sample business plans is *www.bplan.com*. This Web site offers numerous business plans for a wide range of industries. So if you'd like to see what other people have done for inspiration, you can check out plans that will be similar to what yours should look like.

Title or Cover Page

This is the first page anyone looking at your business plan will see, and you know what they say about first impressions. You want to clearly include the name of the company, and perhaps a tagline that will be associated with the company, such as the United Airlines tagline "Fly the Friendly Skies." Don't force yourself to think of a tagline—it's not essential. Let one come to you or your advertising manager. A logo is also nice to include if you have one. Again, don't force yourself to have it if you don't.

It's important that you include all contact information. When creating the cover page, remember that less is more. This page doesn't need to have very much on it. Also keep in mind that first impressions say a lot. With that in mind you might use a more elegant typeface for a more upscale business or a more cutting-edge logo for a company appealing to a young audience.

Table of Contents

A table of contents (TOC) provides an easy way to find key information. In the TOC, you simply present an organized overview of what's included within the business plan. It lets readers go back and find each subject without having to look through the entire plan time and time again. Keep it simple and straightforward.

Your table of contents should not exceed one page. On your initial drafts, you should expect that as you proceed through the plan you'll go back several times to make changes and additions and even delete certain areas, and the page numbers will change accordingly.

Since business plans are not boilerplates of one another (they simply follow similar guidelines), there is no definitive right or wrong way in which to draw one up. Therefore, your table of contents may look different than that of another business. For example one company may have sections 1, 2, 3, 4, and so on, while another may divide each section into subsections with 1, 1a, 1b, 2, 2a, 2b, 2c, and so on.

Executive Summary

The executive summary is the single most important section of the business plan. Generally, it's written last to ensure that you have covered all the areas in your plan. It appears up front, to provide the readers with a concise overview of the business.

In one or two pages, your executive summary should include a description of the products or services offered and what makes your business distinctive. It's important that you discuss your target audience, costs, objectives, marketing plans, and financial projections. The executive summary should express your confidence in the future success of the business and make potential investors want to read more. Don't be afraid to do several rewrites.

Establish a foundation for your business. Point out the current climate and explain what it is that you will offer. For example, you could say, "Last year over 2 million college students traveled during spring or summer vacation," or "According to statistics from XYZ Source, the divorce rate in the United States is over 5 percent." Then explain how this fact or figure opens the door for your business to step in and solve a problem, provide a service, or simply make life simpler for these individuals, your target audience. For example, "Student Discount Tours will offer these students up to 50 percent off on vacations to any U.S. or European destination."

Include your strongest selling point. You may have an ideal location. You may be the first to do something, or the first to do it in a specific way. You may provide a unique service. For example, "GasPedal Ventures is the first Internet Business Accelerator—a next-generation incubator that creates valuable Internet companies, in quantity, by providing startup companies with rapid access to high-level players and by eliminating operational risks." Think concise. If you can say it in fifteen words rather than twenty-five, do it.

Industry Analysis

In this section you present your business in conjunction with the overall industry in which it falls. Here, you take a step back and look at the big picture, the industry as it currently stands and the projected future developments. You will need to do your share of research before putting this part of the plan together. It is important, however, to make note of the size and growth rate of the overall industry. For example, if your business would be part of a $20 billion dollar industry that in the next ten years is expected to grow to over $100 billion dollars, then you would want to include that information.

You can use charts, graphs, or simply text to explain the sales trends culled from your research. Discuss changes in the industry and industry news that will provide your business with an entry point into the market. Also, clearly illustrate the market in your area or region, which could be Baby Boomers in a small town or young executives worldwide. Then tie-in your business with the marketing demands and trends.

For example, if new regional trains will make it faster and easier for commuters to get to work in your city, then there will be an increase in train travel. If this is coupled with a growing need in the region for moderately priced health club facilities, then your company, which designs Riding-the-Rail to Fitness workout equipment for trains, will be on the cutting edge. You will then need to explain how your service will allow commuters to workout while on their way to and from the office, thus better utilizing their time. Of course, you'll need to do market research to determine whether or not people agree with your idea. If 75 percent of the people you survey would prefer to read on the train, then you might not have a feasible business idea.

The end result of the industry analysis should demonstrate why your business will be able to take a piece of the pie. This is important for you, as a future entrepreneur to see very clearly. If you don't have a potential market share, you'll have trouble selling others on what will make your company successful.

Business Overview

This section is also known as the Business Description, Company Overview, Company Plan, or Company Summary. No matter what it's called, this is the place where you can elaborate with a comprehensive description of your plans (within a few pages). Start off with the goals of the business and proceed to explain the legal structure (a sole proprietorship, partnership, corporation, etc.), the resources needed to run the business, the location, the anticipated time until you will be open for business, methods of record keeping, and how the business will operate. You can include who the owners are (or list this in a separate section under Management Team), how they plan to run the business, and perhaps even how this business idea came to fruition. You may also choose to include information on:

- How the business will generate customers.
- Where your database comes from and how you plan to target these customers.
- Which areas you've conducted market research in and how those areas relate to your business.
- The key players that have teamed up to form this company

Use the top five or six key selling points that best describe your company and don't forget to substantiate them with supporting details.

Products and Services

Sometimes this section is incorporated into the business overview. However, you may have a separate page, or a couple of pages, included to describe what you're selling, offering, or manufacturing.

In a business environment, where new innovative products (especially technical ones) and unique services appear almost daily, it's to your benefit to make sure everyone knows exactly what your product or services are all about. What are you selling or offering and why is it better than what's currently on the market? If it's automobile tires, people will generally know how they work, but if you're using a new type of technology for safety purposes or designing the tires in an innovative new way, then you'll need to explain these new features of the product.

Explain your product in succinct, easy-to-understand language. This is not a place to dazzle the reader with high-tech lingo. This is also very good practice for marketing the product or service. If you can explain it clearly in your business plan, you'll have a prototype for future marketing literature that must be discernable to all potential customers.

You should also explain where the product comes from—where you're buying it from or how you're assembling the parts. You can also mention an original creation or patented invention. If you have plans for upcoming products and services, this is also the place to include them with brief explanations of each.

Marketing Plan

The marketing plan is an important aspect of your overall business plan and one that you will need to pay strict attention to. You can have the best product or offer the most useful service in the world, but if you don't spread the word, you won't be successful.

FACTS

You can hire media planners who can provide you with expert advice on where to position your business in the media. This may cost you some money, so you may opt to do this after you are up and running.

In this section, you need to explain who your target market is. Describe this market and why they would pay for your product or services. Most successful businesses are geared to reach a specific market. The size of the market will depend on the nature of the product. Mass marketing to everyone is generally reserved only for major corporations with plenty of money. Keep in mind that if you try to reach too large an audience, you may run into financial trouble and be unable to serve the customers you attract. If you can only accommodate ten customers and fifty show up, you'll be at your peak capacity (with the ten customers) and you'll lose forty potential customers as well. You should also avoid having such a specific, narrow audience that you don't have enough potential customers to make your business profitable.

Next, you will proceed into a market description and analysis. Gather as much information as possible to support why this demographic group will be interested in your product or services.

Finally, you will need to explain how you intend to capture a portion of that market. Detail the methods and media you will utilize to market your business. Will you use direct mail? A radio and television advertising campaign? The Internet? Are you seeking subscribers? Membership? You then need to incorporate how much money you will spend on publicity and advertising. It's very important to justify your marketing plan and show others (and remind yourself) that you aren't throwing money away on a poor marketing strategy. Also, include partnerships you anticipate forming and any strategic alliances.

If you have contacts or relationships with publicists that can help you get your name in the media or discounts on advertising, this is the place to let it be known. It's also important that you list all prices and make it clear where the product will be distributed or the services will be rendered. Also, list your promotional ideas including any special promotional events, giveaways, contests, or anything else that will hype your new business. In addition, if you're looking to create a specific image (which may take some time and effort) you should also include information on that.

A marketing plan takes a great deal of time and careful consideration. It should be the culmination of researching industry trends, your target market, and a careful evaluation of the proper media choices for getting your message to your target audience. Be realistic in your projected marketing plans.

Competitive Analysis

This is the section where you discuss the competition. You'll need to do some investigative research so that you can adequately describe these businesses. You want to discuss how their business operates, their location, products, share of the market, and anything else you think is pertinent—all in a concise form. You may need to visit competitors' stores or sample products of competing manufacturers.

Your next step is to describe and make comparisons to your business and explain how you will improve upon the products and services offered by your competitors. Study what the market wants and show how you can provide solutions in a better way. If you can show that you will draw customers based on what you're offering (whether it's service, products, location, or anything else), then you can gain the upper hand.

While you aren't trying to denigrate other businesses, you're simply trying to separate what you do from what's being done by others. Let people know that you're prepared to carve out your own segment of the market and how you propose to do so.

Operations Plan

This section (sometimes included in the business overview) explains how the business actually works. Who does what and how and where do they do it? Who is responsible for each aspect of the business? Describe how products are manufactured, how the store will be set up or how your service-oriented business will operate. For example, will people be looking at different categories of merchandise on your home page with options to click to nine other pages of merchandise? Will customers be ordering pizza at the front counter with a choice of sitting down to eat in the dining room or at a front counter? What will they encounter first when they enter your spa? Who will greet them and what will they have as options to choose from? What will your business-to-business advisors do first upon visiting a new client's business? Will they do an overall evaluation of the business?

ESSENTIALS

It's very important to include plans for expansion in your business plan. Expansion can be a traumatic time for any business, since the results can be either profitable or disastrous. Investors and others will want to know that you've thought this out carefully and be able to read how and when you plan to expand.

Each business has specific methods by which it's run. Guide the reader through the process from preparing the food or stocking the shelves to the customer or client paying for the service. Will customers be billed in thirty days for their personal makeover, or is there a register in the main lobby as you leave the spa? Perhaps there will be both options for different levels of service. This is the place to explain the program in any manner—from a couple of brief paragraphs to several detailed pages.

Management Team

Here you will list the key players with short bios and what they bring to the table. For businesses seeking capital this is more significant since the potential venture capitalists want to know who it is they're lending money to.

One or two paragraphs should be sufficient to sum up the qualifications and overall background of each key person involved. Don't get into philosophies or include extraneous material. Bios should be short and sweet. Include pictures if you like. You might also mention the board of directors or advisors and include their backgrounds, because they're definitely pertinent to this business endeavor.

Financial Plan

Show them the money. This is where you will need to include all key financial information from startup costs to balance sheets. This section demonstrates what will make your business profitable. It includes all the charts and graphs necessary to illustrate your points, but most significantly it follows a logical trend and tells your financial story, not unlike an annual report provides more than just the numbers. There's nothing wrong with asking your accountant or any qualified financial expert to help you put this part of the plan together.

You'll want to clearly show how much money you're seeking and then explain exactly how you plan to spend it. Marketing? Sales reps? Technology? Make sure it's all spelled out. All expenditures need to be justified—starting with your startup costs.

You then need to explain where your profits will come from. Be realistic. Don't fantasize. Include the next three, five, seven, and possibly even ten years in a profit-and-loss income statement. Break it up by months at first to show how you plan to build the business, and then break it up by years. Include your:

- Break-even analysis
- Balance sheet
- Projected profit-and-loss statement
- Projected cash flow (you need to illustrate that you will *not* run out of cash)

Just as you want to show your projected expenses, assets, and liabilities when starting a new business, you should include previous financial statements of the past three to five years if you're buying an existing business. No matter how brilliant your idea is, if the numbers don't add up, your business will not succeed. The bottom line is just that—the bottom line.

FACTS

Among other key financial indicators, a business plan should include projected sales, operating expenses, and profit margin. You will also want to set benchmarks as indicators so you will know when you reach milestones of some of your projected goals.

Reviewing Your Plan

You will need to review the your business plan carefully. Make sure you've included all key points, the business plan reads clearly, all spelling and grammar is checked and edited, all graphs and charts are easy to read, and the plan is printed on high-quality paper, bound, and has a professional appearance.

A business plan usually runs from twenty to thirty-five or even forty pages in length. Print is double-spaced and there is enough white space (margins) on the page so that nothing looks bunched together. Make sure pages are numbered. Go back to your table of contents and add the numbers (along with correct section names and subsections if you have them).

Attach any supporting documents that you have in an appendix. This could include any research material, articles, graphics, product illustrations, or other data that you might want to attach. Keep the supporting documents to a few pages.

Business plans vary in their style and manner. Some have subsections throughout the plan, while others paint broader strokes. There are numerous variations on the main theme, but the business plan should include, in some manner, the elements discussed in this chapter. Read the business plan in Appendix A, and then do a rough outline of your own. Don't worry about the writing, just do your best to express your ideas and explain your business. Once you have filled in the rough business plan, start sculpting it as you think through and plan out each aspect of your business. Remember, the business plan needs to be a realistic portrait of your business and not an abstract design. If the pieces don't fit together or the numbers don't add up, not only will the plan not work, but neither will the business.

ALERT

Once your business is up and running, you should keep your business plan around because it can help you monitor your progress. It can tell you if you're reaching projected sales figures, maintaining cost figures, doing the marketing you intended to do, or reaching your initial goals.

CHAPTER 6

Regulations and Legal Matters

Determining your business structure is only part of the process when it comes to getting your business started. You also need to file the appropriate paperwork and protect your ideas and company name. This chapter takes a look at some of the preliminary and ongoing paperwork that are part of running a business.

Licensing and Regulations

Financial brokers, insurance brokers, doctors, dentists, veterinarians, attorneys, pharmacists, and certified public accountants are among the professionals who are required to have a license. Likewise, many companies are also required to be licensed in order to conduct their business. From federal to local requirements, it's up to you to contact either the town hall, the records bureau, the Secretary of State, the Department of Consumer Affairs, or any other governing bodies that will inform you of which licenses you need to conduct business. The Small Business Administration (SBA) can also help. Go to *www.sba.gov/hotlist/license.html* for a state-by-state list of Web sites with licensing information.

In most cases, business licenses are not costly, but they can make the difference between staying in business or being shut down—and even a temporary shutdown can cost you a lot in revenues. Certain cities make it clear that you must have a business license. For example, any business of any type in the city of Chicago will need some sort of business license. There are nearly 200 different types of such licenses in Chicago, and your business will certainly fall under one heading if not several. So if you're starting up a business in Chicago, make a visit to City Hall.

Along with having a state or county license, you'll need to address other responsibilities that come with owning a business. Businesses selling or preparing food, including vendors, will need special licenses and/or permits and will have to follow the codes set forth by the Health Department. Outdoor cooking or selling of potentially flammable objects will be closely watched by the Fire Department and you will need to adhere to their local ordinances. The local Sanitation Bureau and various other departments may have regulations that you'll need to comply with—or risk facing fines or even being shut down. The local Chamber of Commerce is a good place to inquire about such local regulations.

Other businesses need to know and adhere to federal regulations, such as radio stations, which need to follow the Federal Communications Commission (FCC) rules. The Internet has presented many gray areas in regard to many of the more standard regulations set forth by governing bodies such as the FCC and Food and Drug Administration (FDA). Thus far, however, it has been very hard to impose restrictions on the Internet because Web sites are based in different states and different countries and can, therefore, cross national and international boundaries. For example, you cannot open up an online casino based in most of the United States. However, if you're outside the United States and open up a casino, U.S. citizens can play for real money online.

The best you can do is to be aware of all regulations and licenses necessary for your profession, your business, and your community. Here's a to-do list for licensing:

- Obtain any and all required federal licensing.
- Obtain any and all required state licensing.
- Obtain any and all local licensing.
- Familiarize yourself with all zoning ordinances and local regulations.
- Make sure you list the dates all licenses must be renewed in a place where you will look in one, two, or five years.
- Post all licenses that require posting, and put all others in a safe place.

SSENTIALS

Except for marriage licenses, most licenses have expiration dates. Don't forget to make note of when you need to come back and renew your business license and what the process entails. That way you won't be scrambling around at the last minute trying to find what you need to get your license renewed.

Inspections

The Fire Department and Health Department are among several agencies that can inspect your business. Code violations can be a fine the first time around, but can become increasingly steep for repeat offenders. Certain businesses, particularly those involving food, plants, or chemicals can expect more frequent inspections. This doesn't mean that other businesses can assume they are exempt from fire, health, or other similar violations, of course.

FACTS

Many states require you to have sellers permits to sell tangible goods in that state. In other states, such as New York, make sure you have proper sales tax forms filed and pay accordingly. Just make sure you know what's required where you live.

Zoning Ordinances

It's no coincidence that all the fast food chains are in one area of town and none are situated amongst a row of private homes on the lake. More than just not wanting to ruin a lovely view, communities enact zoning laws to maintain the structure, property values, and way of life their neighborhood is accustomed to. Zoning laws are primarily designed to separate commercial and residential areas. However, there's often much more to it than that. Zoning laws may also guard against a business opening up that is too noisy, smelly, rowdy, or uses hazardous materials or promotes or sells materials unsuitable for minors.

Beyond the ordinances about which kind of business may or may not open in a certain area, there may be other restrictions. For example, signage may be limited to a certain size or advertisements may be required to be approved.

It's usually fairly easy to get a basic idea of the general zoning laws in a specific neighborhood by simply driving around. A fast food restaurant may not be found on the main commercial street of a residential neighborhood. A topless bar will not be down the block from a school. A bar won't pop up on a quiet residential street.

Even a home-based business can be subject to zoning requirements. If you are anticipating a steady flow of clients to and from your home or have commercial vehicles making deliveries, your neighbors may have a surprise for you in the form of a zoning restriction.

Check out all local zoning ordinances before you set up shop. Some will actually surprise you, while others are those that you would expect. The county clerk, community planning board, or even city hall are places to go for more information.

Leases

Once you find a location that suits you, you'll need to have your lawyer carefully review the lease. You need to know exactly what is expected of you and what you're entitled to expect in return from your landlord.

Keep in mind that just because someone offers you a lease doesn't mean you can run your type of business from that location. Check the zoning restrictions before signing the lease. Conversely, just because the zoning ordinance says you can run a certain type of business in an area doesn't mean the landlord wants you running the business in her building. Landlords don't want a business that will cause their other paying tenants headaches or jeopardize their standing in the community or their ability to maintain a high rental price for neighboring stores or office space.

When looking at a lease, find out if you can sublease the space. This way, if business doesn't grow as quickly as you anticipate, you can fill those empty offices temporarily. You also need to determine the cost of utilities and what other payments will be incurred. Make sure you cover all your bases so you aren't left with any surprise monthly charges.

Fictitious Name Forms

If you choose to run your business under any name other than your own, you will have to file a Fictitious Name or Doing Business As (DBA) Certificate in the county where the business is being conducted (usually at the County Clerk's office). This form indicates that your business is being run under a specific name. Prior to filing the form and paying the fee, you'll need to do a name search to make sure the name isn't already being used by another business. The wider the scope of the business the broader the name search will have to be and the costlier it may become. A local business named Silver Star Cleaners doesn't need to worry about finding another Silver Star Cleaners three states away. But if you're doing business under the name in several states, you will want to do a name search in each of those states.

 Before searching for any name, be it for fictitious name purposes or to incorporate, it's advantageous to think of several names that you might select. This way you can save yourself time and even money by doing a search for several names at once.

Trademarks, Patents, and Copyrights

Incorporating will protect you against another company incorporating under the same business name, but what about your brilliant invention or original work? If it's your business, your creation, or your original idea, you'll want to protect it from being used by another business. The three most common forms of protection for entrepreneurs are trademarks, patents, and copyrights.

Trademarks

A trademark can be a name (one word or several), logo, symbol, design, slogan, series of words, or combination thereof that makes your product or service uniquely distinguishable from others. Companies look for trademarks to help protect the image and brand name presence that they are trying to establish. For example, the name *Pepsi* is a trademark name, as is the phrase *You deserve a break today.* If you're looking to build a nationally known brand or company identity you should consider registering your name or slogan as a trademark.

You can apply for a trademark if you use or have a bona fide intention to use the trademark for commerce that can be regulated by the U.S. Congress. You can obtain an application from, and file it with, the United States Patent and Trademark Office (*www.uspto.gov* or 703-308-9000). Trademarks are good for ten years plus another ten years on renewal terms. Applications need to include the name and address of the person or business filing, a clear representation of that which is to be trademarked, and a list of goods and services. There is also a filing fee.

After the fifth year of having a trademark you will be asked to file an affidavit to keep the trademark active. Don't neglect this or you could lose the trademark. And not only will you have to go through the process all over again, but someone else may snatch up the trademark before you do.

Patents

If you create or invent an original product you might want to patent it. A patent protects the thing you've created from being pirated and created and/or sold by someone else. Not unlike a trademark search or a title search, you'll need to conduct a patent search, which will let you know if your very own original invention has already been invented and patented elsewhere.

You can conduct a patent search at the U.S. Patent and Trademark Office in Washington D.C. or at one of the nation's Patent and Trademark Depository Libraries located in cities all across the country. For information on patents and the locations of these key libraries, go to the Web site for the United States Patent and Trademark Office (USPTO) at *www.uspto.gov.* It may be in your best interest to have an attorney look over and help you fill out your application.

There are several types of patents you can apply for including a utility, design, plant, or international patent. There is also a non-provisional patent that is only good for one year but allows you to obtain a patent more quickly. If you think others may be developing a similar product and you want to beat them to the punch, you could get a non-provisional patent first and then a provisional patent. You must, however, also apply for a provisional patent when you apply for the non-provisional patent. Provisional patents for new products are good for twenty years, except for design patents, which are for fourteen years.

Copyrights

While trademarks protect a name and your image and patents protect tangible products (not ideas), you can protect creative works such as artwork, music, books, brochures, advertisements, and computer software programs with a *copyright*. The U.S. Library of Congress handles copyrights. For $20 you can obtain a copyright by filing the proper application. Go to *www.lcweb.loc.gov* and click on Copyright for more information and application forms. Or write to Copyright Office, Library of Congress, Washington, D.C. 20559. Copyrights are good for up to fifty years after the person who has registered is dead.

Screenwriters and even authors can also obtain protection from the Writer's Guild East or West by following their submission guidelines. You do not have to be a member to register a property with the guild. Go to *www.wga.org* and click on script registration or call the registration department at 323-782-4500. The guild dates and seals a copy of the work in an envelope, which you sign for, and it locks it away in their files. You hold a claim ticket and can use it to open the file in the event of an infringement upon your work.

FACTS

Go to *www.dumblaws.com* for a reminder of the silliness of some laws. For instance, in Waterbury, Connecticut, it's illegal for a beautician to hum, whistle, or sing while working on a customer. In Longmeadow, Massachusetts, it's illegal for two men to carry a bathtub across the town green. And in Harper Woods, Michigan, it's illegal to paint sparrows to sell them as parakeets.

Agencies, Agreements, and Regulations

There are numerous agencies governing various aspects of business—from foreign trade to communications to child labor laws. It's to your advantage to know about such agencies to find answers to your questions and concerns regarding policies, laws, and regulations. The U.S. Business Advisor Web site, at *www.business.gov*, under their laws and regulations section, links to sixty different federal organizations that are designed to assist you with such business needs and concerns. The U.S. Business Advisor was created by the Small Business Administration (SBA), the

National Partnership for Reinventing Government (NPR), and the U.S. Business Advisor interagency task force.

Whether you locate the agency you need through the U.S. Business Advisor Web site or in another manner, it's important to remember they're out there to help you. They also have subdivisions and online research sections that can be of service. The agencies with which you may need to be involved while running your business include:

- Environmental Protection Agency, *www.epa.gov*
- Federal Aviation Administration, *www.faa.gov*
- Federal Railroad Administration, *www.fra.dot.gov*
- Federal Trade Commission, *www.ftc.gov*
- Federal Transit Administration, *www.fta.dot.gov*
- Immigration and Naturalization Service, *www.ins.gov*
- International Trade Administration, *www.ita.doc.gov*
- Maritime Administration, *www.marad.dot.gov*
- U.S. Consumer Product Safety Commission, *www.cpsc.gov*
- U.S. Customs Service, *www.customs.ustreas.gov*
- U.S. Department of Commerce, *www.doc.gov*
- U.S. Department of Health and Human Services: Food and Drug Administration, *www.fda.gov*
- U.S. Department of Labor, *www.dol.gov*
- U.S. Patent and Trademark Office, *www.uspto.gov*

Look for more listings of government organizations, associations, and Web sites in Appendix B.

FACTS

Many companies do work with or for government agencies. To work with the government you should register your business with the SBA's PRO-Net at *www.pro-net.sba.gov*, which has a database of thousands of businesses interested in working with the government. You can also call 202-205-6460 for more information and to request a guide called *Selling to the Government*.

CHAPTER 7

Location, Location, Location

While the world has shrunk through technology and the Internet, it is still important to be in the right place if you expect walk-in or drive-up customers. Although office-based businesses and manufacturing facilities are less often dependent on drawing customers, they also need to be in the right location for a variety of reasons. Web businesses need a Web presence or location that will pop up in Internet searches.

Finding Space

Commercial realtors, advertisements in local papers, and word of mouth are three key ways in which you can find a space for your business. However, before checking out an office or retail space, it's important that you know the needs of your business. Among the questions to ask yourself are:

- How much space does my business require?
- How far away from home do I want to work?
- Do I need to be in the heart of town or can I be in a low-traffic area?
- Will I be able to get there by car or mass transportation?
- How much can I afford to spend for renting or buying?
- Can I share a location or start out working from home?
- How much equipment will need to be in my space, and can my space physically accommodate such equipment?
- How much fixing up and/or renovating am I willing to have done?
- Will suppliers, vendors, distributors, clients, or customers be able to easily get to this location?
- Will the location be able to meet the technical needs of the business?
- What kind of storage space will I need?

You probably have a mental picture of where you see your business located. You know approximately the size of the store or office that will meet your current needs. However, with any luck at all, your business will grow in volume. So you may also want to consider the need to seek more space than you will presently require. Can you find and afford a space slightly larger than you need at present? Can you make use of the additional space or rent it out to another young entrepreneur?

SSENTIALS

Know the demographics of the area before you even considering settling there with your business. A children's shoe store will do poorly in a community of seniors, and a Christmas ornament store will strike out in a Jewish neighborhood. Know the neighborhood!

Most often when searching for a place in which to do business, your options are limited and you have to roll up your sleeves and make the place fit your needs. Remember, you can add paint, put in new windows, and have the wiring inspected and even redone, but you cannot turn miracles. You'll have to say no to certain marginally acceptable locations, even if it means continuing your location search a little longer.

Storefront Businesses

A retail store has special needs, the most important of which is high visibility. The business needs to both fit in and stand out all at once. By fitting in, you want to blend in with the businesses of the neighborhood. An upscale store won't thrive in a poor section of town, while an auto parts store may not fit well on a quaint commercial street with boutiques and restaurants. You also want to stand out in some manner so that people passing by will stop and look.

There are many factors influencing your decision when it comes to opening a store or restaurant including the following:

- Neighborhood competition
- Need for your type of business
- Traffic—both foot and vehicular
- Accessibility of parking
- Storage of merchandise
- Shipping and loading areas
- Regulations regarding garbage pickup, deliveries, snow removal, etc.
- Utilities, including power, water, and gas
- Office and support space
- Heating and air-conditioning systems
- Restroom facilities
- Front window size and signage
- Rental costs and lease terms

These are just some of the key concerns. You'll need to gather up all the information possible and see if you feel that your business will thrive in this location. The roads, off-ramps, and accessibility will play a vital part in your decision process as well. A restaurant that can be seen from the main road but is not accessible unless you turn onto a side road may lose a significant amount of customers who drive past it not realizing they had to make a turn onto the smaller road. The next restaurant on the main road is then the beneficiary of your lost business.

Often a retail business will be at home in a shopping center in which you're one of several businesses and your location comes with built-in accessibility from the main road, plus plenty of parking. You can benefit from other stores and businesses, such as a movie theater that draws customers to that particular shopping mall. Another benefit of a shopping center is security. Often there are security guards for the center or a system already in place that you can utilize.

Sometimes it's difficult to get a location in a shopping center or mall, because they're booked in advance. Often the developers are looking to rent to name franchises or businesses with which they are already familiar. Another drawback is conforming to the rules of the center or mall, which may limit the size of your signs or style of your window displays. You may also have to operate on their daily or hourly schedule.

ALERT

While shopping malls can be terrific places to open a retail business, you must also watch out that your lease doesn't include numerous additional fees. Being part of a common retail location, you may be asked to pay for landscaping, public rest areas, repairs made to the mall itself, parking, and so on.

There are many intangibles and they are all worth checking out when it comes to a retail business or restaurant. Location is always a key factor in your potential success or failure—whether you're selling goods or offering a service, such as hair styling or manicures. Service businesses can often do with less storage space and may have fewer concerns regarding shipping and loading docks.

You might, for example, check with the local Chamber of Commerce and see what kind of reception you get with your news of looking to open your business in the town. Some towns and communities will welcome a new business such as your with open arms. Others are overcrowded and don't want the additional traffic problems, competition, or possibility of attracting what they perceive as "the wrong element," in their (often misguided) opinion. Get a feeling for the people who make the laws and dictate business decisions in the community.

It is advisable to talk with the owners of neighboring shops and restaurants. Will your businesses help draw customers to one another, or are you the enemy? You might also check out the media regarding local advertising rates.

Another important aspect of opening such a business is determining whether you will be able to hire a staff at affordable rates. This will depend on the skills needed to run your particular business. If you can survive with part-timers and college help and are in a town with a young population, you may be just fine. However, if you need a more highly trained level of employee, or individuals with more advanced technical skills, then you'll have to consider whether such employees can be found in the neighborhood where you're considering starting up your business. Run an ad in a local paper and see what kind of responses you get. Also see how much you'll need to pay. Different areas have different wage expectations.

The best retail location is the one that people can find easily, draws walk-in customers, and is easily accessible by car or public transportation (depending on whether you're in a rural or urban area). It's a location where your business can grow thanks to a supportive business community, little direct competition, and a strong demographic base for your products. It's also an area where you feel safe and can attract the high level of experienced personnel you're seeking.

Certain counties or communities still have blue laws regulating the days in which a store may be open. You may be required to be closed on Sundays. Check such local ordinances before opening up your store.

Office Space

Unlike a retail business where drive-by and walk-in customers are essential, an office does not usually need to worry about high visibility. Nonetheless, many of the other concerns about finding a space for your business are the same. You still need to consider utilities, security, rental costs, and how far away the office will be from where you live. Parking is still an issue, although not as consequential, unless you're starting off big. And indoor appearance will generally be more important than outdoor appearance, unless of course the building looks like it's about to collapse and you have clients visiting often.

Much of your business needs will depend on the type of business you're starting. Obviously, you'll put more care into the look of the place and how desirable the location is if you plan to have clients or customers visiting the office. If the business is strictly mail order, and only yourself and a handful of coworkers will be there, the place need not look as refined. Among the common needs and concerns of those looking for office space are:

- Communications and technology capabilities
- Size to meet your needs
- Potential for expansion on the premises
- A lease that has no hidden fees and allows you to rent out space
- Accessibility
- Security
- Heating/air conditioning
- Lunch, lounge, and restroom facilities
- Landscaping and appearance

Some businesses want an impressive address in Beverly Hills, on Wall Street, or in other noteworthy sections of large cities. Many business owners look for the right tone and atmosphere that will enhance productivity from their employees. Most want to know that food can be found nearby. Daycare facilities, health clubs, and other factors are growing concerns for entrepreneurs. The more a facility or area can offer your employees, the more attractive it will be to the highly skilled individuals you are looking to attract. Office parks often offer a host of facilities in a secure setting. They are also hard to get into, since they are custom built for such office-based businesses and highly sought out.

Executive suites, in which businesses share some of the administrative and other support, such as one mailroom or one central reception area, are also common. They can be advantageous if you're sharing with the right business owners. Make sure you feel comfortable and get all the rules and regulations set forth in this type of co-op arrangement before joining. It can save you money.

For a more temporary environment in which to grow, you might lease short-term space from another company that is perhaps slightly larger than your business and has some room to spare. This can prove advantageous if they provide some of the essentials, such as security for the whole office space, a common eating area, and even some technical assistance. You may, however, be asked to chip in on repairs to the air conditioning system or other aspects of the overall space. Cover all the details when you sit down and meet with the owners of the space. Also make sure you know what it takes to get out of the lease. Most offices are chosen because they:

- Handle the size and needs of the specific business.
- Provide a comfortable atmosphere for employees and reception area for clients and guests.
- Are convenient for the owners and staff.
- Meet safety and security requirements.

If you're going to spend forty or more hours a week at the office, choose something that makes you feel good about yourself and your business. An office should have some character and represent the image you're trying to project with your company. Perhaps that's why you'll see mahogany in corporate law offices and modular furnishings in trendy, cutting-edge advertising agencies.

Talk with other tenants about how the building is managed before committing to a lease. Find out what they have to say about service and security issues. Also find out how often the rents have been raised.

Manufacturing Space

If you need to set up a full-fledged factory, you'll need plenty of space, parking for the employees, and a location that can accommodate shipping in a big way. If you manufacture pianos, you need to know that a large truck can get down the street on which you're located and that the elevator can fit a piano. The bigger the products you make, the more size matters—and the more limited your choices will be.

Licenses and ordinances also play a large role in the space you select. More so than retail locations, your location will need to stringently meet the Health and Fire Department requirements. In manufacturing, you will want to determine:

- The square footage and layout of the space.
- How hot or cold the space gets.
- Whether the space can accommodate your technological needs and machinery/equipment.
- The amount of storage space.
- The amount of office and support space.
- Accessibility to ship out your goods.
- Safety issues.
- Security issues.

You will want to look over the area and visualize how you can set up a productive manufacturing business. You want to envision an efficient system where you and your personnel can work with the equipment to create the product in as seamless a manner as possible. Function is more important than appearance, since your goal is to make products and send them out rather than draw customers to you.

The actual location of the plant can range from your den where you make jewelry to a massive warehouse for manufacturing helicopters. It's to your benefit to be within a reasonable distance from whomever you're selling your products to. If you need employees specifically trained with certain skills, it helps to locate in an area where you will be able to find such skilled individuals.

Watch the zoning restrictions carefully. Some areas just don't like it if you're building motorcycles in your apartment. If you plan to be noisy or use hazardous materials, you will need to seek out industrial areas, since other neighborhoods will likely not want your business.

Home-Based Businesses

Many businesses start from home. Working from home is highly desirable for many reasons and plenty of commuters would trade higher salaries and perks for the privilege of rolling out of bed and into the office without so much as shaving.

The success of a home based business centers on you and your ability to self-motivate and remain committed to your work. One person working from home can remain focused and motivate himself or herself to do a productive forty-five-hour work week, while another will stray over to the television set, play computer solitaire, and end up putting in twenty-five hours on the task at hand (building your business).

Setting up your home office means finding a location in the home where you feel comfortable working. You need a place without distractions. You also need a place near electrical outlets for your computer, fax machine, and any other equipment. Include filing cabinets, your phone system, and any other necessities and lay out the space in a manner that makes everything within easy reach. Also, try not to be too far from a window for fresh air, sunlight, and an occasional glance at the world outside.

Advantages of working at home include:

- Saving significant time and money on commuting.
- Home comforts, including your own kitchen and bathroom.
- More time around the family.
- Some equipment already on hand.
- A low-cost starting point.

Disadvantages of working at home include:

- *Losing your motivation*—it's tempting to turn on the TV or do something else that is fun.
- *Working too much*—after all, when you work at home, you're always at work.
- *Loneliness*—working at home can become lonely, as you find yourself missing the companionship and camaraderie found in an office environment.
- *Having to entertain clients*—when an important client is sitting in your living room and Scruffy comes charging out from the den, you'll think again about having an office away from home.
- *Limited growth potential*—if you suddenly find that you can't handle the workload of the business yourself, you may want to bring in an assistant or hire other employees, and most often you can't do this from a home-based office.
- *Liability insurance*—you may need to pay higher insurance in case a client falls on your step and sues you.

The less conspicuous a home-based business is, the less likely neighbors will give you a hard time. Numerous large packages, tons of people hiking in and out of an apartment, or delivery trucks blocking up the street can spell trouble with your neighbors.

The more self-sufficient the type of business is, the easier it will be to maintain a home office. For example, a writer working on a newsletter should not have much trouble working from home. A business in which there is a lot of face-to-face contact with clients and customers will be more difficult to run from home. Determine how much customer/client contact you will need beforehand.

Online Businesses

It is estimated that by 2003, more than 500 million people worldwide will be on the Internet. If that's not a sizable potential market than what is?

There are two manners of doing business on the Web. You can utilize the Web to expand your bricks-and-mortar business, or you can start an entirely Web-based business. Both routes require time and commitment to learning how e-commerce works and what it takes to build and maintain a successful Web site.

Perhaps the most amazing aspect of the Internet is that you can communicate with, and do business with, anyone in any part of the world as long as he's connected to the Web. Internet Service Providers (ISPs) link you to places around the globe in seconds, and doing business is a couple of clicks away. Therefore, your first customers on a Web-based business in Ohio could be from Sydney, Australia, a location you would never have reached through traditional business methods a decade ago.

Additionally, the Internet provides, to some degree, a level playing field between large and small companies. For example, if you put together an excellent-looking site working from your basement, and a multimillion dollar company puts together a site working from its own industrial park, someone looking at the two sites on their computer may not see any significant difference.

So, what do you do to build your own Web business or utilize the Web to enhance your business? First and foremost, evaluate other Web sites and see which ones you do and do not like. Look at each site with a critical eye. Ask yourself:

- Do I like the page layout?
- Do the products or service jump out at me or are the pages cluttered?

- Is the site easy to navigate or do I have to click again and again to find things?
- Is the content crisp and clear or confusing and poorly written?
- Is the site current or does it appear out of date?
- Is there a way to contact the site owner or customer service?
- How easy is it to buy something from selection through checkout?
- Are shipping terms concise and easy to understand?

Next you will need to plan out your site. What will be on each page and how will you capture the essence of your business? Look at prominent Web sites for an idea of how they display products, present features, and walk you through the checkout process. Planning out a site is like decorating an apartment or arranging a store. You need to figure out exactly where everything should go and how you want potential customers to find each item or service you offer.

Give customers several (but not too many) choices. Don't try to overwhelm people when you're starting out. In the beginning, you want to let users get comfortable navigating the site and finding everything easily. When planning a Web site remember the following tips:

- Think concise when creating and writing Web content—less is more on the Web.
- Be visual, show your products or illustrate your services in some manner (with photos or graphics, for example).
- Don't use colors for text and background that are not easy on the eyes, such as blue print against a red background.
- Don't try to dazzle people with high-tech intros.
- Make key features of your products or services clear and inviting.
- Make sure to include a customer service phone number and a toll-free phone number for ordering, for those people who aren't comfortable giving you their credit card over the Internet.
- Include a street address for your business so you don't appear anonymous.
- Include a site map so that everything can be easily found.
- Include a search feature for products and services.

- Include all shipping, return, and other sales related information.
- Make sure to keep the site current with new material, new products and services, new promotions, and key information updated daily.
- Double-check all links to make sure they work.

Studies show that sites that allow users to search have a better chance of holding user interest for a longer time period. Users like the one-click option of being able to find what they're looking for.

Choosing a Web Hosting Service

It is very important to choose a Web-hosting service that can maintain your site in a manner that lets you sleep at night. Too many Web sites have run into great problems because the hosting service didn't do what they were asked to do. There are many hosting services to choose from. Try to get personal recommendations. The technical crew that builds your Website also needs to know exactly what your goals are and what you do and do not want on your site. The same holds true for the Web graphic designers and any other experts called in to help you design and build your Web site.

This is your business, so it is very important to be a smart consumer. Look for long-term contract discounts, services included, and a level of personal attention that meets your needs. If they're trying to sell you on features you don't need, or they're offering all sorts of perks for signing up, then you might look elsewhere. Be careful for anything that looks too good to be true. There are thousands of Web hosting services, and they're competing for your business, so be a smart shopper and compare prices.

Sites such as *www.gomez.com* and *www.sites.com* evaluate other Web sites. Gomez gives an in-depth look at the e-commerce aspect of numerous company sites while Sites reviews the best Web sites in each of a number of categories—not all e-commerce.

Choosing a Domain Name

The domain name is your site's identity, so think carefully before you select it. Your chosen Web-hosting service will usually help you register your domain name, and you will pay an annual fee for having the name you select. The question is, how do you select a name? There are so many already being used that it's hard to come up with something that isn't already taken—so be sure to have a few options in mind.

A domain search will let you know if the name is already being used. Until recently the suffix *.com* was the most common name used by commercial businesses. However, the influx of domain names being gobbled up has opened up new suffixes. Inquire about which suffixes are now available and try your name with some of the new possibilities. When selecting a name, like with the name of any business, think about what will present your image and describe what your business is all about in a few words or less.

ESSENTIALS   You can register at *www.mydomain.com* and for $70 (for a two-year registration) you'll be able to get a domain name—as long as it is still available. The site will search domain names for free.

Marketing

Building a Web site doesn't mean anyone will ever find it. While you can sign up with search engines to help ensure you'll pop up somewhere on the laundry list of sites when people search, it's essential to market your Web site off of the Web. You need to do as much publicizing for your site as you would do for any business—even more. The money you save by not having to pay rent on a large showroom of merchandise needs to be channeled into letting people know your site exists. After all, no one is going to drive by a site in cyberspace. If you have a business and the Web site is an additional way for people to do business with you, promote it to your customers as often as possible. Print the Web address on cards, shopping bags, all company literature, and so on. If you're launching a new site, advertise and market it all over the place.

Taking Orders Online

You'll need to establish a merchant account with a trusted processor such as First Data or Bank America Merchant Services to accept credit cards online. Make sure you're utilizing a secure service and let customers read about the technology involved in assuring them that their transaction is safe and secure. Despite advancements in online security, many consumers are still leery of giving their credit card information online. Also make it clear that you won't sell or distribute their names on any mailing lists, since privacy has become a very significant concern of online customers when asked to provide information online.

Don't ask for too much personal information. While you do want to know about your demographic audience, you don't want them to feel that you're invading their privacy. People are comfortable providing their name and e-mail address and then answering a few questions. Once you start asking for their address or more identifying information, you can lose customers. Also, if you want users to become members, make sure they know what advantages membership offers.

Fulfilling Orders Online

You will need a reliable fulfillment house if you are going to conduct an e-commerce retail business in which you sell products. If orders cannot be fulfilled quickly and accurately, you're in big trouble. Be prepared. If you do mass marketing and your Web site is getting a high volume of hits, you could be in for more orders than you counted on. Make sure you're ready to handle them.

Choosing a Location

You can run a Web business from your home or from an office. Since it's operating in cyberspace no one will really know the difference. In fact, much of the work on Web sites is outsourced and involves people working from numerous locations. It's very important to consider the technical needs when determining whether you can run such a business from your home. Make sure the facility you choose is wired to meet your needs. This may mean checking out what services, such as which Internet companies, are available in the area.

FACTS

Many business owners have taken to building their own Web sites using advanced software programs. They then find a Web hosting service to host their sites. Among the leading Web building software programs are: Microsoft Front Page 2002, Macromedia Dreamweaver4.0/Fireworks4.0, and SoftQuad's HotMetal Pro 6.0.

Web-based businesses sell all kinds of products and services. They provide a wealth of information and offer coaching, consulting, and educational opportunities unparalleled in history. A Web business can be easy to set up, allow for flexible hours (there are no specific store hours), and allow you to reach a worldwide market. Startup costs can be low if you start small. Maintaining the site can also be relatively inexpensive for a small business. The major costs, however, will come in the areas of marketing and promoting the site. You will also need to build a reputation for good, fast service and reliability. If you cannot fulfill the orders quickly, you can lose your reputation in a hurry. Poor customer service has also sent sites tumbling into obscurity.

CHAPTER 8

Show Yourself the Money: Financing a Business

A great idea plus enthusiasm plus no money = A great idea . . . but not a business. A bad idea plus enthusiasm plus lots of money = A business that gets off the ground but crashes shortly thereafter. A great idea plus enthusiasm plus enough money to make it work = A successful business. These are three very commonly found formulas. But as you can see, only one of them works.

Financing 101

Financing a new business means getting the money to make your idea a reality. It doesn't necessarily have to be a huge sum of money. Big businesses have grown from an initial outlay of a few hundred dollars to make a prototype of an invention. Small sums of money have been used to advertise for a unique service, publish a newsletter or magazine, or post a simple Web site. Not every business needs to begin with a business loan from a bank or a large cash investment from an outside source. Your need for financing will depend on the size and projected scope of your business.

The first step is to figure out how much money you'll need to start your business. You'll do a startup cost estimate, followed by an estimate of how much you'll need to spend on an ongoing basis. This information will become part of your financial plan, which then goes into your business plan.

ESSENTIALS Office supplies, a communication system, computers, business cards and stationery, an inventory of products to sell, employees, printed materials, advertising and promotion, office furniture. . . . These are just a few of the many startup expenses that you'll need to consider putting on your list before determining how much you'll need to borrow or obtain from an investor.

The reality is that a service business is usually less costly to start than a retail, sales, or manufacturing business. For example, if you're starting a cleaning service, you'll need to spend some money on cleaning fluids, mops, detergents, and supplies, plus allocate some money for advertising. But your expenses will be fairly limited. Your startup cost estimate might be as follows:

- Cleaning products = $400
- Advertising = $1,000
- Business phone line = $100

- Voice mail setup = $200
- Business cards = $200
- Office supplies = $400
- Web site = $500
- Other = $200

Assuming you're using your own computer and set up your Web site from a software program, you're estimating that your initial cost will be $3,000 to get started.

Next you'll need to determine who will do the cleaning jobs. If you plan to do them yourself, you'll be able to do only one job at a time, and you'll need to take more time to do each job. If you hire someone to assist you, you'll be able to complete a job more quickly, but you'll have to pay someone for the time and hard work—which means you'll need to charge a higher fee. If you charge $50 per hour, you'll need to work sixty hours to cover your initial startup costs. If you hire someone at $20 per hour, then you may need to charge $70 per hour to cover paying your assistant.

This, however, is just the beginning. To keep a business going, you'll need to assess your ongoing costs. If you're hiring an assistant based on specific jobs only, then you can contract someone and pay her based on the individual jobs—and not have to pay an ongoing regular salary. If, however, you hire someone full-time or part-time to answer the phones or do your filing, then you'll obviously need to include that expense.

For the purpose of example, assume you're doing the job entirely yourself for the first year. Maybe you've even found a niche because you're living in a college town and call yourself The Dorm-anizer. You've worked out an agreement with the colleges, and they let you come in and offer cleanup services for college dorm rooms. You not only clean and straighten up but help arrange the space so that it's easier for students to find what they need, and even study (should the mood strike them). Since college kids don't have too much money, you charge $50 for an hour of cleaning and straightening or $405 if they book you for a monthly visit during the nine months they're on campus.

Now, you can look at your annual estimates.

- Advertising in campus-related materials = $1,000 per month, or $9,000 for the school year
- Cleaning materials = $400 per month, or $3,600 for the school year
- Phone (maintained year-round) = $70 per month, or $840 for the year
- Office supplies = $2,000 for the year
- Web site maintenance = $3,600 for the year
- Other expenses = $4,000 for the year

Your total estimated annual expenses are $23,040. This means that to start this dorm-room cleaning service and run it successfully through one year you'll need to make at least $23,040. Therefore, if you're going to use your own money to invest, you want to know you have $23,040 above and beyond your living expenses for the year. This doesn't include buying a computer specifically for the business, which, if the business begins to take off, is something you'll want to do.

Next you need to estimate how many dorm rooms you'll need to clean and straighten to make this money back. Assuming everyone goes for a package deal, which comes to only $45 per hour (and that won't happen, but it's always best to calculate based on your lowest hourly rate), then you'll need to do 512 hours of cleaning and straightening or an average of 9.8 hours a week over a 52-week year (14.2 hours per week if you look at only the weeks school is active).

If there are 32,000 students living in dorms in the town, then even if you never saw the same room twice and worked at the $50-per-hour one-time rate, you would have to visit 461 of these students (or 1.4 percent of the student body) to make back your money in the year. This would be 461 hours or 12.8 hours per week based on the student calendar. You could then use the remaining time to promote the business.

Let's suppose your idea caught on and 3 percent of the students took you up on your $405 nine-time cleaning offer. You'd have 960 students at $405 each, or $388,800 for 8,640 man-hours of cleaning, or 240 hours per week. Guess what? You'd be hiring a staff! Now suppose you hired 8 people at a $32,000 annual salary each to help you clean. You'd now be paying out $256,000 in salaries, but they would cover 30 hours weekly or your entire workload. Add in additional expenses, including social security and insurance costs, and your $109,760 profit (after your $23,040 in initial expenses) would probably be down to $50,000 or $60,000 that you would see in the end and pay taxes on.

Then you'd find ways of adding to your service. (Perhaps you could buy combat gear and try cleaning frat houses.) You could publish and sell an organic guide to cleaning and straightening a dorm room for $2.99, or maybe you'd go into selling trendy room deodorizers. You could add products or services that could help you expand. Since your employees are now doing all the actual cleaning, you're free to handle the business aspect while coming up with brilliant new ideas. More importantly, you can focus on the job of getting new business, which is the aspect of business that many entrepreneurs find more exciting.

In addition to determining what your costs will be, you'll need to figure out how much you can charge—because that directly impacts how much money you'll bring in, and how much you'll need. What rates can you charge for your services that are fair and will keep you in a position to make money? Service rates are obviously harder to determine than products, which are more clearly dictated by the suggested retail price. You can, however, learn the going rate in the market for any services you offer.

Absurd as it may be, this cleaning service example is designed to get you thinking:

- What are your startup costs?
- What will be your ongoing expenses throughout the year?
- How many hours are needed to run the business?
- How many people could you employ and manage successfully?
- What would it take for you to show a profit?
- How can your business grow?
- What products or services could you add to increase business?

If you're selling products, you'll need to calculate how many you'll sell in a given week, month, or year and how much profit you'll make per product. If you'll be selling a range of products, you'll need to determine which ones will outsell the others. This can be very difficult when starting out because you have no prior sales to base it on. So you may want to start with a limited inventory so you don't load up heavily on a product that doesn't jump off the shelves but instead lingers there until it hits the bargain racks.

Study the industry very carefully and know how much you can mark up products and at what price you can still sell them. Be competitive in the market. This includes knowing the product and the area in which you're selling it. A cup of soda may cost seventy-five cents in a small town and $1.75 in New York City. Charge accordingly. At a Major League Baseball game or a movie theater, people may pay $2.50 for that same cup of soda. Similarly, the rent for your shop may be $300 a month in one region of the country and $2,000 a month in another. This will inevitably also dictate your product or service pricing policies.

Business and store hours are also a factor in your overall plan. How many hours can you be operating your business? If you're alone, your time is limited. If you have employees, they can run the show. (They can also steal it, but that's another matter.) You'll also need to pay them for their time. Therefore, you'll have to assess whether it's profitable to stay open twenty-four hours a day if you aren't doing any business after 11:00 at night. A restaurant with a regular dinner crowd may not open until 5:00. Why pay a staff and pay higher utility bills to be open between noon and 5:00 when you aren't doing a profitable lunch business? Other businesses feel that their costs are low enough and that it's important to be open more hours to establish themselves.

An interesting aspect of the manufacturing business, and now the Internet is that these businesses can keep on functioning on twenty-four-hour-a-day schedules without having to stay physically open to the public. A manufacturing business can make use of nights, for example, by running a new line of products. A printing company can have the presses going 24 hours a day even if there is no one answering the phones or running the other aspects of the business. This is a manner of maximizing the expensive equipment owned by the printer. The cost of running the presses and the manpower necessary is factored into the number of additional jobs. One job might not make it worthwhile to keep the presses open for twenty-four hours, but three jobs might make it profitable. Likewise, people can place orders at any hour on Amazon.com, since the Internet doesn't close and the site takes orders around the clock. Arrange your business hours in a manner that maximizes potential business without greatly increasing expenditures.

Work closely with your accountant and play with the numbers again and again. You need to know what it will cost you to start and run the business for one year, three years, five years, and beyond. Focus on the present and plan for the future. Be conservative and realistic in your future predictions. Base your numbers on facts culled from pricing and customer spending research. And don't forget to include marketing and advertising costs in your original expenses. It's often underestimated or left out completely.

If you're in the service industry, it's extremely important that you keep a close watch on the number of hours you put in on a project. Look at the clock when you start and stop working. Time is money.

Getting the Funding

Once you have a grasp of exactly how much money you need and for what you need it, you will have to determine how to come up with the necessary money. According to Roger Abbiss, founder of Sites.com, "Beyond having a good business plan you need to be able to make a good presentation to attract investors. It's very important that you are able to answer all of the questions without stumbling. You need to be well prepared."

Funding can come from any number of sources. Banks, venture capitalists, personal loans, and individual investors can all supply you with your startup and operational funding. You can also dip into your own savings, as most budding entrepreneurs do. However, if you're using some of your own savings, you need to know that the money is available for your business and that you aren't taking away from living expenses or savings earmarked for college tuition or retirement. If you have the money to invest, use it cautiously and follow your own business plan. No matter how much money you secure in loans or investments from other sources, you will most likely have to include some of your own money in getting a business started.

Investors come in any size or shape and sport any personality. You may meet with numerous candidates before finding the right investor. Just like dating prior to getting married, you'll find investors who aren't interested in what you have to offer and investors with whom you don't feel comfortable entering into an agreement. One of the biggest mistakes you can make is jumping at the first offer of money that comes along. In the end, there may be other strings attached, like control issues. It's very important that both sides feel comfortable when entering such a business relationship. When meeting with investors, they're sizing you up. Are you someone they want to put their money behind? Does your plan sound feasible, and can you make it happen? Often more than 50 percent of their evaluation of the investment is their evaluation not of the idea but of the person sitting before them. Many people can come up with good ideas, but few can actually make them work. That's why so many businesses fail in the first few years.

Investors are looking for:

- A sound idea
- A good, comprehensive business plan
- Someone with the drive, determination, and skills to make that plan happen

You're looking for:

- Someone who understands your idea or shares the same vision
- Someone who will let you maintain control of your business
- An individual, or individuals, with the funding to help you make your idea happen

It's worth mentioning before looking at the different ways to raise money, that obtaining financing is often tied closely to control issues. If you get a loan, then you need to pay back the money and interest, no strings attached. If you take on an investor, be it a friend, relative, or stranger, you may be giving up some degree of control over your business and some percentage of your profits. Therefore, whenever taking on investors, determine specifically what they want for their investment. Are they seeking profits, control, or both? Try to reach an agreement that makes you feel comfortable—and get it in writing.

FACTS

In order to build up your credit rating and secure future loans, if you have the money to finance the business, consider taking that money and using it as collateral on a business loan. This will help you build up your credit rating.

Banks

Sitting down at a bank and requesting a loan, knowing you have so much riding on the answer, is never easy. However, it will be much easier if you come in prepared to think from the bank's perspective.

The bank doesn't want any ownership or control of your business. Unlike a partner or private investor, a bank will leave all business decisions to you. Banks operate on the principle of securing whatever money they lend you with collateral on your part. In simple terms, they want to know that they will get their money back. Banks like to know that you have *hard assets,* such as a building or machinery, if not the money itself (as mentioned above), for collateral. The bank is not looking to collect by taking ownership of your building. So they want to be convinced that you have a solid business plan of action and will use the money wisely. As one business owner put it, "If you really don't need the money, they'll lend it to you." Of course if you didn't need it, you wouldn't be there.

Banks want to know specifically what the money will be used for. You must also know exactly how much you want to borrow. You don't want to have a rough estimate or let the bank know you'll take as much as they're willing to give.

Your background, character, and capability to run a business and to repay a loan are the other key factors. Your past financial statements, credit history, and references are all important information to back up your loan application.

Different bankers will weigh the data in different ways. One banker may not be as concerned that you haven't run a business as long as you have the collateral and have a good credit rating. Another may simply not think of the business as a good risk and not see the potential profitability. Therefore, you should try several banks.

Several programs featuring loans for small businesses are also offered through the Small Business Administration (SBA). You can look at their loan programs on their Web site at *www.sba.gov*. Through the SBA, you can obtain a general loan, also known as a 7, which is a guarantee of a loan provided by a commercial bank. Other SBA loans include LowDoc loans for up to $100,000 and a Microloan program.

You can also join a credit union and apply for a loan in that manner. This will usually get you a small, short-term loan. If that's all you need to buy a computer and start your Web-based business, then it's something you might consider.

QUESTIONS?

What is a swing loan?
Also called a *bridge loan,* this is a short-term loan made in anticipation of longer term financing or an equity investment in which a letter of intent has been sent.

Venture Capitalist Firms

In the late 1990s, venture capitalists were kings of the financing hill as they helped finance numerous Web businesses. By 2001, many were licking their wounds as dot-com carnage left venture capitalists holding the bag on a lot of bad investments. As the smoke cleared, the privately owned venture capitalist firms continued to provide capital to businesses, only on a more cautious, conservative basis.

Venture capitalists generally provide funding in a later stage of development, although some will help startups. The more well known the venture capitalist firm, the more you can be sure that they see hundreds, if not thousands, of business proposals every week. Most of these proposals don't look like sound investments. To stand out from the crowd, you'll need a great (*read:* profitable) idea, the skills to back it up, an excellent business plan displaying what you're planning to do and how you're planning to do it, plus a strong in-person presentation that answers all the venture capitalists' questions and concerns. Even in this case, the venture capitalist firm may be interested, but they may let you get individual investors to get the project off the ground. You could then come back to them for a second round of funding. Venture capitalists are generally looking for businesses that need half a million to a few million dollars. So, if you need $50,000 to start with, this isn't the place to go.

You might also note that, unlike banks, a venture capitalist firm may want to have more say in the business. *Remember:* This is not a loan, but an investment—and they may want to keep their hands on their investment, at least to some degree.

FACTS

Entrepreneurs looking for venture capital often hit the road on *road shows.* These are trips arranged through investment bankers or through your own connections, in which you have several meetings lined up with potential investors, sometimes two or three in a day. As the star of the show, you try to sell them on your idea and sound business strategy.

Individual Investors

This is where finding backing for your business gets interesting to say the least. Individual investors can range from friends to neighbors. When dealing with potential investors, whether it's your brother-in-law or a high-powered investor whom you've never met before, you need to present a business plan or proposal in a professional manner. Pitch the idea to friends or family as you would to anyone else. Even if friends or family are not potential investors, you can use them for practice. When you make a pitch, show all supporting paperwork and make a clear presentation that explains the business and how you see it coming to fruition.

It's just as important with friends and family as it is with any other business partners to get any financing agreement on paper. Make sure you differentiate between a loan and an investment. If they're lending you the money, they'll want to be paid back. Perhaps they'll cut you a better deal than the bank, but you'll want to at least pay them some interest. Also set up a schedule of payments.

If, however, you are talking about an investment (which you won't pay back), determine how much input they're expecting to have in your business. Be forewarned: This can lead to major conflicts. Friends and relatives will be very disappointed when you don't use their ideas, put their name on the door, or let them choose the office decor. In short, they may suddenly become your business advisors once they sign the check and place it in your hand. Don't let this happen to you. You must politely set up the boundaries in advance so you will be comfortable and will maintain the lion's share of control over your company. If it looks like a potentially awkward situation from the start, it may not be the best place to look for funding.

Often you're better off dealing with people you know in business and with whom you already have a professional relationship. If you're serious about your business, why not tap into others whom you have dealt with professionally and see if they would be interested in investing. Let them know in advance what you can anticipate being able to give them back for their investment dollar. This will usually be a percentage of the profit based on how much they invest. *Remember:* Plan this out very carefully so you don't end up giving away too much of the pie. Ask for only that which you need and make sure to keep them abreast of how the business is progressing. Also, remember to approach the control issue with some tact.

Roger Abbiss points out that pitching is like telling a story. "Beyond a profitable idea, you have to hold their attention and make them want to hear more." Pitches should be dynamic and *not* simply the spoken version of the business plan.

Angel Investors

Angels are private individuals who make investments, often in new ideas and new companies. Originally, the term *angels* was used for those individuals who invested in a theatrical production. These are often retired individuals with plenty of money and a penchant for getting in on the ground floor of the hottest new invention or business. Some angels invest to better their already strong financial positions; others invest because they enjoy the excitement of being part of a new venture. For some, it's good for conversation at the club and for others it's keeping a foot in the financial world. Whatever the reasons, these individuals play a very significant part in all kinds of businesses—from small retail operations to Broadway shows. They are most often very wise when it comes to investing, which means they ask the tough questions. So if you're planning to meet with an angel, be prepared. Be ready to provide solid answers to any possible business question. If you fumble in your presentation, you immediately lose credibility. You can always say, "We're working on that right now and should have the numbers by next Friday." But this only works once, twice at best.

Because angels are often as interested in the person behind the business as the business itself, it's important that you're both polished and personable. Be straightforward. Even though most angels are well aware of the risks involved, you need to provide as much disclosure as is required by your state laws. Make sure you go over your presentation with your attorney and your CPA to cover all risks.

SSENTIALS

Try to get an in-person meeting. Don't let your business plan do all the talking, no matter how good it looks. If they want to see paperwork prior to the meeting, send them a condensed two- to four-page version and let them know you would like to sit down and give them a presentation of your business ideas.

Since you're meeting with an individual, you should try to get to know something about the person prior to the meeting, just as you would want to know a little about a prospective client, so that you can tailor your presentation ever so slightly to meet the whims and idiosyncrasies of the individual. Much of this type of business dealing is based on subjectivity. A good rapport, a bond, or a business relationship of this sort can be based on any number of factors, even simply common interests. You may be dealing in an area that this angel always enjoyed dabbling in but never had the time to get involved with. This is also why you're looking to meet in person—to make a connection. One investor put up nearly half a million dollars because the budding young entrepreneur was an alumni of the same school he had attended thirty years earlier. Of course, it didn't hurt that the young businessman was an honor student and had a great head for business.

Like all investors, some angels will want to be involved in the business, others will want to advise from a distance, and others will simply be silent and leave it all up to you. While you might initially say that you would want the third option, you might actually want more input. Angels are generally skilled in business, and their advice and expertise can come in handy. Often a young entrepreneur can look to an angel almost as a mentor. In other instances, it's simply good to know you have someone to call on for support and guidance if you need to.

FACTS

BusinessFinance.com, at *www.businessfinance.com,* is a great resource for those seeking financing. The Web site offers a funding directory for businesses. You can search the directory for capital from some 3,600 potential lenders, all in one place, which saves you a lot of legwork and time.

So how do you find an angel? Wish upon a star? Not quite. It's more about asking other business people whom they know. The more you network in both personal and business circles the better your chances of finding someone who invests in various business ventures. It's beneficial to find someone who is geographically accessible in case you want to have periodic meetings to update them on the growth of the business and future plans (and you should always keep angels aware of your plans). Conversely, if you're dealing with a silent investor, he could be located anywhere. One American business owner commented that he appreciated that his investors were in Australia so that they wouldn't be involved in the business. "They don't know anything about this type of business," he added. "So it's better that they're far way".

Be sure to let one angel know if there are other angels on board, and make sure you establish exactly what each angel can expect, if all goes well, in return for his investment. It's unlikely that you'll have more than a few such angels in your outfield. But you can find numerous stories of businesses that were built on a combination of the entrepreneur's own money and that of an angel who believed in that dream.

ESSENTIALS

You can find information on angel investors and more at *www.thecapitalnetwork.com.* The Network offers investor-to-entrepreneur introduction services, seminars, and plenty of information. Be sure to check it out if you are looking for someone to help with the financing of your business.

Stockholders

And then there's the option of going public. If and when you own a company dealing in millions of dollars, you might consider this option. You will need to be a corporation to consider selling stock to the general public. The initial public offering (IPO) is an exciting goal, one that takes a great deal of work to reach. The Securities and Exchange Commission (SEC) has myriad requirements that you must first meet, not to mention paperwork to fill out, before you can go public. You will be spending far more time with your lawyers and accountants than with your family once you decide you're ready to sell stock in your business. Obviously, this is generally not a route you take when first starting a company, since you won't have the millions of dollars necessary.

Once you do go public, you retain control of the company by being the majority stockholder. Of course, you have many stockholders to whom you must provide accurate information about the workings of the company.

ESSENTIALS

A *term sheet* is a one-page sheet that outlines the investment opportunity being offered by your company. This will include a valuation, or fair value estimate, of your company (be realistic) and what can be expected by someone who invests in your company.

When You Have the Money in Hand

Once you've obtained the money from investors or a loan from the bank, it's your money and you can do whatever you like with it, right? Wrong. Your investors invested in more than just a business idea. They invested in *you* because they believed you to be responsible and passionate about your business. Your responsibilities are to follow your business plan, make wise business decisions, and keep your investors informed. If you have an angel in your corner with good advice at the ready, use it. If you have a loan from the bank, don't worry about giving them all the business details. Just concern yourself with making the scheduled payments.

It's important that you watch your investment dollars very carefully. It's easy to let them erode quickly. Make sure you keep excellent records of how these dollars are being spent. It's very likely that you will need future rounds of funding, and how you handle the initial round of investments is vital to obtaining additional money. If you squander away the first half million dollars, don't expect to see the next big round of funding come along soon.

FACTS

The two types of financing that you'll be considering are debt financing and equity financing. Debt financing is where *you're* borrowing the money. Equity financing is where you have *investors* who own a stake in or a piece of the business. You don't have to choose one or the other—you can do both.

Sometimes venture capitalist firms that weren't ready to jump in at the ground floor are more willing to get involved after they've seen how you've done thus far starting the business. The same holds true for individual investors. They're often more likely to invest after you've shown them something. Thus, you need to take first-round funding, apply it to your business plan, use your skills, put in very long days, stay extremely focused on the whole picture, and start off your business in a way that demonstrates why this business is going to thrive

CHAPTER 9

A Look at Taxes

While you may not welcome the taxman with open arms, you do need to know how to prepare for tax payments once you're in business for yourself. There are volumes written about paying taxes and taxation in general. Besides curing insomnia, reading about taxes can enlighten you on how to meet all IRS regulations and help you plan strategies to minimize your tax payments. This chapter gives a broad overview of what you need to know.

Keeping Good Records

One of the most basic principles of paying taxes is doing sound preparation, which entails good record keeping. Studies show that more people run into problems with their tax returns as a result of their record-keeping system than for any other reason.

Your record-keeping system should provide a clear picture of all income and expenses. Keep information on all sales transactions, receipts, and cancelled checks for all purchases made for the business. Make sure all filed paperwork is dated and filed accordingly into categories such as rent, utilities, automobile expenses, advertising, and so on. Your system should be easy to follow and easy to update. It should also provide you with a simple way of locating necessary information by any of several methods, such as by date, subject, or client.

What You Need to Pay and When

You will be obligated to pay federal income tax based on what you earn during the year, minus expenses and deductions. As opposed to individual personal tax returns, which are due every year by April 15, you will be required to pay quarterly estimated taxes. Quarterly taxes are due on April 15, June 15, September 15, and January 15. (These dates will be different if your business is operating on a different fiscal calendar year.) Be sure to check with your accountant to find out exactly when your estimated taxes are due and mark the dates on your calendar.

Your estimated tax payments should be one quarter of your estimated total annual payment. You can use last year's numbers if you anticipate the number for the current year will be similar or lower. However, you must pre-pay at least 90 percent of your total annual tax liability or you can be hit with penalties. If you have any questions about estimated taxes, check out the IRS Web site at *www.irs.gov* or talk with an accountant.

The structure of the business will determine which return you file. If you're a sole proprietor, you file your income tax and deductions on a Schedule C form attached to your 1040 individual tax return. Your tax payments are included as part of your personal income. Likewise, partners are taxed individually on their share of the partnership. Each partner includes his or her income and deductions on a Form 1065, also attached to your individual 1040 tax return. There is no separate partnership tax.

S-Corporations are handled in the same manner as a partnership. C-Corporations, however, are entities unto themselves and taxed as such. Corporations are required to pay estimated taxes. A C-Corporation may have a different fiscal calendar year. In fact, a business with peak seasons may specifically set up a fiscal calendar year that is advantageous to the seasonal business.

SSENTIALS

A company selling winter clothing may have a major seasonal rush that runs from September through February. Not wanting to stop in December, in the middle of the busiest season to prepare taxes, knowing that January and February are also tied to the expenses for that season, it would be advantageous for such a company to have a fiscal year running from April through the following March.

Corporate tax rates are different than those imposed on personal income taxes. It's a good idea to look at the comparative rates when deciding whether to incorporate. In general, if a corporation's earnings are over $335,000, the tax rates may be beneficial from a corporate standpoint. For a smaller business in the $50,000 to $75,000 range, the tax rates may also look slightly more favorable (25 percent as opposed to 28 percent) for incorporating. However, you'll be paying fees to incorporate, as well as legal fees, so you may not be benefiting after all—especially when you take into consideration the additional paperwork. In addition, corporations also lead to double taxation, in which the corporation pays taxes and the dividends are then passed on to the shareholders and taxed. Because you're the majority shareholder, you're obligated to pay personal income taxes on the dividends you earn, because they're part of your personal income. Talk with your accountant about ways of avoiding such double taxation.

Self-employment tax is, as the name would imply, for people who are self employed. When you work for someone else, your employer is responsible for paying half of the combined social security and Medicare payments for you as an employee (7.62 percent of your salary). The other half is withheld from your earnings. In this case, however, since you are both employer and employee, you pay both halves of the 7.62 percent for social security and for Medicare, or a total of 15.24 percent of your salary and wages. This is in addition to your income tax payments.

Taking Deductions

The IRS uses the words *ordinary, necessary,* and *reasonable* to determine which expenses they consider helping you to earn income from your business. The concern is not how much a particular piece of equipment helps you earn, but that the purpose, or reason for buying the item, is business-related. Typical business expenses include:

- Rent
- Salaries
- Employee benefits
- Utilities
- Insurance
- Office and/or business supplies
- Computer equipment and supplies
- Travel expenses
- Advertising and publicity
- Automobile, van, or truck used for business purposes
- Entertaining clients
- Legal and professional fees
- Dues and subscriptions
- Postage
- Telephone (including Internet)
- Professional licenses

If it relates to your business, it's deductible. If it's for personal use, it isn't. If it's for both, such as a car, then you'll have to determine the amount of mileage for personal use and the amount of mileage for business use. For business purposes, you can deduct 34.5 cents for each business mile as of 2001. Keep tallies of how much you use your car, or any item for business and how much it's used for personal needs.

The bottom line is justification. If you put something down as a business expense, be able to justify it with backup paperwork indicating the need to use the item for business purposes. Include the date, the person or the name of the business that received the payment, the total amount and the category of business expense into which you have listed this deduction.

Home offices have increased steadily over the past decade. More and more individuals are working some of the time, or all of the time in the privacy of their own home. Telecommunications and the ease of shipping through companies like FedEx have made this far easier to do in a manner that is comfortable for entrepreneurs and their clients or customers. If you operate your business from your home, and you conduct the administrative or management activities of the business there, you can claim a deduction for the portion of the home used for business. Accordingly, you can also claim a percentage of your utilities and insurance costs.

If you're seeking to deduct business expenses, you need to be engaged in what the IRS considers a trade or business, which is an activity carried out with a profit motive—even if you haven't made a profit in the past year. Generally, the IRS looks to see if a business has made a profit in three consecutive years out of five, meaning you can show losses in those always-difficult first two years. The IRS may also use their nine-step profit motive test to determine whether or not your business is a business and not a hobby. The nine factors include:

- The manner in which the business is run
- Your expertise
- Time and effort involved in running the business
- Appreciation
- Success with previous businesses
- History of income or loss
- Amounts of occasional profit
- Financial status of owner, other than this business
- Whether the activity is usually considered for personal pleasure or recreation

When listing your deductions, always refer to the IRS guidelines, since not all expenses are equally deductible.

ALERT

> Your tax form will include a place where you need to classify your business with a six-digit code, found with your tax forms. If you believe that your business doesn't fall into any of the categories listed, you can put 999999. If you use this code, your return will be looked at more closely and you may be flagged for an audit.

Employment Taxes

Unless you are a sole proprietor, you will need to hire employees. This means that you'll be required to have an Employer Identification Number (EIN). All businesses that employ other people must have an individual EIN. So if you are partners in more than one company or you purchase a new business in addition to your own business, you'll need a separate EIN for each business entity or company. You can obtain an EIN by filing an SS-4, Application for Employer Identification Number, at the IRS service center in your state.

Your principle concerns when paying employees are paying the following:

- Payroll taxes
- Social security and Medicare (FICA)
- Unemployment taxes
- Disability taxes

Payroll taxes are calculated depending on the filing status of the individual and are withheld from each person's salary. You will determine both federal and state income tax payments.

Social security and Medicare (known as FICA) require you to pay 15.3 percent (12.4 percent for social security plus 2.45 percent for

Medicare). You withhold half of these amounts from the employees' pay (6.2 percent plus 1.45 percent), and then you're required to match this amount. You pay the full amount of unemployment taxes. The rate is 6.2 percent for federal unemployment and varies for state unemployment rates (check with your state). Disability taxes are determined by each state.

Paying these taxes can get a little tricky. For example, social security is only paid on the first $82,000 of income. Unemployment tax is paid to the state and to the federal government. However, if you pay the full amount to the state, the federal government only requires you to pay 0.8 percent up to $7,000 in income, for each employee, which is a minimal amount ($56). You'll also find that people working for you get married or add dependents (children) and change their marital or dependent status. In addition, individuals are putting money away in tax-free retirement plans and you need to calculate the taxes after this money is invested into their individual plans. Is it any wonder why you need to hire a good accountant?

ALERT

All full-time and part-time employees should be paid on the books. An IRS audit could prove costly if it is determined that you are paying people and not recording it and reporting it. Likewise, if you're skimming off sales tax amounts, you can be hit with heavy fines.

When you hire an employee, you will ask that person to fill out a W-4 form. The employee will include his or her income tax filing status, and you will calculate the amount of income taxes based on what the person lists.

You're also responsible for having employees fill out I-9 forms, from the Immigration and Naturalization Service (INS), proving that the employee is eligible to work in the United States. Non–U.S. citizens must have work visas. For more information about these forms, contact the INS at 800-755-0777.

Keep in mind that you need to define which individuals are considered your employees and which are considered independent contractors. In general, an individual is considered your employee if:

- He receives his primary income through working for you.
- He receives direction from you on a regular basis.
- He has his pay rate controlled by your decisions.

Also, if you've specifically trained the person to perform a task or job, including procedures and methods in which the work is to be done, this generally indicates an employee.

An independent contractor is hired by you to do a specific job, or several jobs, but has his own established business and pay rate and also works elsewhere to make his income. In short, an independent contractor isn't under your control as an employee, for lack of a better term. If an independent contractor earns over $600 in a given year, you're required to send him or her a 1099 form. There are no withholdings that you're required to pay, and the contractor is, therefore, responsible for including the income in his own personal income taxes.

QUESTIONS?

What is the common-law test for determining the status of an employee?
According to the IRS, you can determine if a person is an employee or an independent contractor based on behavioral control, financial control, and your relationship with the individual. The IRS can provide details of these areas.

Payroll taxes are due either semiweekly or monthly, depending on the size of your payroll, not on when you issue checks. The IRS will dictate the schedule—you can't make the choice. If your total payroll won't come to $2,500 for the quarter, you can file quarterly. You may consider using a payroll software program. Or if your company is growing and you have an increasing number of employees, you might opt for an outside payroll service. The largest service, Automatic Data Processing (ADP), is one among numerous services which specialize in understanding and handling your payroll needs and headaches. ADP provides paychecks to over 30 million workers. You can contact them at *www.adp.com* or 800-CALL ADP or 800-225-5237.

FACTS

If you do not pay your payroll taxes on time, you can be hit with fines and penalties. The IRS takes this very seriously! Today, with modern technologies and wire transfers, there's no excuse for being late with your payments.

Tax Planning with a Pro

You can't avoid paying taxes, but you can strategically plan to structure and conduct your business in such a manner that it reduces how much you have to pay in taxes. While you don't want to focus so much attention on minimizing your tax bite that you neglect other aspects of your business, you can work with a tax professional to choose the best options for your individual situation. The government requires you to pay taxes, but you have numerous options in how you structure your business.

Whatever you do, do it legally. Fraud will result in serious consequences.

A good tax plan evaluates your current situation and looks forward over the next several years to determine what your anticipated earnings will look like. The better you estimate your sales revenue, income, and cash flow over the coming years, the better you'll be able to plan accordingly. Choices of claiming deductions, hiring employees, selecting a business structure, and setting up your fiscal calendar year are all aspects of your business that you can plan, in part, around tax payments.

To successfully handle all your taxation requirements, you should work with a qualified tax professional. You can look in the Yellow Pages, or you can ask for recommendations from others in business. You want someone:

- Whom you can trust implicitly.
- Who has enough time to review your situation and provide you with advice and guidance on an ongoing basis.
- Who has all the necessary credentials in the field.
- Who is familiar with your type of business on a broad level.
- Who knows the state and local regulations as well as the federal regulations and requirements.

A good tax professional can mean the difference between success and failure in business. So take your time and choose someone you believe can help you make the right tax decisions and the best tax plan for your business.

SSENTIALS

As an employer, you must remember to report wages, tips, and all other compensation paid to an employee on the W-2 form. Also report the employee's income tax and social security taxes withheld. You provide copies of the W-2 to the employee and to the Social Security Administration.

CHAPTER 10

Bookkeeping, Record Keeping, and Administrative Tasks

Behind the excitement and anticipation of great business success comes a more mundane, yet vital, task. Bookkeeping isn't glamorous, but it's the backbone of a successful business. Without accurate books and business records, you'll be unable to get a clear picture of how your business is doing.

Why You Need to Keep Good Records

Good bookkeeping and record keeping are essential to operating a successful business. When you start your own business, you need to know why these daily chores are important, so you'll be motivated to keep up with them. (And if you're like most people, you'll need all the motivation you can get.)

To Monitor or Track the Performance of Your Business

Monitoring will tell you whether you're making money. It will allow you to gauge which items or services are selling and which ones aren't. You'll also get a firm understanding of which expenses are necessary and which ones may be higher than you'd like them to be.

All business decisions should be based on where you stand financially. Before you take on new employees, buy more inventory, move to a larger office, or do anything that requires a sound business decision, you'll need to know how it will impact on your business financially. Good bookkeeping and record keeping will provide you with such information when you need it most.

To Pay Your Taxes

It's much easier to calculate tax return figures and pay taxes when you're working from a set of accurate financial records. Besides paying quarterly taxes, you'll be filing tax returns or other returns if you've incorporated. In addition, the many rules and regulations governing sales taxes and payroll taxes will be much easier to comply with if you know where to look for the correct numbers.

To Pay Yourself and Others

They say pay yourself first. But how much? You can't pay yourself or distribute profits to other partners or investors if you don't know what those profits are.

To Sell the Business

Anyone to whom you may sell your business someday will want to know how the business has been doing while you've been in charge. The best way for them to gauge the success of the business is by reviewing the financial statements. The same holds true for merging with another business; you need accurate financial statements.

SSENTIALS

If you're looking for a second, third, or fourth round of investors, or you want to secure a loan from the bank, you'll need to show accurate financial statements. Besides the bank and investors, the IRS and other regulatory agencies will need financial statements from you as well. You can provide these based on solid bookkeeping.

Establishing Bookkeeping Procedures

If you're a sole proprietor, you'll need to take a crash course in bookkeeping basics to gain an overview of these procedures. If you're running a small business with partners and/or investors, you may want to hire a bookkeeper to handle your books. The size and volume of the operation will determine whether you want to have someone on staff or someone coming in periodically to prepare final statements.

Basic bookkeeping starts on a day-by-day, sale-by-sale level. Software packages make much of this work quite simple. Whether you're using a software program or doing the bookkeeping manually, you'll need to keep a journal of sales and cash receipts. This will allow you to see your sales totals, know what items were sold on credit, and keep track of when you received payment for each item. In a retail store, modern cash registers will keep a running total of sales and distinguish between cash and credit card sales. At the end of each day, you'll enter your daily sales total into your sales journal. If you're using sales invoices, you can keep accounts for each customer updated by posting entries to the accounts receivable ledger. File all customer invoices by number and provide one (with that invoice number included) to your customer, so that you and your customer can refer to the invoice when necessary.

Your cash dispersements journal or expense journal will provide you with information on how much you're spending by cash or by check and to whom you're paying the money. You'll also keep a general journal for listing unusual entries or those made annually.

Whether you're actually handling the bookkeeping chores yourself or hiring someone to do it for you (often, you'll want to call someone in who specializes in doing this), you should have a grasp of what's going on financially in your business. The notion that "We'll let the gang in Accounting handle it" or "You'll have to ask my bookkeeper" can lead you into trouble. Bookkeepers are hired to provide you with accurate books and accountants will help you prepare financial statements and make recommendations. But it's up to you to make the final informed decisions. Therefore, it's important that you meet with your accountant and/or bookkeeper regularly for updates on what the books look like. In the case of uncommon situations, such as buying a new building, a merger, or even an audit, you need to spend more time in these meetings and have a firm grasp of the financial picture of your company.

ESSENTIALS   Make sure you save supporting documents to back up your journal entries. For all sales, purchases, and expenses, you want to hold onto any related bank deposit slips, credit card slips, cash register tapes and receipts, invoices, credit card receipts, cancelled checks account statements, and petty cash vouchers.

Choosing an Accounting System

There are two basic types of accounting methods: the cash method and the accrual method. In the cash method, you record income only when you receive it from your customers or clients. Likewise, when you write a check or pay cash, you record that as well. This system is very simple, since you're only keeping track of cash in or out of hand. However, the problem is that most businesses are not cash-only businesses. It's very common today to extend credit to customers or to buy on credit. These types of transactions aren't accounted for in a cash accounting system. Therefore, you don't have the whole picture of what you've actually earned or spent. It's not unlike those outstanding checks that haven't yet cleared when you balance your own checkbook.

Much more commonly used today is the accrual method, whereby each transaction is recorded when it occurs, regardless of whether you've received the cash or spent the cash at that moment. This will generally provide you with a more accurate picture of your profits and losses, especially in an age when invoices are paid 30, 60, and 90 days later and credit is extended to customers in a variety of situations. To get the best picture of where you stand, you'll benefit by using the accrual method. If you have an inventory, you do not have a choice: The IRS says you must use the accrual system.

Another choice you may have is whether to use a single-entry or double-entry accounting system. The reason you *may* have such a choice is because most software programs will come with the double-entry system already inside. On these programs, you make one entry and the program makes the other. The basis of the double-entry system is that both a debit and credit entry is made for each transaction.

Single-entry accounting has you just record one side of the transaction in your sales journal and a separate entry in your accounts receivable ledger. In a double-entry accounting system, however, you make debit and credit journal entries. This is the most common accounting system because it provides you with a checks-and-balances system (after all, credits equal debits) and allows you to find errors more easily.

ALERT

Be leery of accountants, bookkeepers, or any online offers that offer dramatic shortcuts to handling the tasks of record keeping. While technology can speed up your accounting methods, anything that appears to be too fast or taking too many shortcuts is probably missing some vital steps that will come back to haunt you later on.

What to Keep Track Of

Choosing an accounting system is one thing. But after you've made that decision, you need to know what to keep tabs on—otherwise, your accounting system won't do you any good.

Accounts Receivable

You'll need to keep track of all *accounts receivable,* the money owed to you by customers. For each customer, you'll keep an individual list of accounts receivable. This will allow you to know how much you're owed in total and how much each customer owes you.

Accounts Payable

The money that you need to pay (your bills piling up) are your accounts payable. You may owe money to suppliers and vendors or others from whom you've purchased merchandise, equipment, or services. If you keep a separate ledger account for each supplier or vendor to whom you owe payments, you'll be able to see exactly to whom you owe money and how much you owe at any given time. This will be especially valuable when you receive bills and second invoices, and you can look back and see if you've already made a payment.

General Ledger

The general ledger is the place from which you can start to organize your financial statements. It summarizes data from other journals, including cash disbursements or your expense journal and your sales and cash receipts journal. Here you'll find the balance between debits and credits when you finish posting your entries.

Balance Sheet

One of the key financial statements you want to be able to prepare, based on your bookkeeping and accounting procedures, is the balance sheet. This will provide you with an overview of your business at the present time. Included on a balance sheet are all your assets and liabilities. The balance sheet will result after postings to the general ledger, adjusting entries, and the trial balance have been completed.

As the name would imply, the balance sheet will need to balance, meaning your assets will equal your liabilities plus your capital. If the totals don't balance, you'll have to look for a discrepancy or error.

Asset accounts on the balance sheet include current assets, which include anything that can be turned into cash easily. The balance sheet usually reflects how you list your categories, starting with assets that have the most liquidity, such as cash and petty cash, and extending to the fixed assets, which include equipment, vehicles, furnishings, and so on. Also included, although not on the following list, will be intangible assets, such as a patents or trademarks. The balance sheet will likely include the following assets:

- Cash and petty cash
- Cash in the bank
- Investments (short-term and long-term)
- Accounts receivable
- Bad debts
- Merchandise or inventory
- Prepaid expenses
- Prepaid insurance
- Prepaid rent
- Office supplies
- Vehicles
- Land
- Buildings
- Equipment
- Furniture and fixtures

Also include categories for the depreciation of buildings, vehicles, and equipment. Among the liabilities you will include are the following:

- Accounts payable
- Salaries payable
- Sales taxes payable
- Federal withholding taxes payable
- FICA taxes payable
- Self-employment taxes payable
- Property taxes payable
- Unemployment taxes payable
- Short-term loans or notes payable
- Interest payable
- Dividends payable
- Mortgage payments payable

Essentially, this list will comprise all that you're obligated to pay, but haven't yet made a payment on.

Profit and Loss Statement

This is the statement that will generate the most attention from perspective investors. It's also the one that you're most eager to read, simply because it shows your net income or loss and gives you an overall perspective on where the business stands in terms of making money and reaching your goals.

Also known as an *income statement,* this is very simply a final, rounded-off (not down to the penny) summation of what you've spent in each of several areas and what you've earned. Generally you will list the following:

- Net sales
- Cost of goods sold (This will include the cost to you for buying the goods sold during the period for which you're preparing the statement, less any discounts offered by vendors for businesses with an inventory; start with your beginning inventory and add the sales purchases, then subtract your ending inventory.)
- Gross profits (The gross profit is the difference between the net sales and the cost of goods sold.)
- Expenses (This includes salaries to your employees, advertising, rent, payroll taxes, insurance, depreciation, repairs, office supplies, and all other expenses.)
- Net income (Your net income from the period is your gross profit less your expenses.)

If nothing else, you will learn from profit and loss statements how quickly expenses can cut into your profits.

Besides finding a competent, trustworthy bookkeeper and accountant, you'll very likely need to have administrative assistance in your office. It's very important that you find someone whom you can trust with confidential information, including personal data on employees and client contact information. Anyone violating such trust should be dismissed.

Accounting Software for Your Business

Modern technology requires the right software for the right task, whether it's for project management, inventory, graphics, or communications. An accounting software package should be easy to learn and include features pertinent for your particular business. You should also discuss your choice of software with your accountant to make sure you're using the same program, or at least one that's compatible with your computer.

There are numerous programs and online services available, ranging from ones under $20 to high-end programs costing several thousand dollars. In the following sections, you'll find some of the more popular programs that should cover most of your small business accounting needs while not costing you a fortune.

Quickbooks 2002 and Quickbooks Pro 2000

One of the most popular accounting software programs on the market, Quickbooks includes many key accounting features. You can navigate between reports and documents easily, e-mail and fax invoices, enjoy online banking privileges, manage files, modify reports, and essentially handle all your bookkeeping needs with one program. The Web site, at *www.quickbooks.com,* lets you view each feature and click for support and service help. To order Quickbook supplies, call 800-433-8810.

Peachtree First Accounting 2002

From the general ledger to your accounts payables and receivables right through to advanced accounting features, this program should meet all your needs. The popular Peachtree accounting programs have been among the top-selling products in a competitive software field. Peachtree First Accounting includes more than fifty predefined reports and statements designed to provide you with a comprehensive look at the financial picture of your business. Support and services are also offered. To order, visit *www.peachtree.com* or call 770-724-4000.

MYOB Accounting Plus, Version 10

This program helps you "mind your own business" (MYOB) with a variety of powerful features including multiuser capabilities, professional time billing, a fully integrated payroll system to take the headaches out of payroll calculations, and multi-currency accounting features for international business needs. The program is easy to navigate and MYOB provides support. Visit *www.myob.com* or call 800-322-MYOB to order.

Oracle Business Suite Accounting

An online accounting system, Oracle offers a 14-day free trial of this comprehensive service. All the necessary components of the accounting process are featured, including the general ledger, budgeting, bank reconciliation, expense reports, purchase requests, accounts receivable ledger, and more. You can customize the suite to fit your needs as you prepare your financial statements. The online accounting system allows you to easily transfer data from Peachtree or Quickbooks. After you pass the 14-day free trial, you're billed monthly ($99 per month at the time of this printing) and don't have to worry about downloading or upgrading software. Visit *www.oraclesmallbusiness.com* or call 800-SMALLBIZ.

ACCPAC Simply Accounting Pro 8.5

This program is designed to be simple to use and powerful all at once. Offering up to six multiuser capabilities, Simply Accounting allows you to have flexibility with customizable forms and reports. The program also features online banking and electronic payment capabilities. ACCPAC offers Advantage Series business solution programs for medium to large sized businesses as well. Visit *www.accpac.com* or call 800-773-5445.

 **ESSENTIALS**

In your haste to get your bookkeeping into your computer system, don't forget to carefully review the systems requirements for any software package you purchase. Do the same for upgrades. The last thing you want is to invest a lot of money in software that your computer is too outdated to run.

Record Keeping and Administrative Needs

Besides all the financial records of profits, losses, and expenditures, you'll need to maintain other records, including the names and addresses of your suppliers, accurate client records, and up-to-date employee data. It's important that all your files be accurate and updated on a regular basis. If you're keeping inventory and other such records on your computer, it's in your best interest to also keep hard copies of key information as a backup.

Your personnel files should include:

- All necessary tax information for each employee, including social security number
- Personal contact information, including emergency numbers in case of illness
- Employment history (resume, initial job application, and so on)
- Employment record with your company, including pay rate and vacation days accrued

For clients and customers, you will also need to maintain files, including:

- All up-to-date contact information
- Correspondences
- Record of transactions

Other files that should be on hand include:

- Permits, licenses, and registrations
- Equipment leasing contracts or receipts for purchases
- Correspondences with landlords, regulatory agencies such as the FCC, and any government officials
- Contact listings for all local and industry governing bodies, including the local Chamber of Commerce, zoning committee, and so on
- Legal papers including claims you've made and claims made against your company

One of the biggest, yet least discussed, causes of business failures is poor record keeping. This doesn't mean strictly financial records. Businesses have been shut down because they let licenses and registrations lapse. Companies have found themselves in financial trouble because they neglected legal matters. It's vital to have a solid record keeping and filing system.

Even though a lot of business is transacted through e-mail, it's very important to take the time to run hard copies of all key documents and have them stored safely in your files. Businesses that rely solely on their computers are taking enormous risks. Have backup data available at all times!

CHAPTER 11

From Chairs to Copiers: Furnishings and Equipment

N o, it's not rocket science, but there is more to furnishing and properly equipping your office then meets the eye. Unfortunately, most business owners pay little attention to such details. They're too busy figuring out on their $90,000 state-of-the-art computer system why their profit and loss statement shows them at $90,000 in the red.

Assessing Your Needs

Before you break out the office supply catalogs or go to the Office Max Web site, make a master list of what you need. In an effort to prepare such a list, you might start out by asking yourself a few questions.

Will Clients Be Visiting Often?

This is the old form-versus-function decision, based on how important it is for your business to present a particular image. The more often you plan to be entertaining clients, the more important it will be to project the right image and furnish accordingly. Whether it's trendy (for a company dealing with Gen X or Y apparel) or more formal (for a legal or accounting office), you'll need to look for furnishings that make the desired impression. If, however, your office is just for you and your ten employees and not the outside world, you may think of ways to create a comfortable work atmosphere while cutting some corners.

FACTS

Many offices today are more sparsely furnished—not for lack of budget (although that may also be the case), but because people appreciate having room to stretch their legs, talk with coworkers, and even do yoga or other activities together. Less can be more when it comes to furnishings.

How Many People Will Be Working in the Office?

Not everyone needs a workstation with a computer. On the other hand, you don't want to be three computer monitors short. You need to carefully review what each position that you intend to fill will require, and then add a little extra in case you experience technical failures or your business grows and you need to take on new people. Also keep in mind that some people may work off-site and other tasks may be outsourced.

Just because you hope to be so successful that you can increase from three employees to a staff of forty, doesn't mean you start out with forty computers sitting in the storage room waiting for the mass expansion. Buy or lease sensibly and know you can always buy or lease more.

How Much Space Do You Have to Work With?

Pay attention to fire regulations and other such rulings when you consider cramming 20 people into a space designed for 10. Additionally, consider that people won't work as productively if they're tripping over each other. Remember, equipment takes up space, so measure accordingly and leave some empty spaces.

Take note of the dimensions of the freight elevator if you're in an office building. Don't just assume that because the building has a freight elevator it will accommodate anything you plan to stick in your office. Also, consider the width of hallways and doorways before you buy.

What Is Your Budget?

Make sure to research prices in advance so that you can make reasonable estimates. Once you set up a budget, stick to it as closely as possible. Prioritize your list and decide in which areas you do and do not need top-of-the-line equipment.

What Equipment Do You Consider Absolute Necessities?

Typical major equipment includes:

- A communications system, including telephones and voice mail
- Computers
- Computer software
- Printers
- Fax machines or fax software programs

- Filing cabinet
- Desks or workstations
- Postal meters and mailroom necessities
- Various chairs for various needs (computer chairs, conference room chairs, and so on)

Retail outlets will also need cash registers, display cases, shopping carts, and much more. Manufacturing companies will need to house the necessary machinery to build or assemble the products. Security systems will also be necessary for all types of businesses (see Chapter 16).

 **ESSENTIALS**

> The first consideration of many entrepreneurs starting their home office is their chair. It's one feature that you shouldn't overlook or skimp on. The right chair for working at your computer station or at your desk is essential. Take extra time to make sure you have the right chair to meet your needs.

Comfort, Layout, and Personal Space

An increasing number of studies show that work environment is tied closely to the level of productivity. The right layout and design of the office, coupled with the right furnishings and equipment, can make a world of difference in the success of the business.

It's very important that you assess the space and the number of people who will be occupying the premises during the workday. People need a degree of personal space and with that in mind, you can only fit a certain number of people into an office without overcrowding and creating an unproductive—and even unhealthy—work environment.

Keep in mind that certain tasks can be outsourced while others can be performed by employees telecommuting. In some instances, you can have more than one person at a desk, because each person is only working from the office one or two days a week.

Cubicles and workstations have become very popular in the modern business world, eliminating the need to build walls throughout the office space. The open feel of cubicles often creates a better team atmosphere than you might find with traditional offices (with closed doors). However, the personal space and privacy issues also need to be addressed. So if you're going to set up cubicles, make sure they're roomy, comfortable, and allow for individuals to add their own personal touch. Employees who've invested the time and even money to design and spruce up their work area are more likely to feel a greater sense of loyalty to the company.

Customized workstations help employees work more efficiently. For the sake of comfort and efficiency you need to consider:

- *Distractions:* Think about whether there are any distractions from either outside sources or inside sources, such as office machinery or equipment.
- *Acoustics:* You don't want sound from radios, computers, or even phone conversations bouncing off the walls, so consider the type of paneling or soundproofing that will create a quieter work atmosphere.
- *Lighting:* It's essential that everyone has sufficient lighting at their workstation or in their office.
- *Accessibility to shared equipment:* If everyone needs to use the copy machines, then have them in a central (but separate, for the sake of noise) location.
- *Electrical wiring:* Since most offices require cables and numerous wires, it's important that wires be carefully handled and unobtrusive for safety purposes; have an electrician review your wiring needs.
- *Common space:* It's important that there is a place where employees can take a break from their daily routine and socialize with their coworkers or just read quietly over a cup of coffee for a few minutes.
- *Temperature and climate control:* Remember, you don't want your high-end computer equipment next to the window that gets the most sunlight.

Consider using modular furniture, which can be re-arranged as your company grows. Modular furniture is put together piece by piece and you can build vertically for storage needs, rather than horizontally. This allows you to have more free space.

Whether they're called coffee breaks or latte breaks, those few minutes away from the computer screen have been shown to be very productive. Employees who stay glued to their computer terminals for five, six, and seven hours straight make far more mistakes than those who get up every couple of hours and take a short break.

Taking a Look at Cost-Effectiveness

You need to determine how much buying for a product will increase your profitability and productivity. Increasing either or both can justify your need to purchase specific equipment. Even a television for the lounge can be a productivity booster if people enjoy watching it on their lunch breaks. Look at how each purchase works for the best interests of the business as a whole. Keep in mind you most often don't need to buy top-of-the-line products. Top-of-the-line products are necessary when you need the features (on a regular basis) or need to present a certain impression to clients. In this case, however, you can often fool most of the people most of the time with near-top-quality furnishings.

It's very important to make a list of your office supplies. Include model and serial numbers as well as the cost and date of purchase for major equipment and furnishings. This will come in handy if you ever need to call your insurance agent following a robbery, fire, or natural disaster.

Deciding Whether to Buy or Lease

As you take a look at the cost-effectiveness of your office equipment, you'll need to consider whether to buy or lease. Obviously, leasing or renting smaller items is not cost-effective. However, you may want to lease some of your larger equipment, including copiers, fax machines, furnishings, and computers. If you're starting out and don't want or can't afford to make large purchases, this may be a way for you to meet your equipment needs without a major cash layout up front. However, over the course of a one- or two-year lease, you may end up spending as much as or more than you would if you purchased the item.

Leasing has advantages and disadvantages. First, the advantages:

- While you may be required to put down deposits up front, you don't need to spend as much money when you're starting out as you do when you purchase items.
- You can get better equipment for your money.
- You aren't stuck with plenty of obsolete (useless) office equipment after a couple of years.

Here are some of the disadvantages to leasing:

- You may spend more on the item, over time, by leasing than if you purchased it.
- For items that don't depreciate greatly, such as furniture, you don't have any resale possibilities and can't claim the items as assets because you don't own them.
- Leases are very difficult to get out of.
- You're responsible to someone else, which means if you damage leased equipment, you may find yourself paying additional money.
- You can't take advantage of the tax deduction that comes with depreciation of equipment that you own.

Deciding whether to buy or lease is a matter of evaluating your startup budget and determining what you can afford to buy and what you can't. Many companies lease a copier. It's an expensive piece of equipment to buy (and service) and after a year or two it will often be obsolete. Computers, on the other hand, while they also become obsolete quickly, are often so integral to the company that the investment in purchasing such equipment is worthwhile from many aspects, including tax purposes. Furnishings, such as desks, chairs, and filing cabinets not only can be purchased in a wide range of affordable manners, but can be resold, making them assets.

ALERT

Be careful that you consider the long-term use of equipment that you're purchasing for short-term projects or needs. If you'll only need a particular piece of equipment for a month or two, consider leasing, renting, or borrowing rather than tying up capital.

Cutting Costs

You can furnish and equip your office in a wide range of manners. Besides your local Office Depot, Staples, or office furniture store, you can also check in with the folks at eBay *(www.ebay.com).*

Used, remodeled, refurbished, or recycled furniture, as well as used office equipment, can help you save significantly on your budget. As is always the case, you'll need to be a savvy shopper and know the cost of a new version of the same item. You also need to evaluate the condition carefully before making a purchase. In the case of equipment, you might be able to get the original warranty, if the item isn't too old and allows for a transfer of the warranty.

Some places to find used office furniture or equipment include:

* Auctions—both online and in the real world
* Estate sales
* Businesses that are remodeling, relocating, or going under
* Classified ads

On occasion you might find someone who has outgrown his or her home office and has some items that would help you get started, especially if you are trying to furnish your own home office. It's also advantageous to look around at what you already have and make use of what is already in your possession. A desk lamp, for instance, may be sitting in your closet— or at least a lamp small enough to use as a desk lamp.

Also, don't overlook the barter system of furnishing your office. Depending on the nature of your company, you can trade goods or services for what you need. One law firm received payment for their legal services from a furniture company in the form of an entirely furnished office. This saved the law firm the time and effort of finding, buying, and shipping the new furniture to their location (plus the taxes), and the furniture company was able to save on their high legal bill, since they manufactured the furniture or purchased it at cost.

Whenever you read about a company moving to another location, check to see if they may be selling off some of their equipment to make the move easier. Contact the office manager and see whether you can strike a deal.

Stocking Up on Office Supplies

Once you get the furnishings and equipment in place, you'll need to fill the drawers and stock the shelves. Stores, manufacturers, and corporate offices all need a wealth of supplies. Commonly needed supplies include paper for copiers, fax machines, and printers; legal pads; notepads; pens and markers; paperclips; postage stamps; rubber stamps; envelopes of various sizes; staplers; calculators; calendars; printer cartridges and toner; rubber bands; various tools; numerous preprinted forms, including invoices and/or receipts; and file folders. For presentations, you may need projectors and/or microphones for speakers. Retailers will need credit card forms as well as boxes, bags, and packaging supplies. Manufacturers will often need a variety of specialized tools. And everyone will need a coffee pot, coffee cups, and some kitchen items.

Keep supplies well stocked and put someone in charge of them so they don't walk off in great quantities. Ask whomever is in charge of supplies to make sure to order new supplies before the old ones completely run out. Let specific departments, or even individuals, fill in their own needs and order accordingly. Keep tabs on office-supply expenses so that they stay within the parameters of your budget.

Shipping and Shopping

If you can fit it in your car or van, then by all means avoid unnecessary shipping or delivery charges. If, however, you're ordering via the Internet, keep tabs on the shipping costs. Some Web-based office suppliers will provide shipping values or wave the fees altogether on larger orders over a certain amount.

Office supplies and equipment are very easy to locate. You can look in the local Yellow Pages for the nearest locations or find the major suppliers online. Here are some great resources to turn to:

- Office Depot, *www.officedepot.com,* 800-GO-DEPOT
- OfficeMax, *www.officemax.com,* 800-283-7674
- Staples, *www.staples.com,* 800-3STAPLE
- eBay, *www.ebay.com*
- Chair Pricing, *www.chairpricing.com,* 800-922-4401

Shop around, compare prices, review customer service and other store policies, and make smart choices.

SSENTIALS

Many companies buy equipment and furnishings from other companies that are moving or going out of business. Examine the equipment carefully. If it's a computer or another piece of technical equipment, have someone with a technical background evaluate whether it can serve your needs.

Remembering Ergonomics

Ergonomics is the office buzzword at the start of the twenty-first century. It's the effort made in offices to recognize and structure the office environment with a focus on employee safety. Furniture, particularly chairs, is now being designed with safety in mind. The increase in back, wrist, and forearm injuries has become increasingly significant among office employees working at computer terminals thirty-five, forty, or forty-five hours a week. The results have been decreased efficiency, lower office morale, and increased disability payments. The number of office-related injuries has risen drastically in recent years, as many employees are not working at properly designed workstations. It's no surprise that uncomfortable employees, or those with sore backs or sore wrists, aren't likely to be as productive as happy comfortable workers are.

The ergonomics issue has not only benefited chiropractors and office chair manufacturers, but it has drawn significant attention by the Occupational Safety and Labor Administration (OSHA) in the U.S. Department of Labor *(www.osha-slc.gov)*. There are 200 OSHA offices around the country; look for one in your area. There are also several proposals for guidelines being discussed that employers may need to adhere to in the near future. Just as the issue of sexual harassment in the workplace drew concern and guidelines were drawn up in recent years, office safety is the current issue of growing concern.

While OSHA provides various safety guidelines for specific industries, some basic information can benefit all employers:

- Seek out ergonomically designed chairs.
- Make sure all employees know how to adjust chairs and other workstation features to best fit their height and reach.
- Provide for necessary protective equipment such as wrist pads.
- Encourage employees to discuss work-related physical strain or other injuries with employers.
- Instruct employees on proper lifting techniques, good posture, and the need to take periodic breaks.
- Observe procedures and find ways to reduce repeated motions.
- Review the records to see if there are common causes of injuries.
- Seek out employee comments and suggestions and look for patterns.

There are several simple things that can be done to improve posture and decrease the chance of strain and injuries. If you're working in a home-office environment, you might take particular note, because it's very easy to lose sight of such concerns in the relaxed environment of your home.

While this may not suit everyone, and there is some debate, the 90-90-90 posture position is often recommended for working at a desk, or workstation. In this position, your ankle, knee, and hip joints are all at 90-degree angles and your shoulders are straight (not flexed). Elbows are also at 90 degrees, and the wrist is straight.

Consider foot rests, back rests (or a small pillow), and wrist protection if you're already feeling discomfort. The keyboard should also be adjusted to your height and you should keep your arms at your sides, with the elbow joints at 90-degree angles and your wrists straight. Make sure you have proper lighting in your work area as well. Consider glare guards and try to stay 15 to 18 inches way from the monitor.

FACTS

According to studies, nearly one-third of all occupational injuries or illnesses are the result of overexertion or repetitive bending, lifting, or other motions. As a result, workers compensation costs are more than $20 billion dollars. It pays to make sure your workplace is safe for your employees.

Naturally, these are just a few of the precautionary measures you can take to help avoid work related injuries. It's also important if you own a retail establishment or manufacturing business that you consider safety precautions necessary for your employees including padding, goggles, and work breaks.

CHAPTER 12

Technology: Computers and Telephone Systems

One of the most essential aspects of running a business is utilizing the right technology to meet your specific needs. No, you may not have the latest state-of-the art computers, DVD players, and wireless technologies at your fingertips, but you may not need them.

What You Need

Technological efficiency results from:

- Carefully assessing your needs
- Smart shopping
- Effective and ongoing training
- Sound policies regarding the use of technology in the workplace

The two primary technologies that most businesses require are computers and telephone or communications systems. Fax machines are also still in vogue and for retail businesses, the modern cash register and price scanner are a necessity. Projectors, presentation tools, and manufacturing technology may also come into play, depending on your business.

When it comes to technology, you need to be a good shopper. This includes:

- Comparing prices
- Looking for first-rate service policies and tech support
- Checking to see what's covered under the warranty

Computers

Before buying a computer, it's important to assess your needs. Make an initial list of how you anticipate using your computers and how many people you'll have on staff working on them. Ask yourself:

- Will you use the computer for inventory control and bookkeeping?
- Will you need the computer for word processing?
- Will you be managing projects?
- Do you need to have graphic design and layout features?
- Are you planning to have an e-commerce business, with customers ordering products or services?
- Will you need a computer network for interaction between several users?
- Will you need to run advanced, highly technical programs?

You'll also need to consider your office layout and space as well as the technical capacities of the facility. Then you'll need to assess the technical know-how of your employees, or the time needed to train them. And don't forget the price factor.

Finding the Right Computers for Your Needs

It's not hard to find computers. Every major office-supply company has plenty of models and all the popular manufacturers—Dell, Compaq, Gateway, IBM, Apple, Hewlett Packard, and so on—have Web sites and plenty of advertisements touting brand-new products and special deals. If you browse the computer magazines, you'll get an idea of what's out there. Of course, the newest, hottest, most hyped model isn't necessarily the one you need. Quite often, the second or third in line from a manufacturer is better for your needs. It may be easier to obtain, and you may find it at a good price, since the newest models are the high-ticket items. Don't pay for a host of computer features that you do not need. Shop for your specific needs.

Speed is also a relative factor that often fools computer buyers into spending more than they need to. The fastest machine on a dialup ISP will be slower than the third-fastest computer on a T1 line. No matter when you buy your hardware, something will come along that's faster by the time you've got the computer set up in your office. So don't get overly concerned about comparing speed between models. The speed is important, but your Internet connection is also a major factor.

For anywhere from $500 to $10,000 you can have a desktop computer up and running in your office. Most often you should land between $1,200 to $2,000. If you're buying several computers, you can work out a bulk rate. In the following sections, you'll find information on the key areas to concern yourself with as you're shopping around.

Random Access Memory (RAM)

You should look for 128 MB of installed memory and the capacity to add more. The greater the RAM, the better your computer will be able to operate more memory-intensive programs.

Processor Type

The processor, or CPU (short for central processing unit) is the brain of the computer. It will determine how well the computer handles programs and at what speed. While speeds range from 300 MHz to 2,000 MHz, some systems will work better than others at the same speed. A Pentium III 600, for example, will meet the needs of most small businesses, unless you have extensive graphic needs.

Drives

You need drives for inserting disks for storage or CD-ROMs for either storage or running programs. You might seek out a recordable CD drive if you are planning to store large amounts of data or are planning to make CD presentations. DVD drives are the popular new feature. However, you'll need to seriously determine what need you'll have for a DVD at work and why you want to spend this extra money.

SSENTIALS

Protect yourself. Assign security passwords for everyone using a computer and change the passwords periodically. When an employee leaves or is dismissed from the company, make sure to change the password on that person's computer. You don't want a former employee coming back to haunt you.

Operating System

The operating system is the program that manages the programs, so to speak. Windows 98, 2000, Me, or XP, along with Mac OS, are the most popular operating systems. But there is growing interest in Linux. Computers come with an operating system in place. If you buy a Macintosh computer, you get the Mac OS. And most PCs (non-Mac computers) come with the latest version of Windows. If you want something other than Mac or Windows, you can get it—you'll just have to ask.

Hard Drive Capacity

Your hard drive determines how much data your computer can hold. You'll find anywhere from around 6 to 80 or more gigabytes (GB).

The price will rise as the size of the hard drive increases, so consider your needs for stored applications and documents. You may not need the biggest hard drive out there, so why pay for it when it may just sit empty?

Monitor

You can do fine with a 15-inch monitor. But a 17-inch monitor is just that much better on the eyes, and not much more expensive. A decent monitor is also much less susceptible to becoming obsolete than other computer components.

Shopping for a Computer

Like anything else, you should compare prices when shopping for your computer. Whether you plan to buy in a local store or online, spend some time browsing computers in-person to get a feel for the latest models. The more comfortable you are, the more likely you'll be able to do some mixing and matching and not simply buy the configuration as presented by the manufacturer.

Don't wait to set up your computer equipment. You may only have seven to ten days in which to return it—and that starts when you receive it, not a week later because you didn't have time to set it up. Also keep the tech support number in a safe place from day one, in case you need help.

Shopping Online

You'll probably get the best prices if you go directly to one of the manufacturers sites such as *www.dell.com*, *www.gateway.com*, or *www.ibm.com*. You can also do well with the top computer online e-tail sites, such as *www.buy.com*, *www.computers4sure.com*, or *http://computers.cnet.com*. You'll also find many Web sites selling reconditioned or discontinued models. Make sure you shop on reputable sites. Search carefully, take your time, and check out customer service and shipping policies.

Computer Stores

Often, you'll pay a little more at a computer store, but you should get better service. (The operative word is should.) A good computer store has knowledgeable salespeople working to fit you with the best models to suit your needs in an effort to get your return business. A poorly run computer store is trying to push whatever they have in stock and provides insufficient answers to your questions. Pay attention to the kind of service you're getting, and move on if it doesn't meet your needs.

Shop at major name stores or Web sites. You have a better chance that they'll still be in business when you need to contact them for servicing. Many small shops boast of great deals on machines that they assemble themselves. Watch out! Often these machines aren't well built or are lacking quality parts, which explains the too-good-to-be true prices.

Office-Supply Stores

Generally, you'll find a more limited selection at office-supply stores. However, you may stumble upon a good deal, often on the last model, which they need to roll out since their shelf space is limited and they have newer merchandise to fit in. You also may be limited to buying a specific configuration.

Some stores charge you a fee to put the computer back on the shelf if you return it—even unopened. You may also be required by a retailer or e-tailer to return an item in the original packaging. Inquire about both before you purchase, because you never know when may need to return some computer equipment.

Searching for Software

Once you've found the computer to meet your needs, then comes the software. You'll be able to find software to meet just about any need your business has, including accounting, presentation, inventory, and graphics needs. From word processing to detailed project management, numerous programs exist.

Although there are more software programs promoted for Windows users, Mac enthusiasts have been glad to see the rebounding of Apple and more Mac programs on the way. The current market has a wide range of products available. Being an astute shopper means reading up on the various offerings in each category and reviewing their features. When shopping around, compare prices, look over the system requirements, and read user reviews. Word of mouth is also an important source for computer information, because you can talk with people who are actually using the programs and see what they think.

Popular sites for software shopping include the following:

- *www.egghead.com*
- *www.cnet.com*
- *www.beyond.com*
- *www.chumbo.com*
- *www.softwarebuyline.com*
- *www.amazon.com*

You'll also find a site for downloading software at *www.buyonnet.com*. Although the models are continually upgraded, some of the software to look for includes:

- *Accounting:* QuickBooks Pro, Peachtree Complete Accounting, Accounting Plus, and MYOB Accounting Plus
- *Planning and contact management:* Day-Time Organizer, Lotus Organizer, Franklin Planner, and Microsoft Outlook
- *Office suites:* Microsoft Office, WordPerfect Office by Corel, IBM/Lotus Smart Suite
- *Business presentations:* Microsoft PowerPoint, AllClear, Flow Charting PDQ, and Corel Presentations
- *Spreadsheets:* Microsoft Excel and Lotus 1-2-3
- *Word processing:* Microsoft Word, WordPerfect, and WordPro

- *Project management:* Microsoft Project, SureTrak Project Manager, and FastTrack Schedule
- *Graphics:* Adobe Illustrator, MacDraw, Freehand, and CorelDraw

Along with the many e-tailers, you can go to the manufacturers' Web sites and buy directly. When shopping online, make sure you check the in-stock availability of the item, look for product features, compare prices and return policies, and take note of shipping charges. Well-known manufacturers and e-tailers have an edge in the marketplace because they provide customer service and have been proven reliable. Before you go out and buy software, though, check out what comes with the system. It can save you from buying unnecessary software.

Computer crashes and Internet viruses have made it more than necessary to back up your software programs as well as your data. Most people don't make backup copies because they claim they don't have the time. Make the time! You'll be glad you did.

Networking

Businesses that use multiple computers often set up a computer network. The network allows them to share and exchange information. For example, you can have common files that several people can access and work on with relative ease (although not at the same time). Networks eliminate the need to save files onto disks for someone else to use. One main schedule can be posted and everyone in the office will have access to it. Computers on a network can also share a printer and a modem for Internet access. In a business in which people are frequently interacting and collaborating on a project, a network can be very valuable.

While networks can be very helpful, there are also some problems with them. If the network is down (and anyone who has spent any amount of time in a busy office has heard people complaining that "the network is down" from time to time), then it slows everyone down, not just one person working on a file. So it's advantageous to have people doing work off-network and then transfer the files onto the network. It's also important that case-sensitive materials, which aren't for everyone's eyes, don't end up on the network. Personnel information and other sensitive data needs to be kept off the network as well.

Setting Up Your Computer System

If you're not sure how to set up your computer (whether for a network or individually), then get help from someone who's well-versed in the area. It's not hard to find a computer expert these days, whether it's a real consultant or someone you know who just happens to work in the field and is kind enough to help you out.

While it's tempting to put all the components together in a hurry and fire up the new computer, like taking a new car out for a spin, it's to your advantage to be meticulous and follow the directions to the letter. Set up a surge protector, have an antivirus program ready to load, and make sure you put the computer in a location that's dry and won't get too much heat.

Take your time when setting up your computer. Getting it set up correctly the first time is a tremendous time-saver. Save all documentation, installation disks, and even the box in case you need to return it.

An antivirus program is a must for any computer that will be hooked up to the Internet or loading any software programs. Norton and McAfee are two of the most popular makers of antivirus programs on the market. Check out *www.mcafee.com* or *www.symantec.com* for information on these antivirus programs, or look for the software in computer stores and e-tailers.

Getting Online

Even if you aren't planning to have your own company Web site in the near future, you'll most likely benefit from the multitude of resources on the Internet. Therefore, you'll need an Internet Service Provider (ISP) to join the million of other people on the World Wide Web.

There are numerous ISPs to choose from. While you might be tempted to go with the first one that sends you a free CD in the mail, remember that the most popular, widely known company may be in that position because millions of teenagers and college students are using it for chatting—and the connection may be slow and cumbersome. You may find yourself getting a busy signal, being bumped offline, or sitting through numerous advertisements. Because this is your business, and you take it seriously, you may be better served by one of the other players in this very competitive circle. A good ISP can provide several local dialup access numbers, a fast connection, and good service and customer support. Local ISPs may meet your needs but they may not have the latest technology to give you the best connections. You'd hate to lose a business deal because you can't connect to your ISP.

When comparing ISPs, look for 24/7 accessibility, unlimited local service (so you're not paying for long-distance phone calls every time you dial-up), and a good monthly rate. If you aren't anticipating that you'll need the Internet for more than a few hours a month, you can go with a plan that offers just a few hours for a low rate. However, it's always better to overestimate your Internet needs, because hours add up quickly and you don't want to end up paying by the hour once you've exceeded your maximum. Therefore, if you expect that you'll use the Internet thirty hours a month, bump that number up to forty. Always add on about 33 percent.

ESSENTIALS

Unless the Web is your business, you should be able to function when the network is down, your ISP connection is failing you, or your computer crashes. In short, don't rely entirely on your computer system. Machines aren't infallible. Have backup materials and contingency plans in place—or you could lose a significant amount of business.

Your business and how much you'll use the Internet will help you determine which method of connectivity you'll need. Dialup service is the most popular, whereby your computer modem connects at 33.6 Kbps or 56 Kbps. Millions of people rely on dialup service for their daily needs.

However, if your business depends heavily on the Internet, you might select a digital subscriber line (DSL). DSL is more expensive, but it's faster than dialup and makes uploading and downloading easier. Cable modems are also a popular method of connecting. If you're already hooked up to cable for your TV, you can use this same cable for your Internet needs. Cable lines allow you to be constantly hooked up to the Internet. Like DSL, they're costlier than a dialup, but faster and more reliable. They can, however, slow down if numerous people are using the cable.

For a company using the Internet frequently for daily business needs, it's recommended that you consider DSL or cable if they're offered in your area. If your business is an Internet-based business or if a portion of your business is dependent on Internet sales, you should have a T1 dedicated line, which is all yours and not shared with anyone. This is a dedicated connection that provides constant service. Naturally, you'll pay much more for it. However, you'll have greater bandwidth. And if your business depends on your Web site, you'll need it.

Computer Policies

Just as it's important to buy your hardware, install your software, and train your employees on how the system and the network works from a technical standpoint, it's important to establish computer-related policies. Set up your guidelines from the outset. Computers in the workplace are not for solitaire, personal e-mails, or checking out "the articles" on Playboy.com. While you may want to allow your employees some freedom to check out the latest news stories, stock quotes, or sports scores, you do want to maintain a level of professionalism. Setting up policies and even blocking access to tempting online activities such as chats, may be necessary. While you don't want to become Big Brother, you also need to let it be known that you may occasionally monitor to see what sites are being visited. You should check the system and Web logs periodically to see what activities are going on. This will also help you guard against hackers. Don't let unauthorized individuals have access to your server. If you encounter suspicious activity, monitor usage more closely and have employees change their passwords.

You also need to make it clear who the "computer person" is in your office. Every business has someone who handles the computer problems that arise and integrates any new equipment. Having one person handle the computer configurations and the network is advantageous.

Set up guidelines regarding what does and does not belong on the network. For several reasons, you may also want your employees to have passwords. It's very important that you establish your computer policies before you hit the power buttons.

ESSENTIALS Make sure everyone understands how to use the e-mail system and remind them not to abuse it. E-mail is a marvelous communications tool externally. Internally, it's a great way to communicate important information with everyone in the office or for sending a quick memo. However, be sure to maintain some degree of human interaction— it's good for morale.

Telephone Systems

Along with computers, your telephone system will generally be your most important technological need. If you're working from home, you should consider a two-line phone or a separate line for business calls. When you set up an office, as your business grows you'll need to consider setting up a phone system. As with computers, it's important to meet your own business needs and not simply buy the latest model with excessive features that you won't be using. Consider the following:

- How many phones you'll need
- The price of the overall system
- Servicing from the company from which you're buying the system
- Ease of transferring calls
- Ease of using the voicemail system

It's very important that your employees are comfortable using their phones, which includes recording and receiving their messages. If the phone systems takes 40 minutes to explain and confuses everyone to the point where people are intimidated, then it isn't worthwhile for your purposes.

Next, you'll want to review all phone-related features closely and determine which ones you need. Call forwarding? Call waiting? Speakerphones? Speed dial? Many of these are standard features along with caller ID and, of course, the ability to put people on hold. (Remember what they say: The key to determining how successful you are in business is how many people you have on hold at any one time.)

Shop around and compare prices. Then establish some telephone policies and let it be known that you'll monitor long-distance calls or excessive personal phone use.

If possible, you might try to get a phone number that's easy to remember, but don't count on it. As for spelling out words such as 800-DUCKSOUP, remember that, in general, people hate having to slowly look at their phone to find letters as they dial your number.

Select a long-distance plan that has a solid reputation, has a good offer for weekday usage (which is when most of your business calls will probably take place), and has quality service, including service calls when necessary. If you can't reach the service department or they don't come when you need the phones repaired, you should consider switching long-distance carriers. The competition is fierce, so you shouldn't have to stand for inadequate service. Also make sure that the bills come promptly and are understandable. Complicated phone bills often result in your paying too much money. Make sure you aren't billed for features or services you don't have or want.

Because there are now over 60 million cellular phones in use in the United States, it's worth mentioning that you'll likely need your own cell phone and possibly several for key personnel who will be traveling. Don't hand out cell phones as a rule, or you can incur very high costs, but arm your sales staff who are in the field. Limit personal cell phone use in the office. These popular new business toys are very addictive. Curb the addiction before it starts. The more time employees spend on their cellular phones, the less time they're working. Also, keep your own usage in check.

And finally, don't forget your fax machine. Despite the advent of e-mail, there is still a need to fax invoices, take orders, and send (or receive) other important documents to clients, vendors, and others. Look at brand names such as Brother or Hewlett-Packard, compare prices, and make sure the features you're getting are the ones you need. Select plain paper rather than rolled up, and stock up on cartridges, because they don't last very long.

ALERT

The long-distance carriers make a variety of claims and have all sorts of offers. If you see offers that seem too good to be true, be wary: They might be. If the price for one feature seems too low, then they're likely making up for it somewhere else. Read all offers very carefully before jumping at some great long-distance rate.

CHAPTER 13

Hiring and Handling Employees

Once you've outgrown your home office, you'll need to hire employees. Whether you need retail sales help, skilled engineers, graphic designers, sales managers, administrative assistants, or Web content specialists, hiring employees presents new challenges and requires preparation. You want to start by listing your personnel needs and then prioritizing them. Ultimately this should give you an idea of which positions you want to fill first.

Knowing What's Expected of You

Prior to hiring anyone, you need to prepare, and preparation means focusing on a number of details. If you're going to hire someone, you'll need to be prepared to do the following:

- Get a federal ID number as an employer.
- Find qualified individuals, review their skills, and contact their references.
- Be ready to train and supervise others.
- Adjust to various personalities.
- Be ready to delegate responsibilities.
- Recognize that some things may be done in a manner that differs from yours.
- Make sure you're a good communicator and listener.
- Know the going rate and how much you can afford to pay employees.
- Pay employees on a regular basis no matter how business is going.
- Establish rules and guidelines so that your employees have a set of parameters and so that you don't find yourself being taken advantage of.
- Pay unemployment taxes, social security, and Medicare.
- Have desks, phones, computer terminals, and other supplies ready.
- Offer health benefits.
- Know how to lay people off or fire them.

Are you prepared to do all of this? Can you handle conflict between employees? Can you motivate employees to work at peak levels? All of this is part of being an employer.

There are numerous books, lectures, articles, and seminars offered on the subject of leadership. As an employer, you'll have to set the tone and lead by example. You'll need to determine your own style and be consistent and fair to all employees. Hone your leadership skills in advance. Learning as you go can result in poor business practices and even lawsuits. You want to project an image of professionalism.

Finding Qualified Employees

They say good help is hard to find. True, but not impossible. It's all a matter of clearly defining what your needs are and screening the applicants accordingly. The better you know what you're looking for, the more likely you'll be able to find someone with those skills. Take your time and assess potential employees very carefully. The human element of your company is more significant than the brand of computer you're using.

Classified Ads

If you're a local business, place ads in local papers. Also consider classified ads in trade publications. Keep the ad brief and make the job description (and list of requirements) clear. Explain the basic skills you require and the experience you would prefer. Don't ask for unreasonable amounts of experience, like ten years in the Internet field. Include any technical know-how that a person should have and exactly what you want to see (for example, a resume, work samples, and cover letter). Also include how applicants should get their information to you (e-mail, fax, snail mail, carrier pigeon). Give a few options—not everyone has e-mail (or carrier pigeons).

If you're looking for someone with ten years of skills, knowledge of a dozen software programs, plenty of energy, enthusiasm, creativity, leadership skills, dozens of personnel attributes, and the ability to leap tall buildings in a single bound, you may be overdoing it. Don't intimidate good applicants with endless copy in your ad or posting.

Web Postings

You can post a job opportunity on your own Web site or on any of the many employment Web sites. Monster.com, HotJobs.com, and Yahoo! Careers are among the many places where individuals look for work—which makes them excellent places on which to post. Keep in mind, however, that the Web is worldwide, so put your location up top in the ad. You don't want people from Paris overlooking the fact that you're located in Paducah.

Employment Agencies and Headhunters

Employment agencies generally sign up far more applicants than they can find jobs for, so they may have someone to place in your business. Few agencies are very creative, so you'll need to be extremely clear as to what your needs are. If the job isn't easily defined, you may run into trouble. Headhunters, however, take a more professional approach and deal with higher-level executives to place them accordingly. They can sometimes be helpful if you're looking for top-level talent.

FACTS

Very often, someone you've hired knows someone else who can do another job for your company. Don't just go by their word, of course. Interview the person carefully (people tend to exaggerate about their friends and family). It can be good for morale to have people bring in others that they believe in.

Friends and Family

The business world is largely run based on the "who you know" principle, especially in certain fields such as the entertainment industry. Consider those people you know and trust—but remember, when friends work for friends, trouble can ensue. Establish a business relationship in the office that is separate from your personal relationship.

School Internship Programs

Whether through local high schools or colleges, internship programs are great places to find young energetic young talent willing to learn in exchange for course credits. They can often be your future full-time employees in training.

Job Fairs

Job fairs are good places to get numerous resumes and business cards. Keep in mind that you need to present yourself well to attract plenty of possible applicants.

Knowing the Components of a Job Posting

A job posting can not only help you hire a person for a specific job, but it can serve as a blueprint for the tasks associated with that job. Here are the key elements of a job posting:

- Date of posting
- Name of company
- Brief description of company
- Job summary, with the primary functions described

- Compensation
- Necessary background and skills for doing the job
- Benefits
- Contact information

Interviewing the Candidates

After you decide on your method of searching, you'll have to go through the task of evaluating resumes and determining which individuals you want to call in for interviews. The job market in the past year, with many corporate layoffs, has caused employers to become flooded with resumes. It might be worth your money to hire someone to read through the resumes and narrow down the field to find the best candidates.

You should also keep in mind that experience in the workplace counts. While the young whiz kids fresh out of school may be found for less money and prove marvelous training material, there is often a lack of basic work experience. A marvelously talented young computer genius who spends an inordinate amount of time making personal calls or doesn't grasp the true meaning of hard work may be costing you money rather than he's helping your business earn. Weigh the benefits of knowledge and experience in the field along with basic work experience and an often-overlooked strong work ethic. In short, you may be best hiring a mix of people fresh out of school and people who've been in the work force for a while. They can balance your company and benefit from one and other.

Many people think that it's easier to be the interviewer than the interviewee. However, because you're the one representing your business, there is a lot of pressure on you to act in a professional manner and in a way that adheres to proper protocol. In other words, there are questions you can ask and questions you cannot ask prospective employees.

For example, you can ask all about past jobs, past responsibilities, favorite tasks or work-related activities, and why they've left their last job. You can't ask if they're married, have kids, or about their sexual orientation. You can ask about goals, dreams, special skills, strengths and weaknesses, long-term plans, and preferred work style (team, individual, and so on). You can't ask about religious beliefs, a person's age, political affiliations, or disabilities. In short, personal questions are out and work-related questions are fine.

ESSENTIALS

Read the candidate's resume again shortly before the interview so you sound prepared. You'd be surprised how many interviewers haven't looked at the resume since the person sent it in two months earlier. Not only does that reflect poorly on you and your company, but it leaves you ill prepared to conduct a solid interview.

When interviewing, stick to the subject (the job), explain the company, make no judgments, and use common courtesy. You should be able to evaluate and determine whether you want to hire someone based on two interviews. Sometimes, individuals are asked for samples of their work such as a portfolio in advertising. Take good notes when interviewing someone so that you can go back and compare candidates later.

It's often advantageous to ask someone how they would handle a certain responsibility or how they would act in a specific situation. The answer to these types of questions may prove more valuable than the standard "Where do you see yourself in five years?" Get an idea of how an individual solves problems. You can, and should request references and have a resume from the person's initial contact in front of you as a guide during the interview.

Once you do decide to hire someone, establish a start date (usually a new employee will start in a week or two). Provide each employee with the W-4 form for the IRS, any benefits information, the I-9 form from the INS and any employee handbook if you have one.

You should also get all pertinent information for your files, including an emergency phone number. This may already be available if you have had the applicant fill out a standard job application.

Running Background Checks

You don't have to check up on everything, but a little checking can't hurt. In this day and age of people making gross exaggerations, it could prevent you from hiring the wrong person.

Get the applicant's permission to call previous employers. Then check on the previous jobs, dates, salaries, and skills. Specific references given to you by the candidate are also fine to call, but they're always someone who will obviously say good things about the person. These types of references should therefore be taken with a grain of salt—call one and that will usually provide you with all the praise you need for this person.

If the factual information the applicant provides is incorrect, be suspicious. Make sure, however, that if you call a company to ask about someone who worked there seven years ago, that you're talking to an individual who can look back in the files (assuming the company keeps files that far back). Just because someone working there at that moment never heard of the person, that doesn't mean they didn't work there in the past.

Be consistent and check up on all potential employees in the same manner. This way no one can accuse you of discriminatory practices.

FACTS

As your company grows, it becomes more imperative that you know the laws and regulations administered by the United States Department of Labor. Pay them a visit at *www.dol.gov* and go to the Laws & Regs page. This way, you'll be able to focus on the candidates instead of worrying about whether you asked a discriminatory question.

Creating a Worker-Friendly Environment

Significant turnover in a business can slow down productivity, curb your profits, and squelch morale. The more time spent on training new people, the less productive work is getting done. Therefore, you want to make an effort to keep your employees happy. Besides additional compensation (which isn't always possible), there are other ways to attract and hang on to talented people:

- Allow for flexible working hours.
- Allow for some telecommuting.
- Encourage employee suggestions and feedback—and pay attention to it.
- Help with childcare.
- Encourage and set up social outings.
- Offer fitness activities, such as a lunch-hour yoga class or a fitness room.
- Be understanding in the case of emergencies and extenuating circumstances, and allow for a paid leave in certain situations.
- Set up an ergonomic office or business.
- Consider job-sharing situations, where two people do one job by dividing up the tasks and splitting the schedule.

There are many things you can do to make your business the kind of place that attracts and keeps talented employees—and many of these perks won't cost you very much, if anything at all. It shows that you respect your people and want them to stay with your company for a long time. Company outings, social gatherings, and buying lunch on occasion are all effective ways to build your business's family atmosphere.

FACTS

Statistics show that in the past five years, there has been an increase in the number of people seeking part-time work. This is due in part to an increase in working seniors, working moms, and working students trying to offset the high costs of tuition. Consider part-timers to handle jobs that you don't see requiring a full forty-hour week.

Establishing Rules and Policies

Whether your business has an official handbook outlining the rules and procedures of the company or simply a list of policies, it's important that you establish basic rules and guidelines that people are expected to follow. Put rules and regulations in writing in case someone ever questions company policies.

More and more employees are jumping at the chance to sue their former employer. Don't make it easier for them to do so. Spell everything out. Such policies should include information on:

- Vacations
- Holiday pay
- Sick leave and disability
- Reviews and raises
- Incentives and bonuses (if you offer any)
- Hours and work schedule
- Defined work status (full-time, part-time)
- Discounts on merchandise services

- Pensions and retirement benefits
- Safety regulations (including those imposed by outside agencies)
- Specific grounds for termination
- Sexual harassment
- Drug use, drug testing, and smoking
- Theft or misuse of company property, equipment, or funds
- Inappropriate use of the computer and/or Internet (or other technological equipment)

If you have more than twenty people working for your business, you should consider putting all this information into a booklet or handbook to distribute when an individual is hired. Having such a book (or at least having the rules and policies in writing) can help you if you're ever sued.

ESSENTIALS

You should spell out (in writing) employee responsibilities and evacuation procedures. Review these plans with a safety inspector (and possibly a fire inspector). Establish plans that suit your geographic area, such as hurricane response measures if your company is based in Florida or earthquake response measures if you're based in California.

On the other hand, don't get carried away and start making up rules that confine and hinder the ability of your employees to feel comfortable in the workplace. Stick to the basics as outlined above. Don't let your personal views get in the way. If you look at old laws that were once on the books in towns, cities, and states, you'll see some absurd ones, many of which were nothing more than someone's own point of view on an issue that they decided should become a law. Keep this in mind when making rules and regulations for your office, store, or factory. And even if you're hiring someone to work from your home-based business, set up some informal ground rules.

Compensating Your Employees Fairly

You'll have to do some research to find out what the average salary is for the type of job you're offering in your geographic region. Pay rates vary in different parts of the country. A magazine editor in New York City, for example may be making $60,000, while an editor with the same amount of experience in a small town in the Midwest may be making $35,000. The cost of living in New York (and other big cities) is higher, and the salaries are higher, too. Know the going pay rates before you interview, and be sure to pay people based on their expertise, abilities, and level of experience.

Many jobs are based on hourly rates. Know these rates as well. Make competitive offers but give yourself some leeway to negotiate. If you know you can afford $50,000 for a specific position, offer $42,000. If the candidate was hoping for $50,000, tell them you can pay $45,000 plus a $5,000 yearly bonus. This gets them to the $50,000 they were looking for and gets you an employee with incentive to stay at least one year and hopefully longer.

If you can't match the going pay rates, make up for it in other ways, such as telecommuting possibilities, additional vacation time, and so on. Someone making $50,000 with three weeks' vacation and two days a week of working from home may be happier with that setup than someone else making $60,000 with two weeks' vacation and a five-day-a-week commute to and from the office. See what you can offer.

You should also set up some system of raises or additional incentives. Be consistent, though. Employees often find out what other employees are offered and are resentful if they haven't been offered similar perks.

Be very clear with all offers that you make. Put compensation, entitled vacation, reviews and evaluations, and so on in writing. And above all, don't offer what you can't provide.

ESSENTIALS

Many companies pay their employees biweekly, which makes life a little easier on the payroll department (as opposed to having to issue paychecks every week). Establish when employees will be paid and check with state laws to make sure you are adhering to their guidelines.

Offering Employee Benefits

Employees today want benefits—and can you blame them? The cost of medical insurance on an individual basis can be staggering. You're not required to provide medical insurance (although there are regulations if you do offer it), but if you're a growing company looking to attract quality personnel, you'll want to be competitive. And that will mean offering health benefits.

Health maintenance organizations, better known as HMOs, and preferred provider organizations, also known as PPOs, are the most popular forms of health benefits offered. An HMO will cost you less money but only allows for payment for doctors who are within the HMO network. A PPO is more attractive to employees, and more costly to you. It will allow for a minimal payment by employees who see doctors within the plan, but it will also allow them to visit doctors outside of the plan. You'll need to review and assess the costs and benefits of each and shop around. Dental coverage is frequently included as well.

Savings and retirement plans are also in vogue these days, particularly 401(k) plans. The 401(k) came into prominence over twenty years ago and is now widely utilized by companies today. An investment vehicle, the 401(k) is set up by an employer to allow employees to put away money, tax free, toward their retirement. The money is invested in any of various investment vehicles, including stocks and most commonly mutual funds. Plans generally give the employees a selection of five or more choices of where they want their money invested. You should encourage employees to take their time and decide what the best options are for their unique situations, based on the current market and the economy.

While these plans are very often handled within a company, if your company is getting large (twenty or more people) you may want to look for an outside company to handle your 401(k) plan. The 401(k) plan transfers money into investment vehicles directly from the regular weekly or biweekly paychecks of the employees, who can elect to contribute up to a certain percentage of their salaries, but not more than $10,500 per year (as of 2000). The amounts change annually with inflation. The employer can then match a percentage of the money invested by the employee.

This may not be possible for a growing young company. However, it is very attractive to potential employees if the company is contributing 10 or 20 percent. Since this plan is designed as a retirement plan, there are penalties if the employee takes out the money before age fifty-nine and a half. If the person works past that age they can keep the money in longer. As an employer, you must allow employees to roll over their 401(k) plans when they leave the company. For all the details on 401(k) plans go to *www.401k.com*. Other benefits that might attract top talent include tuition payments for job-related education, a relocation package, additional health benefits such as prenatal care or CPR training, adoption assistance, child care, and benefit plans that cover life-partners who are not married.

FACTS

Studies show that, after more money, the second most attractive perk is being able to work from home. If you can't show your employees more money, show them the keys to their own front door. They'll thank you for it.

Using Contractors and Freelancers

There are many online listings where you can post positions for freelancers or contractors. There are an equal number of freelancers and contractors who have posted their qualifications on the Internet. You can also find qualified contractors and freelancers through word of mouth. It's important to get good references and check the work and background of such independent workers, since you don't have a personnel office in their last company to turn to for information.

Here are some things you need to know when hiring a freelancer or independent contractor:

- How soon can this person commit to the project?
- Can he meet the deadline?
- What are his hourly rates?
- How many hours does he anticipate the job taking?
- Does he work onsite of off-site?
- How does this person expect to be paid?
- Does he mind signing a confidentiality agreement?

Research other rates for the same job to make sure their rates are in line with what you can expect to be paying. Writers, graphic artists, and most other professions in which people often do freelance work have associations, unions, and/or Web sites where you can find salary information.

Once you've established the boundaries and guidelines for the job and how your company works, write up a basic contract agreement. Don't get too elaborate with your contract or you may box yourself into a corner. Include outs for both parties. From the contractor or freelancer, you want sufficient notice if he can't finish the project, and make sure it's clear that he will only be paid for the work he's done. If you, however, need to end the project at a certain time or cancel, you should also give notice and pay the person for the work they've done to that point.

While contractors and freelancers are not employees and do not get the benefits of the individuals on staff, you should still treat them in a proper, professional manner if you want them to work for you in the future and let others know you are an employer worth working for. Contractors and others who are self-employed do a lot of networking and you can get a bad reputation very quickly, which will make it harder to find good people.

Be careful not to give freelancers and outside contractors too much information about the inner workings of your company. A week after they have finished a job for you, they may end up working for one of your competitors—and taking that information with them.

Firing and Laying Off Employees

It's not easy to let people go, especially if it's not through their actions but simply a matter of funding (or lack thereof). Nonetheless, you'll have to handle the situation professionally and get it over with—unlike Mary Richards on the old *Mary Tyler Moore Show*, who said, "I couldn't fire my cleaning lady . . . so I moved."

There are a number of reasons for letting someone go. If you're firing someone because of his actions, you must let him know the grounds on which you're dismissing him. Your reasoning should be supported by company policy (which should be in writing). If, however, the person is simply not working up to the capacity that you had hoped for, simply let him know that the situation is not working out.

People react in many ways to being fired. While you cannot know for sure how a person will act, you want to take some precautions. Have someone else alerted to what's going on so that the individual's access to the computer and or company files can be shut down when necessary. Let the person respond, which may include venting their wrath. Let them talk, and be positive and understanding. Answer their questions to the best of your abilities. Arguing will get you nowhere.

In most situations, the employee will want to know what he's getting. Almost every company provides its employees with some type of unconditional severance pay. This can be higher or lower depending on the specifics of the termination agreement, but they should get something unless they've broken company policies and/or the law.

You also must be careful when terminating someone. Today, the moment someone is told that he's being let go, the thing that enters his mind is not "severance package" but "lawsuit." Minorities, women, individuals over forty, people of particular religious affiliations, and just about everyone else can come up with a reason why you wrongfully discriminated and let them go. This may mean reviewing your own termination practices over months or even years. If the last ten people you let go were all over forty, the forty-two-year-old woman sitting in front of you may have a pretty good case against you.

Try to fire or terminate everyone in the same manner. If you act in one way with one employee and in another manner with another employee, it can come back to haunt you. Work out your termination plan of action in advance. If you have proof that the person has violated company policy, broken the law, committed fraud, or acted in a violent manner, then you have just and legal cause in your favor. Don't go by hearsay in any of these situations and make sure you're correct with your information. If you fire someone for stealing and it turns out that the items were lost in the storeroom, you may be headed for court.

Laying off employees is becoming more and more common as the economy struggles to right itself. Like all termination procedures you need to prepare in advance, which may mean brushing up on company policies and procedures regarding severance pay, vacation days owed, and so on. You will also have to read up on the Worker Adjustment and Retraining Notification Act. Under this act you may be required to provide sixty days advance notice.

When planning layoffs, have very specific reasons for the layoffs clearly established. Communicate exactly what the problem is within the company that mandated this decision. Set a policy that determines which employees will be laid off. Stand by your policies and never let there be any room for questioning your motives for selecting employees for layoffs.

Do your best to make a difficult time easier for employees. This may mean writing reference letters, providing job placement opportunities, and even offering counseling. Be helpful in supplying information employees will need when filing to collect unemployment insurance. If your employees are part of a union, make sure you comply with policies outlined in any agreement made with the union.

It's important that you handle the situation of laying off employees as professionally as possible. You want to protect yourself and your company and also let others know that you're human and have a heart. Don't forget that those employees who aren't being laid off will be watching your every move. You'll need to boost their morale or they're likely to update their resumes out of fear that they'll be the next ones to go. Explain the situation to all employees and let them know that you hope business turns around. Be honest and be supportive.

CHAPTER 14

Insurance

If you've worked long and hard to start a business, you should make a serious effort to protect it. Being uninsured is taking a major risk that could, in as little as a few seconds, destroy all that you've worked for. In some instances, as with loans and leases, you may be required to carry insurance. In all states you're required to carry workers' compensation insurance and will need to pay unemployment insurance for your employees.

Protecting Yourself and Your Business

There are many types of insurance and an aggressive insurance agent may try to talk you into buying all of them. Business insurance, property insurance, and general liability insurance head an ever growing list of types of insurance offered for business owners.

The best way to approach insurance is to determine what you need coverage for and then find the plan that meets your specific needs. A company based in an area that hasn't been hit by a hurricane in fifty-three years need not be paying extra for coverage against hurricanes. On the other hand, a business based solely on the operation of its computer system might take out a new form of insurance called *hacker insurance,* as a safeguard in the event that a hacker breaks into the business's Web site.

There are basic business needs as well as needs specific to your industry or business. For example, all business owners will want to protect important property from being destroyed or stolen and safeguard themselves against lawsuits. A limousine-rental service will also be far more concerned about their specific auto insurance needs. A childcare facility will need to be more heavily insured against possible injury than a five-person Web operation.

FACTS

Another form of insurance that has become very popular in recent years is employment practices liability insurance. This important insurance can help protect you from lawsuits by your employees for discrimination, wrongful termination, sexual harassment, and various other potential legal actions that can be taken against you and/or company management.

Business Insurance

Business insurance is offered in a wide variety of forms and meets various needs. For example, some policies include liability insurance and others may not. Interruptions in business, whereby the business was forced to close or discontinue operation for a period of time (but was able to resume) may also be included in the policy. Extra-expense insurance may cover relocation needs if your business was forced to operate from another location. Property needs will generally be covered, but there may be limitations. You'll need to review a business insurance plan carefully to assess what is and isn't included, and then determine what additional insurance your particular company could benefit from adding to its coverage.

ESSENTIALS

Insurance companies are rated, so while you're shopping for coverage, you should check the rating services. Standard & Poor's, A.M. Best, and Duff & Phelps are among several companies that provide ratings of insurance companies. They can tell you how financially sound the insurance carrier is.

Property Insurance

Property insurance will cover your actual location, or facility, and everything you have inside for operating your business, including furniture, inventory, files, machinery, and so on. You may opt *not* to take a general business insurance plan, but to take out property insurance to cover losses by fire or theft. If, for example, your home base is in Southern California, you may take out specific earthquake insurance. Or if you're in the Texas panhandle, you might opt for insurance against tornados. The bottom line is that you need to look at what makes up your business and how you can protect it from being taken away from you.

General Liability Insurance

The other important aspect of buying insurance is covering yourself from legal action brought against you as a business or an individual. Today we're surrounded by individuals and companies taking legal action. The courts are overloaded with cases due to what has been termed *lawsuit abuse*. Everyone is ready and waiting to sue someone. Don't let that be you. Take all reasonable precautions, and get liability coverage.

Liability insurance protects a company's assets. Your need for coverage is based on your potential risk. This can range from someone slipping and falling in your place of business to selling someone a faulty product or providing a service that caused someone emotional stress. Any type of injury sustained by someone deemed to be the fault of the business, or damage to someone's property, can result in a lawsuit against your company. Professionals such as doctors, dentists, and financial planners carry malpractice insurance, which is their own form of insurance against a lawsuit stemming from their work or even their advice.

Liability insurance will cover you to a particular amount, and after that, your business or you (if you're a sole proprietor) will be responsible. For example, if you're sued for $1.2 million and your liability insurance only covers you up to $1 million, your business is responsible for the other $200,000. If you're running a small company, this could put an end to your entire business.

The greater your odds of being hit for personal liability, the more liability insurance you may want to carry. It's better to pay on premiums to keep your business afloat than risk losing it all. Weigh the risks carefully.

Many people believe that because they're working from home, they're covered under their homeowner's insurance. But this isn't necessarily the case, especially if clients or customers are coming to visit you for the express purpose of conducting business. Review your homeowner's policy carefully and then look for some additional insurance, particularly liability insurance, for your home-based business.

Getting Insurance Mandated by Law

Along with unemployment insurance, which is paid at both the state and the federal level, you're required to have workers' compensation insurance. It's designed to cover all medical costs and damages, as well as pay for lost wages if an employee is injured while working for your company.

State laws differ in how workers' compensation insurance needs to be purchased and what it covers. States also set up their own guidelines for who is and who isn't covered. For example, a contractor working at your facility may or may not be covered, depending on the laws in your state.

The cost of workers' compensation insurance is determined on an individual state basis based on the particular job. You'll obviously pay higher rates for someone working in construction on a beam some forty stories off the ground than you will for someone answering the phones in the branch office.

Because jobs are classified, you'll pay according to the types of jobs your employees are doing. To save yourself from paying higher amounts than you should be paying, check to make sure your workers are classified correctly. If you feel that you're paying too much for a particular employee, you might request an inspection from your workers' comp insurer to determine if the risk is as high as they've deemed it to be.

Studies show that behind salaries, health benefits are, along with telecommuting, among the most significant considerations for potential full-time employees. So you want to be sure to put together a package that will attract people to come and work for your company.

Offering Your Employees Insurance

The most commonly offered insurance benefit is medical (which often includes dental) coverage. Some companies still offer life insurance plans as well. Medical benefits, however, are the perk that will attract more skilled employees.

Managed care is the type of health insurance most often offered by businesses. This includes the HMOs and PPOs. HMOs are less expensive but offer your employees fewer choices than PPOs. It's up to you to look into group insurance plans and determine how much you're willing to spend and whether you feel your medical plan will attract top-quality personnel. No matter which type of medical insurance you offer, it's very important that someone, whether it's the office manager or a benefits manager, be very well versed in the process for filing claims and receiving reimbursement when necessary. Employees find the red tape and bulk of paperwork administered by some of these providers to be infuriating, and they need to know that someone in your company is able to help them deal with HMO or PPO bureaucracy.

Make sure that all benefits are spelled out in writing. Produce a benefits manual or at least some paperwork that explains the medical plan so there is less confusion. Medical plans are, by their very nature, complicated. Insurance companies have many loopholes to jump through to avoid paying claims. It's up to you to shop carefully and find someone who specializes in benefits to assist you if necessary.

QUESTIONS?

What's the difference between a PPO and an HMO?
A preferred provider organization (PPO) requires employees to make a minimal payment when they visit doctors within the plan, but it also gives them the opportunity to visit doctors outside of the plan. A health maintenance organization (HMO) only allows your employees to see doctors within the plan.

Doing Your Part

If you think insurance premiums can really add up, you're right. So it's important that you take all necessary steps to avoid accidents, theft, and lawsuits. What can you do? Plenty!

Taking necessary precautions can help prevent your business from being wiped out by theft, disaster, or a lawsuit. It can also make the difference between having a claim accepted or rejected. While most of the following suggestions sound like common sense, it remains quite astonishing how many businesses don't adhere to these basic recommendations:

- Install a good alarm system and make sure whoever leaves last knows how to activate it.
- Make sure smoke detectors, fire exits, sprinkler systems, and other safety equipment are in working order, and check them periodically.

- Take necessary safeguards against likely natural occurrences in your area (for example, buy hurricane-resistant windows in an area that is hit with frequent hurricanes).
- Keep all equipment, including company vehicles, well maintained.
- Make sure all employees are taught proper safety methods for handling or working any equipment or machinery (this also includes teaching people—and reminding them—how to bend to lift things).
- Make sure you have working locks on all doors and windows (more than 50 percent of thefts occur because doors were left unlocked or windows were left open, inviting trouble).
- Consider hiring a security guard for retail businesses or larger companies (make sure you review their credentials carefully before hiring them).
- Strongly consider installing security cameras, especially in a retail store.
- Review safety records of employees who will be working machinery or driving company vehicles, and make sure they have the necessary licenses.
- Have an ergonomically designed office, meaning furniture built to reduce injuries such as back strain.

FACTS

The vast majority of major companies offer health-plan coverage not only for their employees but for their employees' families. Those who only cover the employee often find that they lose good people when their young employees suddenly get married and start having families.

- Make sure to have antivirus protection for your computers, and update such protection often, because new viruses appear frequently.
- Keep an inventory list of all key items.
- Do background checks when hiring employees (*www.usmutual.com* offers retailers a database of reports on employee theft, including names of employees fired for theft in your area).
- Keep up-to-date records and a watchful eye on bookkeeping.

- Include disclaimers on contracts and spell out exactly what you are and are not responsible for if you're providing a service.
- Make sure all employees know that you have a zero-tolerance policy for thievery, drug use, sexual harassment, or violence in the workplace (outline all such policies in an employee booklet or handbook).
- If you're in the retail business, be alert for recalls or complaints about unsafe items.
- In any industry, keep abreast of the latest government rulings and local ordinances, and make sure employees know about changes in laws, policies, or regulations that affect your company or industry.

The idea is to consider any and all scenarios that could cause you to lose property or money. You want to prevent injuries, theft, and cause for legal action to be taken against you or your business. You also want to minimize potential loss due to fire or other types of disasters. All of this will help you keep your premiums down. Your own awareness can often be your best insurance plan. Nonetheless, buy the insurance you need to cover everything you've worked so hard to establish.

ALERT

Many businesses lose great sums of money because they believe their insurance policies cover occurrences that they don't cover. Read the policy carefully, ask your insurance agent questions about various securities, and buy riders if you need additional coverage.

CHAPTER 15

You and
Your Inventory

I f you plan to sell anything in your business, you're going to have to purchase the items and price them accordingly so that you're making money on the deal. From tacos to transformers, if you're not making them, you've got to get them from somewhere—and if you're making them, you still need to buy the parts or ingredients.

The Importance of Inventory

Your inventory is your lifeline if you're in the retail business—and access to your "alleged inventory" is your lifeline if you're in an online-only e-tail business. It is important that you decide carefully:

- From where to order
- How much to order
- Which goods to order and which ones to avoid
- When to reorder
- How much to have in inventory at a given time
- What to do if the merchandise you receive is unsatisfactory

How well versed you become at buying and merchandising will factor heavily on your level of retail success. Larger, more established companies will hire buyers, versed in the area of sales, to stock the shelves and track the sale of goods. When starting a retail business, this will be your job, along with anticipating upcoming trends and knowing what to buy and what not to buy.

Today, an inventory software program can expedite the process and keep you up to date. You can use a perpetual inventory system, which continues as you make sales. Whether you use an advanced or basic inventory system, make comparisons as you go to previous months and eventually, to the previous year's sales totals.

Stocking Up

You're opening a store, but where do you find the merchandise to sell? You have a few options. You can attend trade shows, which are one of the most significant opportunities for retailers to meet representatives from major manufacturers, get business cards, and establish a relationship. Nearly every industry has trade shows either regionally or even locally, if you're in a major metropolitan area. You can also contact manufacturers directly. It's easy to find a number, or Web site for any leading company and then locate the buyer for your region. Find out whom the sales representative is or if the company sells through a distributor or a wholesaler. You may also want to get a hold of the trade magazines for your industry and read them thoroughly. You'll find listings and articles about manufacturers. Finally, there are general directories for suppliers, manufacturers, and distributors as well as industry-specific directories. Look for them at business libraries and online.

Buying from Reps

You'll be making your purchases from either the representative working for a specific company, an independent representative handling several manufacturers, or through the manufacturers themselves. But first, become a savvy buyer. Read up on the sales trends in the industry. Learn which items are hot, and which are not. If, for example you were opening a toy store, you'd attend toy trade shows and read up on the latest toys in trade magazines and journals. You'd scour toy-store Web sites and browse the shelves at actual toy stores with an eye for what's prominently displayed and at what price. The best way to learn about your new business is to immerse yourself in it.

When you buy items for resale you need to consider:

- What are the sales terms?
- Is there a minimum order?
- Can you return items that don't sell?
- What is the method of shipping?
- How long must you wait to receive the items?
- Are there additional shipping charges?
- How quickly can you restock if something sells out?
- What can you do if the items show up damaged?
- What happens if the shipment never shows up at all?
- Can you buy on credit, and if so, what are the terms?

Be leery of distributors who are too anxious to sell you a line of products that you're not familiar with. Just like an experienced poker player who is bluffing, a good sales pitch may take you. Know the brand

and the products before buying—do your homework. And if you take item A, don't get suckered into taking items B and C, too. An old trick is to pawn off poor merchandise with the good merchandise you're buying.

Your relationship with sales representatives and vendors is very important. If you establish a good working relationship, you can then trust each other and work together for many years. The bottom line is, you need each other. Vendors make money if you continue to buy from them and you make money if their products sell to your customers.

After you become established as a retailer, you'll find that reps contact you. Be selective in what you order, since after all, you only have so much shelf space. If you overstock, you're prepared should an item be in heavy demand. On the other hand—and this is more often the case—you're stuck with an item that isn't moving as fast as you would have hoped, or has gone out of style.

Selling Online

Internet retailing, or *e-tailing,* is a new concept. Born in the 1990s, it's still growing despite the demise of many Web sites. Established retailers use it as another means of marketing themselves and selling goods to customers in areas where they don't have an actual bricks-and-mortar location or to reach customers who want the convenience of shopping at home. The fulfillment houses for these companies stock a supply of goods, which varies based on the demand for the product. If you have a new Web-only e-tail business, you might stock only a few of any given item, and in many cases zero quantity of certain less popular items. This, of course, means that you're able to order the products as you need them. You'll save on the need for a warehouse, but you may spend more per item because you aren't utilizing the savings you get when ordering in bulk quantities. Hot selling items that take up little space are good to stock up on because you can buy in bulk quantity and carry an inventory without having to use physical space for storage. All of this is relative to your business and products.

If you're maintaining an inventory, you'll need to establish how often to restock the shelves and how much to keep on hand. You may want to always have 20 percent of your total order on hand at any given time. For example, if you order 500 units of a new Scooby Doll and are down to a total of 100 on the shelves or in the stock room, you'll be ready to reorder.

If you keep inventory numbers up to date, you'll be able to look back at when you ordered an item and how well it has sold over a month, a quarter, or a year. This will help you determine whether or not to reorder. Turnover rates will depend on numerous factors including:

- Advertising and marketing—both yours and that of the manufacturer
- Display in the store
- Trends and overall popularity of the item
- The drawing power of your store, based on location, store marketing, reputation, and word of mouth

You will generally need to turn your stock over a few times a year. Besides how well an item is selling, you'll need to consider how often new models or styles come out and how much you want on hand at any given time. Naturally, if you're dealing with perishables, your turnover will be daily or every few days.

From Web pages to catalog layout to the design and layout of your store, how well you present the goods you're selling will impact heavily on their sales. Different schools of thought will suggest that best-selling items be up front so people will be drawn into the store to buy them. Another theory is to have hot selling items further back in the store so that people will have to pass your other stock and possibly buy other items. You can put one or two samples or demo items in the window to draw customers in. However, if a customer sees the one in the window and then doesn't bother to look around, you can lose the sale and your trick will backfire. Study the layout of other stores to get an idea of how you want yours to be set up. Then work hard on a logical traffic flow that will create an easy-to-navigate store whereby customers will see the merchandise.

You can also take advantage of your lack of a physical need for space when you're selling online. Your graphics of ballpoint pens or grand pianos can be the same size. It's easy to display two dozen styles of sofas that you might not be able to fit in a store. Don't get fooled by how easy it is to post items on your Web site—you still have to deliver them. Make sure it's worth the trouble. Web sites have gotten carried away offering everything including kitchen sinks and realizing the cost to order and deliver some items was impinging upon their profits. Set shipping order benefits, so that if customers order over a certain amount they won't pay shipping charges. It's worth it to you to get a larger order and pay the charges yourself, as opposed to having tons of small orders to fill.

If you're a manufacturer, you'll be looking to house a smaller inventory and ship out as much as you manufacture. You'll need to gauge the size of the orders you can fill and how long it will take to fill them. You'll also need to establish a shipping policy that's beneficial to your business and to your customers. Make sure you know the cost of transporting the items you're manufacturing and take that into consideration.

ALERT

I once called a computer store looking for an ink cartridge. They said that they had it in stock, but when I got there, they didn't actually have it. Instead, they tried to sell me a similar brand that was $10 more. The Better Business Bureau and I weren't amused. Don't try the old bait-and-switch game—it can cost you.

Buying

When you start out, you won't be making many deals. You'll be writing checks and buying merchandise C.O.D. As you build your retail business and establish relationships with vendors and/or sales reps, you will have greater negotiating power. You'll discuss the terms of the deal, such as a discount for a cash purchase, specific details of delivery, and possibly additional merchandise. In some cases, vendors will even split the cost of advertising with you on one of their products, in a cooperative advertising arrangement. Rarely, outside of the book industry and a few other industries, do deals include returns to the manufacturer of unsold merchandise.

Of course, you'll need to prove yourself a good retailer and build your reputation to forge relationships with vendors, sales reps, distributors, and manufacturers. Over time, you'll go from looking for goods to stock to turning products away. A retailer like Amazon.com has practically everyone who publishes a book, creates a software program, or develops a toy or game contacting them. Amazon.com can accommodate many of them because they don't need to stock the shelves. They can order just a few copies of a book and wait to see how it sells before ordering more. Their reputation helps them maintain ongoing relationships with an enormous number of publishers and manufacturers. New businesses should start small and increase their orders as sales increase. However, unlike a Web-based store, if you need to stock shelves, you'll become more and more discerning as numerous salespeople try to sell you on their latest products.

As the buyer for your retail business:

- You must consider the cost per item and determine the markup. (Is it worth your while to buy the item? Can you make enough money on it to warrant putting it in your store?)
- You need to read up on the latest trends and newest products in your industry, and stay ahead of, or at least keep pace with, your competitors—every time your competitor has a new product available and you don't, you're losing a sale and telling that customer that you aren't as up-to-date as you should be.
- You must consider the seasons and place orders in advance, making sure you buy far enough in advance that you have items on hand for peak sales seasons such as the end-of-year holidays.
- You will make decisions on style and image—you will want to create a certain image for your store and order items that fit that image.
- You should look for unique items that other stores may not carry—even if you only carry a few and cannot mark them up as much as you would like, these may draw customers or grab their attention once they're in the store.
- You need to have a good eye for quality merchandise—this means knowing your industry and knowing the real thing and imitations of the real thing.

- You need to know the types of products that will sell to your customers—study the demographics of your industry, your location, and your store or Web site.
- You should also know which products can be sold with accessories or other related items (a model train set, for example, comes with numerous pieces that are sold separately).

Being a good buyer is all about knowing the industry, thinking ahead, establishing relationships, and working good deals. If you open a restaurant, you'll be buying food on a daily basis from suppliers. You may be down at the fish market at 6:00 in the morning or have deliveries made regularly. Either way, you'll need to learn about food quality and how to get fair deals.

FACTS

If you attend trade shows, put your name on mailing lists. Once you spread the word within the industry that you're selling a product, sales reps and manufacturers will begin to find you. The more established you become, the more they'll want to be in your store.

It's fair to say that you can learn a lot from others who have run retail businesses for many years. Successful retailers love to talk about how they built up their empires, and as a future empire builder, you need to soak up as much of that collective wisdom as possible. Join associations or the local chamber of commerce. Look at trade journals and gather as much information about retailing as you can. *Stores Magazine,* at *www.stores.com,* has a wealth of retail information plus an Industry Buying Guide that will help you put your store together from the sign in front to the bags customers carry out when the leave. You'll also find links to some 700 retail based sites at *http://retailindustry.about.com.*

Keep good records of the cost for each product so that you can know your bottom line amount in case you need to sell off an item at rock-bottom prices to clear it out without taking a loss. This means that if you order from different distributors, you know the various costs and can come up with a cost average. For example, if you purchased a brand of dog food for your pet shop for $0.69 per can from one distributor, $0.67 from another, and found someone else selling it at $0.65 per can, and each time you bought 100 cans, your total expenditure for 300 cans is $201. Therefore, if you had to reduce your selling price to $0.67 per can to be competitive, if you sold them all, you'd break even (less any delivery cost).

Pricing Your Goods and Services

How much you charge for goods or services is crucial to your success as a businessperson. Your pricing decisions will affect your sales volume, profits, image, inventory, ordering decisions, and more. Prices that are too high can alienate customers, while prices that are too low can hurt your profits and ultimately your cash flow.

Products

In a retail business, you're concerned with the cost of the merchandise and the retail price at which you can sell the product. The difference between these two amounts is your markup. Therefore, if you're buying toys at a cost of $12 per item, and selling them for $19 each, your markup is $7 per toy. As a retailer, you will always need to concern yourself with this basic calculation whenever you're buying for your store.

There are numerous factors that come into play when you're pricing goods and services. However, you'll generally use these factors to adjust the pricing, since you will most often be guided by:

- Suggested retail price by the manufacturer
- Competitive prices on this product as found in other stores

Be careful not to get into a price war with a larger store. They can order in larger quantities making it hard for you to beat their prices. They can also take a loss on one product if it means keeping customers from coming to you. Try to win a potential price war by offering services or specialty items.

Consider the costs of running your business. You need to pay your rent, your employees, and other bills. If your rent, bills, and other expenses add up to $10,000 per month, and you expect to sell 5,000 units a month, then you need to average $2 each on whatever it is you sell to cover these additional expenses.

Consider the popularity of the item. Is this a hot selling item that will move off the shelves just as quickly at $20 as it would at $17?

Consider your customer base. Do your customers look for high quality? Are they shopping at your store for convenience and personalized attention? If so, they won't mind spending more. If, however, they are looking for bargains and are very price-conscious when they come to your store, then you need to provide them with prices that match or beat the competition.

ALERT

Review laws and regulations. The FDA and various other organizations (and local laws) may restrict how much you can charge or mark up an item. Be aware.

Think about drawing additional customers to your store. This ties into the popularity of the product and the competition. If a lower price will draw more customers and increase overall traffic in the store, then you might price an item at close to cost, which will result in less profit per item but more overall sales—plus more store traffic.

Think accessories. Hobby items are perfect examples of areas where you make plenty of potential sales on accessories. If you have any type of item that offers numerous accessories, you can take a lower markup on the main item. A dollhouse itself can sell at close to cost. Then you can get a higher markup on the furniture and other accessories needed. You can also work a deal that if they buy item A, they get a percentage off on items B, C, and D if they buy the entire set. Be creative. You can think accessories in almost any type of retail business.

Know your neighborhood. This goes in line with your customer base. If you're in an elite part of town, you'll be perceived as a high-end store, so price accordingly.

Think about seasonal and holiday shopping. The Saturday before Mother's Day, the price for a dozen roses at local New York City fruit and vegetable markets suddenly jumps from $10 to $15 or even $20. Funny how that happens. Also, as seasons approach, you will see more demand for certain items. Likewise, as the season passes and you're left with items on the shelves, you'll need to mark them down to clear them out.

Consider who sets the prices. If you're working for a franchise, you may not have the final say in determining the prices. Manufacturers often suggest retail prices, but generally they can't hold you to them. However, they also don't have to continue to sell to your store.

Think volume. Consider whether the item is one that you expect to sell in large quantities, producing a good overall return or if it's a rare item that will only sell a few units, meaning you'll have to make money off of each one to make it worth your while.

Consider the trends. If you're dealing with clothing or other items that will change in style within a few months, then be ready to mark down the item so that you'll be able to move them out as the trend fades.

ESSENTIALS

Remember supply and demand? Just like the New York flower shops that are aware of the demand for flowers around Mother's Day, you can benefit from knowing the supply and demand of a particular product. If you're the only store around selling the new glow-in-the-dark bell-bottoms, you can mark them up higher. If, however, they're easy to get on the Web, you can't. The Internet has made goods and services once scarcely found in many regions accessible worldwide. However, there is something to be said walking into a store and taking the product home immediately.

Determine what else you can offer. If you charge more but throw in gift-wrapping or other services, you may attract customers for the added perks. While you're spending money on wrapping paper, you're also building an image and satisfied customer base with each purchase made.

There are numerous methods and theories regarding retail pricing. Keep in mind that it's an ever-evolving process, one that will change with new products, higher costs, more or less competition, and the economic picture. Don't stick to one hard-and-fast rule for pricing. Unless you're a very specialized retailer, you probably will have various markups for various products. This is quite common in what has become a greatly diversified market place.

QUESTIONS?

Should you ever sell merchandise for below cost?
Yes. If you're otherwise going to be stuck with a product and have no way to get rid of it, or if you very badly need to draw people into the store and see one loss as potential gains for other products.

Services

People in the service industry are always pondering the question of what to charge. Rates vary based on numerous factors. First, the service providers must consider the overhead costs including rent, legal fees, accounting, bookkeeping, and so on, plus the materials needed to do the job.

Then the specific service must fall into the range of competitive prices. This can be tricky because service providers offer different specialties. Also considered is the reputation and background of service providers. An established financial planning company can charge more because they have 40 years of experience and people are willing to pay more for that expertise.

When determining how much you will charge for services, consider the competition. Know the range of competitive prices in your industry. Know how much your operating expenses are, including overhead costs, material costs, and marketing costs. Consider your profit goals. How much are you trying to make and how much do you need to charge to get there. Set realistic goals based on national figures for your industry. Factor in your own level of experience, specific expertise (including degrees or certificates), and your region or area. A New York–based service provider, for instance, may charge 25 percent more than the same type of business based in Columbus, Ohio.

Create an hourly rate. Even if you quote a flat fee, determine it by how many hours the job will take and how much you can bill per hour, factoring in all of the other variables. Always estimate that a job will take 20 to 25 percent longer than your initial calculation.

Consider selling accessories. If you own a hair-cutting salon, you may set a price for hair cutting and styling, but you also may make extra money by doing a little retailing of styling gel, special brushes, hair clips, and so on. Many service-based businesses today are making money off of such peripherals.

From $5 to $500 per hour, you will need to evaluate your service and what it is worth on the market. Whether you're running a personal training service, beauty salon, accounting service, or dog walking service, you need to evaluate what the market will pay you for your service and how much profit you're making above and beyond your expenses.

ESSENTIALS

A good service provider generally has more than one rate in this modern, often-confusing marketplace. While you need to have set prices for the sake of avoiding legal hassles and claims of discrimination, you can consider lower hourly rates for longer-term projects or higher rates for more specialized projects. Keep in mind a range to stay within when quoting prices.

Even if you're brand-new in the market, don't let that intimidate you from charging competitive rates. If your rates appear too low, it can be a signal to potential customers that something is not right.

In the manufacturing business, like the retail and service businesses, you will need to weigh your costs and your competition when determining prices. The cost of equipment (buying, maintaining, and servicing) as well as manpower (and specific skills), raw materials, product testing, and shipping will be factored into your pricing equation. While you seek quality in your products, you're often looking to sell in quantity to be cost-efficient.

It is also advantageous to stick with one product line for as long as possible. Depending on the industry, this can be years—like the VW

Beetle—or months, when you're manufacturing an ever-changing high-tech item. It takes time to switch from making one model or design to another and, therefore, slows down your production. You still need to account for such downtime in your pricing.

FACTS

The Thomas Register is the most complete directory of U.S. and Canadian manufacturers, including over 150,000 industrial products. The register is available in print, CD-ROM, or online. You'll find the register and numerous publications at *www.thomasregister.com.* Biz Web is a Web guide to nearly 47,000 businesses in over 200 categories. You can search for companies by industry at *www.bizweb.com.*

Establishing a strong reputation for making quality products quickly and delivering them on time will factor into your ability to charge more. Supply and demand factors into the equation as well. If everyone is clamoring for what you make, you can charge more. Don't get greedy, however, because trends change very quickly and foreign (and other domestic) manufacturers will find a way to make the same product, or a reasonable facsimile, for half the price.

In all aspects of pricing, for any kind of business, make sure you think out a strategy for your prices very carefully. Do your competitive analysis and be ready to change your prices when necessary.

CHAPTER 16

Protecting Your Business Security

O ne of the most frequently neglected areas, when starting a business is that of security. For some
inexplicable reason, entrepreneurs often
believe that it won't happen to them. But
it's worth taking some time to consider
precautions, even if you opt for common-
sense techniques over high-tech security
systems. Either way, you could be saving
yourself a lot of money in the long run,
not to mention protecting yourself against
the potential of personal injury.

Paying Attention to the Neighborhood

You won't find a crime free neighborhood in which to open your business. However, you should check out the crime statistics for any neighborhood that you're considering. Look at the types of crimes that take place and the frequency. Find out how fast the police have responded to calls in that particular neighborhood. Consider the traffic in the area, especially at night. Then consider your work hours and those of your employees. Will working late at night pose a safety concern? Is there a high incidence of car theft in the area? If so, can you secure a parking facility for your employees? How well lighted is the area at night?

Consider the safety of your personnel and your property in a selected neighborhood. Many business owners use a combination of statistics, interaction with neighboring businesses owners, and consultations with local police to assess the safety of the neighborhood in which they plan to do business. Knowledge is power.

SSENTIALS

Don't forget the human element. You can have the greatest alarm system in the world, but if no one hears it ring or responds to the call then you've wasted your money. Criminals get wise to alarms that do not elicit a response. Make sure someone is responding quickly.

Securing the Premises

Whether you're operating a storefront or an office, you'll need heavy doors with secure locks, window guards (maybe even a gate for a storefront), and some type of security alarm. There are a wealth of modern alarm systems available, and depending on how much you want to spend, you can find the one that fits your needs. Motion detectors and silent alarms to the local police precinct are frequently-used security devises.

Retail businesses also benefit from:

- Security cameras hooked up to a video recording system or watched by a security guard
- Dummy security cameras (a low-budget alternative)
- Secure safes for keeping cash and valuables
- One-way mirrors for watching the sales floor from the office or storeroom
- Well-placed mirrors watched by security personnel
- Electronic article surveillance with pedestals for customers to walk through as they exit the store
- Locking display cases
- Guard dogs or signs that imply such dogs are on the premises

These are just a few of many suggested security measures you can take to protect a retail outlet from theft. Other tips include:

- Watching customers who linger or browse for an excessive amount of time without buying anything
- Having higher-priced items in an area that is easier to watch and less accessible to the main exits
- Keeping the store, or certain sections of it, well lit when closed
- Making sure you have good external lighting
- Training personnel not to leave cases unlocked, to put inventory back where it belongs, and to follow other basic security measures
- Familiarizing yourself with the local police patrol and making sure they're familiar with your store
- Taking secure measures when opening and closing a store
- Not keeping a significant amount of cash on the premises
- Allowing only reliable employees to have keys, access to money, or the combination to the safe
- Changing locks and even the combination to the safe periodically
- Making sure to do background checks when hiring employees
- Not trusting anyone to handle significant amounts of cash except yourself, your business partner, and *maybe* your mom.

From security-tagging your merchandise to hiring armed security guards (check your insurance policy before doing so), you'll need to think through many areas of security when opening a retail business. Any area you neglect may be the one a potential thief considers.

One important place you might consider checking out is *www.lossprevention.com* for a wealth of information on protecting your business. Robert Blackwood, who runs Loss Prevention Strategies Group (407-816-9601) with partner Reid Hayes, strongly suggests that you do a risk assessment before opening a retail operation, or any other type of business. "You need to look at zones of influence," says Blackwood. "You need to draw a ring around the box (your facility) and look at the community at large and consider the types of potential risk. Then look at physical security from the outside, including the parking lot. Then go inside and consider theft from shoplifting (in retail) or internal theft by employees." Blackwood points out that the needs for security determined from an assessment will vary depending on numerous factors including location, type of merchandise, and size of the facility. He does emphasize that you carefully assess all possible means of loss.

Blackwood also points out that state laws are different regarding shoplifting. He notes that most retailers are conservative, giving customers the benefit of the doubt until they have passed the last possible point of sale, which is generally the register closest to the exit. Within the store, customers can still claim that they're planning to pay for the item and threaten to sue you if you accuse them of shoplifting. This is why electronic article surveillance with radio frequency–tagged merchandise and pedestals that customers walk through upon exiting have become increasingly popular in retail locations.

Don't forget to secure the loading docks, storeroom, and other areas of a store. Just because these areas are off-limits to non-personnel doesn't mean they won't be the first places thieves will strike. Lights, alarms, and security cameras should be part of your plan for securing these areas as well.

Securing Your Office

Many companies are lax in the area of office security. Office equipment is valuable, especially high-tech computer equipment. Thieves are looking for laptops, PalmPilots, and other high-end items that they can carry out easily and make money from selling quickly. In addition, while it's nice to think of the gang at the office as one big happy family, you should remember that most families have a black sheep or two. In other words, not everyone working in your office can be trusted.

With those sobering thoughts in mind, consider a security system—including an alarm and possibly a security guard. You may also consider employee ID cards and security cameras for entrances to areas with valuable equipment or important documents. You should also:

- Limit access to key areas or files.
- Have individual passwords for computers.
- Have sign-in/sign-out registers, and specific policies regarding outside visitors.
- Check packages entering and leaving the facility.

Keys are also an important issue in office security (or any security for that matter). Office keys should not be labeled, should never be allowed to be duplicated, and should not be left unattended. Only trusted personnel should have keys to the office, and they should be informed of the responsibilities (and potential repercussions) that go along with being given a set of keys.

It's advisable to change the locks and subsequent keys periodically. Keep a list of who is supposed to have the keys. You'll be surprised when, after six months, you collect all the keys to issue new ones and you find out how many people who should have keys don't have them anymore and how many people who shouldn't have keys somehow have a set. That presents a perfect time to remind everyone about the policies you have about not duplicating or lending keys.

Other office security tips include:

- Report any broken windows, damage to the front door, broken lights, or suspicious articles found in or around the premises to the building maintenance office.
- Have all laptops and other technical equipment securely stored when the offices are closed.
- Let employees know that they shouldn't leave valuable items at their desks including their wallet or a purse.
- Check identification from all outside repair and delivery people until you're familiar with them.
- Make a serialized list of all key office equipment including computers, technical equipment, and office furniture.

No one wants to work in an environment where they feel like Big Brother is watching their every move. On the other hand, you don't start up a business to watch it slowly walk away from you, item by item. Find a happy medium. Be alert and cautious without stepping on people's freedom to act in a comfortable manner.

It's also very important that you guard your profits. Make sure you exercise some control over all bookkeeping, including invoices and purchase orders. You'd be surprised how easily your most "trustworthy employee" can drain money from your company by taking advantage of your complete trust. You should also open all-important mail yourself and review the bank statements carefully. If you put all your trust in someone else, that person can abuse your trust and you'll never know it.

Other means of security are those that are found on paper in the form of non-disclosure agreements, confidentiality agreements, non-compete agreements, or forms mandated by the government. Certain industries such as the Securities and Exchange Commission, in an effort to prevent insider trading and other illegal activities, will also require signed agreements. Make sure all such forms are kept on file in the event that you will need them in the future.

FACTS

It's very common practice today that businesses require all outside contractors or freelancers to sign confidentiality agreements. Remember, the next job for these individuals could be with your competition. So make sure you get these agreements before outside contractors do any work for you.

Security in Manufacturing Facilities

While shoplifting is not an issue, theft remains a serious problem facing manufacturing businesses. Tools disappear often in the hands of workers, and the products you're working hard to manufacture can be at risk if your facility doesn't employ adequate security measures.

It's important to secure all entrances to the facility with surveillance cameras and/or guards on duty. Checking bags and briefcases of everyone entering and exiting the facility should also be considered. You might even consider metal detectors if you're worried about loss of products and tools. Keep in mind that this can obviously be taken as an implication of mistrust by your employees and may not be the best way to increase morale.

Within a factory, inventories must be closely watched and numbers of products should be recorded. Any report of your merchandise being sold or distributed illegally outside of your factory can be traced back to your company and should then be investigated. Often the source of black-market goods is someone working in the factory.

In the manufacturing business, you'll also have a great deal of shipping concerns. It's important that the drivers of your trucks or vans keep a log or you use a plastic seal indicating how much inventory is in the vehicle and how much is delivered to each merchant or customer. If the numbers on the log or seal and the physical count don't match up, then there may have been tampering with the vehicle's contents.

The best advise is to use sound judgment and determine how much security will prevent loss and make you feel comfortable. Know where to draw the line so that employees feel that you do trust them.

Staying Safe Online

Computer hackers have hacked into FBI files, so why couldn't they get through to your site? Chances are they can. Setting up a firewall to prevent outsiders from getting into your computer is essential for business, and not a bad idea for personal use as well. A firewall is used to prevent unauthorized access to a network. It's designed to make sure that communication between an organization's network and the Internet, in both directions, conforms to the organization's security policies.

There are two types of firewalls commonly used. An application-level firewall determines whether a requested connection should be made between the computer on the internal network and the outside computer. A network-level firewall determines whether a packet of information should be allowed to pass through or blocked, as based on rules set up by the firewall administrator. Many businesses use a combination of both.

FACTS

Many companies find that multiple passwords including one for access to the computer, one for the network or a company intranet, and others for case-sensitive files can be helpful. This way if someone learns one password of an employee, they can't access all of that employee's information.

Besides hackers getting into your system, there are security issues regarding online transactions that can make or break an e-business. When it's widely believed that your business is not conducting secure transactions, you might as well pack up and call it quits. Consumers' number-one concern when shopping online is the security of the transaction.

The key to secure transactions online is encryption. Protecting the entire transaction in this manner protects the contents, which can only be accessed by the intended parties, even after the transaction is completed. Using advanced encryption technology (128-bit SSL), you can protect sensitive data. If you only encrypt the traffic between the browser and the server, and not the entire transaction, when it's completed, it's fair game for hackers or even your own employees who may be less trustworthy and more computer-savvy than you know.

It's more than just e-tailers or e-commerce sites that can be penetrated. It's very likely that much of the significant data pertaining to your company (any type of company) is stored on files in your hard drive. This information needs to be protected and the best protection is, not unlike dressing to prevent the cold weather, using layers. These layers include a firewall, password logins, encryption, and antivirus software. A layered security system can not only prevent outside hackers from gaining access to your data, but can make it harder for employees who already have the passwords to get through to sensitive materials.

Another major issue of concern is online privacy, which differs from security in that customers are willingly providing information on membership forms or in surveys, expecting this information not to travel elsewhere. As soon as word gets out that as an entrepreneur, you're selling lists or personal information, your reputation will take a significant hit, along with your credibility—and you might even face serious fines. If a customer purchases a product or service from your company via the Internet and suddenly finds twenty-five e-mails in his inbox the next day, you'll be suspected. Surveys show that more than 90 percent of Web users feel that companies that violate an individual's online privacy should be disciplined. Nearly 90 percent are in favor of only using e-mail marketing that requires the user's permission.

Go out of your way to emphasize to your customers and your employees that the privacy issue is of paramount concern, and anyone caught violating the privacy of a customer or client will be fired.

Billions of dollars are lost each year due to online fraud. Online transaction-screening software products are combating this growing epidemic, and they're well worth the cost. However, a layering system is again worth looking into for the best possible protection. A few effective tools as determined by a survey from the folks at Merchant Fraud Squad.com include the following:

- Address-verification systems
- Real-time authorizations
- Card verification codes
- Customized rules

Computers and the Internet are the way of the business world today. Therefore, online safety is a growing issue and one that business owners must take very seriously, especially if you're dealing with sensitive material over the Internet. Some places to turn include the following:

- For a wealth of information and the latest news on hackers and the fight to keep them away from your Web site, go to *www.securitynewsportal.com* and read the articles and special reports or browse a listing of top books on Internet security.
- For firewalls and antivirus protection, go to *www.symantec.com* or *www.zonealarm.com*.
- For secure server IDs, encryption tools, and all means of Web site security, go to Verisign (*www.verisign.com* or toll-free at 866-893-6565), or check out TruSecure Corporation, which specializes in security for the Internet (*www.trusecure.com* or call 888-627-2281).
- You can also join the Merchant Fraud Squad for valuable information on e-commerce fraud by going to *www.merchantfraudsquad.com*.
- For real-time behind the firewall monitoring, you can go to *www.sitescope.com* for the latest in site monitoring systems.

ALERT

If you have no further need for any collected information, get it off your database and off of your files. Too many companies are lax about deleting old files or destroying old disks and they fall into the wrong hands. Even old paper listings of names should be files under lock and key or destroyed.

CHAPTER 17

Marketing Your Business

Ever wonder why some wonderful products and services fail while other products and services sell widely? The answer is simple: marketing. Marketing means building a base of potential customers and ultimately turning them into satisfied, regular customers. It means reaching out and making your product or service the one that customers want to own or use. Marketing focuses on the wants and needs of the customers.

Doing Market Research

If you plan to sell to a particular market, it's important to know all about that market. Research means finding out what customers want, don't want, and why. Surveys, questionnaires, and focus groups are a few ways to find out the needs and desires of your potential customers. You may be able to tell a lot about your customers by watching them and taking note of who they are and what they're interested in when they're in your store. Get some basic information when they call for your services or browse your Web site. When customers make a purchase or any kind of inquiry, you can ask them where they heard about your business.

There are many factors that will impact on your marketing plan including the following:

- Your budget
- The type of products or services you're selling
- Your scope (are you selling locally or going on the Web to handle worldwide sales?)
- The amount of volume you can handle
- Your methods of distribution
- The amount of personal service you can or cannot provide

Each business will present the unique attributes of that specific business and then have to consider all such attributes while designing questionnaires, surveys, or any other type of research-gathering materials. For example, if you're planning to do business worldwide, then you'd better plan to ask questions and conduct surveys in other languages.

Market research can tell you many things. You can learn about the pricing, trends, and competition. You can gain a greater understanding of the actual value of what it is that you're selling in the market. You may also encounter changes in the marketplace that can be advantageous. For example, if surveys indicate that healthy foods are the hottest items on the menus for the lunch crowd at the competing restaurants, then perhaps you can have a special price-fixed health lunch and even offer calorie counters and other health-related information at your dining establishment.

It's very important to look at trade magazines and reports from organizations and groups in your industry to get the latest industry news. Visit Web sites and subscribe to such industry publications. It is also important, if your business is local, to know what's going on in your community in regards to sales trends. Libraries, Web sites, company reports (annual or quarterly reports from public companies), and the local chamber of commerce are just a few places to look for local business information. Manufacturers will want a broader picture, depending on how far-reaching they anticipate their customer base will be.

When you conduct your research, you can use primary research or secondary research—or, if you're like most businesses, a combination of the two. Methods of primary market research are covered in the following sections.

Surveys

Keep surveys short (ten to twelve questions maximum), whether they're online, in-person, or by telephone. Phrase questions in a straightforward (nonjudgmental) manner, with neutral language, and keep questions one sentence long. Keep it relatively simple and even entertaining if possible, so readers will want to continue. Get the age, sex, and approximate income level (give them ranges to select from) of participants. People are more likely to fill out a written survey or answer questions in person than they are likely to want to be bothered with yet another annoying phone call. Internet surveys can get responses, but it's often hard to determine the validity of such results.

Focus Groups

Focus groups are wonderful ways to get insightful answers to questions and opinions about your product or survey. You will want to have a neutral group in a neutral location with a neutral host and provide a pleasant atmosphere—sometimes including snack foods. Often focus groups are watched through a one-way window or mirror or taped for future evaluation. Keep them to an hour and a half or two hours at the most. The drawback is that such groups can be hard to pull together and can be time-consuming and even costly. If you do get a focus group together, remember that it this isn't the final answer to all your marketing needs, but a means for gathering opinions that might benefit you. Often companies swear by a focus group that didn't adequately reflect a good cross-section of the overall population.

It's vital that your market research studies provide a close representation of your target audience. In fact, by your third focus group or series of surveys you may be intentionally including 90 percent men or 90 percent women because that percentage most accurately profiles the population buying your product or using your service.

Know your product, know (or learn) your market group, and then test the product on the right group. For example, if you're testing your new wedding-planning Web site, test it in front of engaged couples or engaged women but not in front of a room with 50 percent divorced men who have no interest at present in getting remarried.

For the best results hire professionals, whether it's graphic artists, publicists, or copywriters. Don't try to do everything yourself. Good advertising, marketing, and publicity is not the place to cut corners. Be careful, however, and get referrals and review the work of the company or individual before you hire them.

Monitoring

Keeping close tabs on who buys what product or service is a way of gathering information. Are all your credit card receipts from the same zip code? Do customers always seem to visit the same pages on your Web site? Simple statistical information can be gathered by monitoring your business transactions. This can provide market research information and help you define your target audience. You might simply notice on your store video camera that the last sixty-one customers who bought items were males in their early to mid-twenties. Pay attention and you can gather inexpensive marketing research.

QUESTIONS?

What's the difference between primary and secondary market research?
In primary research, you go out and gather all the information from surveys, questionnaires, tests, focus groups, and other means. Secondary research uses other sources, such as data services, the Census, books, magazines, or Web sites. Primary research is more accurate, but secondary research is faster and cheaper.

Identifying Your Target Market

Just as children's games say clearly on the box what ages the game is geared toward, nearly every product or service has some demographic group that will be most interested in spending money to own it, use it, or rent it. The number of businesses that have failed because the owners haven't taken the time to determine their target audience is staggering. Know your target market, and remember it doesn't have to be twenty-year-olds. In fact, the group with the biggest buying power in this country is over forty, not sixteen to twenty-three. A particular growing market with people living longer is the over-sixty-five demographic, particularly women. There are almost 40 million people in the United States over the age of 65, and more than 55 percent are women.

Yes, a store selling air would have a target market of everyone, since we all need air, but our interests, likes, dislikes, tastes, and needs are different based on many factors—including age, location, income level, ethnic culture, marital status, and so much more. There are many reasons why the one-size-fits-all approach usually doesn't work when marketing a product or service.

Some questions to ask yourself when outlining your target market or demographic group include:

- What is the age range of the customer who wants my product or service?
- What is their income level?
- What level of education do they have?

- What is their marital or family status?
- Is this a product or service they need or a luxury item?
- How will they use this product or service?
- What will draw them to my product or service?
- Which sex will be buying my product or service more often?
- What special features or attention are they looking for?
- What do they like or dislike about the product or service in general?
- Is this an impulse buy or something they are saving up for?
- Where do they gather their decision-making information?

These are just a few of numerous categories into which you can break down your target market. While you don't want to make a marketing plan that is ultimately so narrow that it limits your sales to a small few perfect customers, you do want to narrow down the field from that elusive "everybody" response that generally spells trouble.

Don't forget to properly expose your product to the public and get feedback. Test marketing, focus groups, or even on a smaller level, showing the prototype to friends and family for their honest opinions are important ways of getting feedback before taking your product or service before the public.

Reaching Your Market

Let's say you've established that your ideal customer is a single woman between the age of twenty-five and forty-two, with an income in the $35,000 to $55,000 range, who resides in the suburbs of a large city, drinks diet soda, watches *Friends* on television, speaks to her mom twice a week, dates men three to five years older than herself, and has a cat. Well, perhaps you didn't get that specific (you generally don't need to), but the point is, once you've established who your audience is, you need to know how to reach them.

FACTS

Some refer to it as a lifecycle; others see it as highs and lows (since products sometimes rebound for various reasons). The bottom line is that products and some services have periods where they are at high points in popularity. Price accordingly—follow the popularity curve of the product or service you're selling.

Pricing

Before venturing into the methods of getting your name out there, it's important that you consider your pricing strategies. In a new business, you may need to establish your reputation and brand name with potential customers by keeping your product or services below average market prices. Otherwise, you'll need to provide special services or incentives that your competition cannot provide. If a new product and an established brand-name product are priced the same, the established brand will most often be the choice of the customer.

You might also use time-factored pricing as a promotion point. For example, you can promote a lower price if customers buy before a particular date. Be careful not to lower your prices below cost or make prices so low that customers don't return when you're selling at your regular prices.

Pricing is also linked to perceived value. If someone is expecting to pay a certain amount for a product or service, he won't question that amount. If you're able to cut costs, you can lower the price. However, you don't have to. For example, if you're selling soda at $1 per bottle and buying bottles in mass quantity at $0.59 each, you're making $0.41 per bottle sold. If everyone is used to paying $1 for a soda in your area, then no one will think about the price. If, however, you can suddenly get bottles of soda at $0.49 each from a different distributor, it doesn't mean you have to lower your price to $0.90. If you stay at $1 per bottle you're staying at the market price, which means more profits for you. If, however, you want more volume because there aren't enough people coming into your deli, you might lower your price—and promote the fact that you did so through fliers, signage, and word of mouth. Keep in mind, though, that people can become spoiled by lower prices.

Some stores offer major sales so often that customers wait for those sales, causing the store a great drop-off in business on non-sales weeks. Plan sales accordingly and make sure customers are drawn to the store by promotions in-between such sales.

Promotion and Advertising

The concept is simple, if you have a product or service and you want to make money from it, you'll need to promote it. This includes promoting a new business, new products, services you offer, and keeping your name in front of the public. Promotion includes selling, sales promotion, and advertising. Selling can include talking with customers and sales calls. Sales promotion can include anything from how you arrange the sales items on a selling floor or set up the home page on your Web site to attending trade shows.

There are numerous ways to get your name out there, and once you've done your market research and established who your target audience is, you'll need to put together your promotional budget.

If you send regular mailings to customers, it's more effective than a one-time deal. Often it takes three or four mailings for the person to notice you. In essence, they become familiar with seeing your logo or slogan and finally pay attention to what you have to say.

Direct Mail

Often referred to as *junk mail* by its recipients, direct mail can yield a greater response if you target the consumer for your product or service correctly. Magazines seeking subscriptions have long been relying heavily on direct mail, and today numerous products and services also seek significant returns from direct-mail marketing. Direct mailing differs from a mail campaign to your regular customers because it involves buying or compiling a specific list that best suits your target market or demographic needs. Certainly, many people will toss what you send into the garbage. However, if you send out 100 direct mail pieces at a cost of $100 and make three sales at a cost of $60 each, you're making $180. You've also put your name in front of the other ninety-seven people, four or five of whom may remember you at a later date or have a friend who needs whatever it is that you're selling.

With direct mail, your goal is to at least make enough profit to cover the entire cost of the mailing including printing, postage, the cost of the list, and so on. Study other direct-mail pieces and create (or hire someone to create) a professional-looking direct-mail piece—one that appears personal, presents the benefits of what you're offering, and makes them an offer they can't refuse.

Postcards can be effective direct-mail pieces. They're cheaper than letters and can grab attention immediately.

FACTS

Companies often buy mailing lists that are ultimately much larger than the mailing they will send out. It may be advantageous to buy a list of 5,000 names and narrow it down to the best 1,000 that you can afford to reach.

Timing is everything when it comes to direct mail. Plan your mailing for opportune times. For example, you won't want your direct mailing piece to get caught up in the holiday postal overload. Make your piece stand out. Use color, a photo, or a clever quote. Avoid mixed or confusing messages. Use a tone that reflects your readers. You don't want to sound pretentious. If your piece has too much to read, people will toss it.

Don't insult or put down your audience. Don't tell them why what they're doing is wrong or stupid and why you have all the answers. Tell them you can improve upon their way of doing things.

E-mail

E-mail marketing is a popular yet tricky way of reaching a worldwide audience. Internet users hate *spam,* or the electronic version of junk mail that comes from buying lists of unwanted participants. The same people might not mind junk mail in their mailbox—in fact, they're used to it—but e-mail is considered more intrusive. The delete button is easy to hit before ever looking at anything you send.

It's to your advantage to market yourself clearly on your Web site or even on another Web site of a similar nature. You want people to sign up for, or agree to receive, e-mails from you. Blind e-mails from massive lists generally annoy people. Although you may still get a 2 percent response rate, you may also have gained a negative reputation with the other 98 percent.

If you do plan to use e-mail, keep the message concise and make sure people can get off the list if they want to. It's one thing to reach them with a message and another to bombard them. Also, keep your messages in text format to best cross over into different e-mail systems.

FACTS

Some of the ways in which people waste their time and money on direct mailing is by not following up on responses. Many people will not respond, but those who do are the potential customers you're seeking. Don't waste the leads you receive.

Signage

If you have a store or even an office, your sign or signs are more important than you think. Signs draw people into an establishment and keep your company name highly visible to new and old customers alike. The lettering, the colors, a logo, and anything else that makes your sign stand out is significant. Remember that passersby are not stopping to read your sign—they're catching it at a glance as they drive or walk past. A simple three- or four-word sign is easier to comprehend than posting two sentences.

Along with your actual signs, you can take advantage of inexpensive but effective advertising with posters and fliers. In major cities, there are numerous construction sites and other such areas that have advertisements posted all over them. As long as the posting of bills is allowed, this is an inexpensive way to be seen by numerous people. The traffic that passes by in a major city is tremendous. College campuses are also great places to post fliers.

Handouts can also be an effective way of letting people know about your hottest products or specialized services. Instruct those handing out such materials to be courteous and not stick them in people's faces.

Be clever. Anywhere you think people who are prospective customers might see your company name is where you want to have it placed. Abide by laws, rules, and regulations—or you could be fined.

ALERT

Be sure to check local ordinances before putting up your signs. Your city may have restrictions about how big the sign can be, what colors can be included on it, and where you can post the signs. Your effort will be wasted if the signs are torn down by the city—and you're issued a fine.

Advertising

Posting bills and posters is advertising, so is direct mail, but it's a less expensive method than major newspaper or magazine ads. And they pale in comparison to the cost of a TV advertising campaign. Depending on the nature of your business, you'll need to evaluate the types of media available. If you're planning and promoting an annual one-month festival held every October, then you'll use your ad money to advertise in a big way in August and September. However, if you're selling products or services year-round, you'll want the budget to last.

Newspapers provide a means for reaching a particular region (or the nation, if it's a paper with a wide circulation, such as *USA Today* or *The New York Times*). You can time your ads to run when you choose and reach a large audience. Keep the ads simple and make sure they provide a means by which customers can reach you—phone number, e-mail address, and so on. Remember to place your ad in the section best suited for your product or service, such as Sports or Lifestyle. You can also include perks like coupons. Be forewarned, however, that photos and artwork don't always look good in newspapers.

Look at the ad rates carefully and measure the size of ads that you might want to buy (ads are sold by column inch). Generally you will need to advertise more than once so people become familiar with seeing your ad. Sunday papers can be good because people save them. Pennysavers aren't newspapers but can also be good for small inexpensive ads, depending on your product.

Magazines allow you to reach a more targeted audience. Also, your ad will have a longer shelf life than a daily paper, which gets tossed or lines the litter box by evening. Select magazines that are best suited for your product or services, and remember that they usually have a long lead-time. Magazines allow for marvelous artwork, so you can be colorful and creative. Trade magazines can be beneficial for business-to-business sales or industry recognition. Get a calendar of when ads are needed at the magazine. Provide as close to camera-ready art as possible so the art director doesn't have to make significant changes—some of which you won't like. Make sure the copy suites the magazine and its readership.

Radio is an excellent way to reach a targeted market, since different demographic groups listen to different formats. Radio allows you to be creative with sound effects and you will spend a lot less money than advertising on television. Be concise and conversational in your tone, get to the point quickly, don't be obnoxious, and try to be entertaining and snappy—whether the copy is produced or it's read by on-air talent (naturally a thirty- or sixty-second produced commercial is more effective). Make sure the location of your store or Web site is clearly stated and the phone number is repeated twice if you're a one-location business. Look for high-traffic times like morning or evening drive times.

You should also consider easy listening stations or light music stations, which are played in establishments where many people will be listening, such as restaurants or even over telephone lines when people are put on hold. The listening audience for such stations is often larger than the ratings reveal because of all these secondary listeners. Also remember that radio stations love to do giveaways—your product or service can be one such giveaway or you can stage your own contest.

Be creative when it comes to television. For example, if a local talk show needs a hotel for their guests to stay at, you might provide rooms free of charge in exchange for a promotional announcement. If you run a limousine service, provide free transportation for all guests in exchange for a daily mention of your company. Such deals are worked out all of the time. And then there are infomercials. They're expensive, but they can be very effective for certain products.

Some businesses dedicate 30 percent of their operating budget to advertising, others set aside just 3 percent. How much you spend depends on the size of the company and how you can reach your market. Think about how rapidly you'll grow, how much competition you have, the amount of word-of-mouth advertising you can generate, and the size of your market.

Billboards are a great way to put your brand name in front of the public. Be creative and keep it simple. Remember, they're driving by and have no time to read five lines of copy at 60 miles per hour.

Trade shows are another great way to be seen. Design a booth that grabs people's attention and displays your products or services. Have plenty of literature and friendly, smiling faces on hand. If you can't afford to be part of a trade show, at least attend and make sure you put your business card in the hand of everyone you meet.

Other forms of advertising are all around you. The tops of taxis and sides of busses, the outfield fences at the ballpark, and numerous other places have advertising. You can promote yourself with T-shirts, sweatshirts, pens, notepads, or baseball caps. CD-ROMs or in-house newsletters (online or offline) can also spread the word about what you're up to and what you offer potential customers. Put your name on a takeout menu, or sponsor a local event. Putting your name before the public—preferably your target market—is your goal. Advertising can be one method of doing so, but there are other means of getting publicity. Keep in mind that repeat advertising is more effective than one-time advertising so budget accordingly.

Make sure to monitor your ads to be certain that they run when they're supposed to and look—or sound—as you wish. If the ad didn't run properly, or at all, you must make sure the media source knows it.

Advertising is designed to increase your business and put your name and image before the public in a positive manner. It is generally less effective to slam your competitors (even if you're a politician).

ESSENTIALS

If you utilize various forms of media using a cross section of advertising methods, and maintain your message through slogans, catch phrases, characters, or in any other manner, it can be very effective. You'll reach a wider audience through various types of media.

Specialists in advertising can be helpful but some will try to sell you anything including a campaign that *they* like. Get recommendations before signing up with an ad agency or consultant.

Look into co-op ads with vendors, merchants, or manufacturers (depending on which side of the fence you're on). You can get plenty of coverage for half the price, or less.

You can trade advertisements for products or services by working barter deals.

If you're operating an online business, you may benefit from online means of exposure, which include:

- Linking with other sites
- Registering with several top search engines
- Using specific keywords to increase your likelihood of your company name coming up during a search
- Swapping ads with other sites
- Joining Internet organizations and getting yourself written up in newsletters and on other sites
- Getting your name around by mentioning it on newsgroups, in chat rooms, or in forums
- Offline marketing and promotion

One of the biggest reasons for the downfall of several major Web sites was that they overextended their advertising beyond the value or profitability of their product. This can be the downfall of any business. If you're spending an average of $10 to promote a $7 item, you're in trouble.

Publicity and Public Relations

You need not always go out and spend top dollar on advertising and promotional ideas to get your name before the public. Stories about your business in newspapers, magazines, on the Internet, or as part of radio or television newscasts can be remarkably successful ways of increasing business. Unlike advertising, you don't pay for these directly, but you may pay for a publicist or public relations agency to help put you in the limelight, or at least in a few key stories.

When you're starting out, you can do some of this work yourself through writing and sending press releases to anyone and everyone whom you think might find a story of interest in what your business is doing. Send information about new products, upcoming events, new technology or inventions, interesting news, mergers, or anything else that could potentially become a story. Look for a clever attention-grabbing hook. Think up an eye-catching title and include the who, what, where, when, and why of the proposed story. Double space your press release, keep it to one page (two maximum), and make sure you include specific contact information.

Press kits are important and should include a collection of recent press releases, clips from stories that were written about you or your company, and an overview of what the company is all about, plus bios of the key players. A nice-looking, professional-looking press kit is a very important business tool. You can start by having a few kits printed to serve your immediate needs, but as your company grows you will want to look at places like *www.presskits.com* for a selection of professional personalized kits. The kit should reflect the image of your business.

Public relations is more than trying to place your name in front of the media. A good public relations firm can help you maintain a positive image through damage control. This includes cleaning up negative publicity that may result from incidents, activities, or accidents involving your business. If one of your products was recalled, you'll need to spend time and work with your PR department to reassure the public that your company has addressed and dealt with the problem. Your reputation and how it plays in the media is very important. If you're a media darling, you can thrive. If David Letterman and Jay Leno make jokes about your company, you might still thrive. However, if your company has a seriously bad reputation or is part of a negative news story, this could cause you to lose significant business.

Another great way to promote yourself is by sponsoring local activities or events. From a local track meet to a major golf tournament, sponsorship can be a marvelous way to put your name before the public in a positive manner. You can also host seminars, classes, or other such events. Joining trade associations, attending conferences and seminars (press kits in hand), and putting yourself and your company name in front of groups of people who are in your industry or interested in what you do can help you spread the word.

ALERT

If you're being interviewed for a story, prepare in advance. Make sure you offer positive information and limit your answers to the subject. If you go off topic, you may put your foot in your mouth and end up with a negative story. Be careful. If you think the interviewer is digging for dirt, cut the interview short.

Word of mouth is another way of gaining free publicity, one that you can get started by getting people to talk about your product or service at anyplace from cocktail parties to boy scout hiking trips. Tell your friends and family to talk you up! Remember charitable work can't hurt either.

CHAPTER 18

The Human Element

Technical sophistication can only take you so far in business. Without the human element, you fail to build relationships. While there are many who embrace new technology and utilize each advancement for the betterment of their business, few, if any, businesses can survive strictly on technology. Consumers today demand attention. They no longer want strictly automated phone responses or one-size-fits-all boilerplate service providers.

Customer Service

Customer service is not just being there to respond to the complaints. It is, as the name implies, providing a service. It is the way you can show your customers or clients that they're very important to you. Customer service can help enhance your reputation in a way that far exceeds hiring even the best public relations firm. For every customer that tells his friend how well he was treated by your company, you'll be saving money on advertising and PR. Retaining customers is just as important as attracting new ones. Too many businesses take their regular customers for granted and only realize their value when the competition lures them away. Companies of all sizes need to maintain their steady customers.

Part of your product-pricing policy will include the service you will offer. People will readily pay more to eat in a nicer restaurant that costs more, because the food is of higher quality and the service is good. A quality product coupled with arrogant service won't work in the restaurant business—or anywhere else. Unless you're the only store in town selling shoes, another shoe store will gobble up your customers if you don't provide good service.

ESSENTIALS

In the early 1980s, a company called Crazy Eddie sold electronics in the New York area boasting (in loud obnoxious television and radio commercials) that they could beat any price. They did as advertised. However, they treated customers poorly. "So what do you want to buy?" was their greeting. In time, Crazy Eddie was out of business. Why did things fail? Simply put, people were turned off by the bad attitude, poor service, and ultimately the mismanagement of the business.

For a long time, an uptown New York City shoe store was a favorite for buying children's shoes. The sales help were given a bonus for selling a certain number of shoes and were hired on the basis of being able to work well with kids. It wasn't that the city didn't have plenty of other locations to buy shoes for kids, but this store had excellent service and activities for children to play with while they waited. The prices were not the lowest in town, but people shopped there regularly. And, the storeowner decided to benefit returning customers, knowing that children's feet grow steadily and their need for new shoes is frequent. They started a policy that after buying ten pairs of shoes the next pair would be 50 percent off.

To establish a successful business you need to know not only what products your customers want, but also how they expect to be treated. Your customers expect:

- Consistency: If you're known for doing something in a certain manner, you need to be consistent.
- Fairness: If you treat customers differently, you can put yourself in deep trouble.
- Assistance: You know more about your products and services than they do, so you need to provide assistance.
- Responsiveness: Customers expect prompt service—don't keep people waiting for great lengths of time and expect them to return to do business with you again.
- Competence: If you continue to bring them the wrong order or incorrect shoe size they won't be back.
- Fair policies: If something needs to be returned, let them return or exchange it.

Customers also want something more. From gift-wrapping to e-mails of new products when they come into stock, you can provide the little things that make your business stand out.

Customer service isn't relegated only to retail and e-tail businesses. Client relations are tantamount to success in corporate America as well. Note the number of company box seats at the ballpark. While you don't want to spend excessively to indulge your clients, you do want to keep them smiling. This often means doing the little things—from remembering birthdays to sending thank-you notes to not billing them for every photocopy you run on their behalf.

Also keep in mind that prompt correspondence and replies to letters and e-mails from customers or clients is very important. If it takes you a week to e-mail someone back or you send them a perfunctory form letter or e-mail, you can be sure they've lost confidence in your company.

Training Employees and Hiring Personnel

There is nothing worse than losing business because your employees simply don't know how to do their jobs. This is ultimately a reflection on you and your leadership. Training entails:

- Properly assessing the person's skill level when you hire them.
- Clearly explaining what is expected of them in their positions.
- Offering an open line of communication and encouraging trainees to ask questions.
- Clearly explaining policies, including explaining when a policy might not fit the specific situation.
- Re-training when advanced technology or new products or services are introduced.

Before you can train people, you need to hire the right person for the right job. This includes politely placing, or not placing, family members in specific roles (if you have a small business and are relying on your family for help). Don't be conned into letting your nephew handle your books if he has no bookkeeping background whatsoever.

At the two ends of the spectrum you can:

- Hire people who have years of expertise in an area—but they will cost you more and may not last, as they will want to move up.
- Hire people and train them in an area—they'll cost you less initially, but may end up costing you more depending on how long it takes to train them.

You, therefore, need to assess a person's general skill level and see how close he is to meeting your needs. Too often employers are seeking the ideal candidate with many years of experience and all the skills imaginable. This prolongs the hiring process and costs more money in advertising and recruiting. Unless you're in the business of rocket science, training individuals in most industries is not rocket science.

Remember, skills alone, such as computer skills, are not as important as having well-trained individuals who know how to act and interact with others and deal with a variety of circumstances. You should seek out individuals who:

- Offer new ideas
- Have problem-solving skills
- Meet deadlines
- Understand the need for professionalism in the workplace
- Can make a commitment to the company and their assigned role

Well-rounded employees are more valuable than just finding specific skill sets.

QUESTIONS?

What does employee rotation mean?
It means having employees rotate and do different jobs and tasks to learn more about the business. In some types of businesses, this can be done effectively and allows people to back one another up if necessary.

Your Business and the Community

Whether you operate a local or national business, you will be a part of some community at large. Your business will be based somewhere and you will be responsible for following local ordinances, paying local taxes if necessary, and so on. But there is more than just setting up shop or opening an office. It's advantageous to your company to seek out help from local business organizations and to network with members of such groups. The local chamber of commerce and other such groups can provide leads for businesses and help you extend your name throughout the community.

Community involvement is also a way of helping you to build a strong relationship. Local, and even national programs may ask businesses for support. Support from the right leaders in the community can help your business draw attention, as can donating to local charities or sponsoring a local event.

The media can also help or hurt a business depending on the stories they broadcast or articles they write. A positive relationship with local media is helpful when it comes to potentially controversial stories that could involve your business. The media can paint a picture of you that is positive, negative, or neutral. Some ways to establish yourself with the media include:

- Sending press releases and information about community activities that you're involved in.
- Offering input as a business owner when business-related issues arise (just try to speak as an expert rather than taking a side).
- Providing interesting story angles and suggestions to local reporters and journalists.
- Being available for interviews or letting your place be a central location should the media need to conduct interviews.

A Comedy Club gained a foothold in the media by letting all of the local television stations know that if they wanted to use the facility for casting calls they could do so. Back scratching with the media can be to your benefit—just keep it clean.

It's advantageous to get involved in community activities. However, if you're asked to take a side on an issue or back a politician, make sure your partisanship won't jeopardize your business. If you're afraid taking sides will hurt your reputation, then remain neutral.

Making Sure Your Needs Are Being Met

So, you treat your employees well, and you try to create a positive attitude around the office, the store, the factory, or wherever your business resides. You lead with both a gentle touch and a forceful hand. You try to maintain a steady base of customers while constantly seeking to expand upon that base. The business is growing but not for lack of effort. You put in 40, 50, 60, 70, or even 170 hours a week (okay, there aren't 170 hours in a week, but you're working so much it feels like there are). Are you overworked? Yes. Underpaid? Yes. Under appreciated? Yes. It goes with the territory.

One of the hallmarks of a successful business is (dot-com madness aside) that it is built on a foundation of very hard work. There is no way around it. Anyone who has built a successful business will tell you "It's not easy. It's exhausting"

QUESTIONS?

What can you do to take care of yourself?
Walk away once in a while. A few hours for a round of golf is nice, but a weekend away is nicer. There is a burnout factor that will take its toll on you if you overwork yourself and/or your staff. If you kill yourself starting up a successful business, you won't be around to enjoy the benefits.

It takes just as much self-discipline to tell yourself to stop working as it does to do an all-nighter getting the software properly set up. Whether you walk away for three hours on the golf course, spend a day at the beach, or take a weekend away, you need to shut off the cell phone and clear your head. Make long lists before you go if necessary, just to get the workload out of your mind and onto a piece of paper or into your PalmPilot. Put someone else in charge and instruct him or her to reach you only in an emergency, like flood, fire, or major computer virus. Time spent away is time to refuel your body and your mind. Don't think about the office. Read a good book—and not one about business.

The only type of person who can start a business and see it to success is one who is driven. It can take three to five years for the average business to turn a profit. It's during those years that you're getting no write-ups in business journals or awards for local entrepreneur of the year. All you're doing is working to keep the business going and, hopefully, growing. You need to set realistic goals and try to meet them. You also need to appreciate the baby steps you take as your business grows. If you train yourself not to think of only profits as the measure of success, then you're making your life easier. A businessperson needs to stay in present time but keep thinking toward the future. That's not always easy when customers aren't calling, showing up, or contacting you through your Web site. If you can accept the fact that you'll be living off of your savings, loans, or your spouse's income until the business is off the ground, you'll be in a better position to handle those lean years.

Here are some ways to remain sane during these trying times:

- Enjoy what you're doing—if you don't like a business, don't enter into it.
- Look for humor—if you take it all too seriously, you'll end up with an ulcer.
- Don't compare yourself to everyone else—reading the Business section to find out about each entrepreneur who made a killing may be killing you inside, so give it a rest once in a while.
- Don't over analyze—there are only a certain number of business options, solutions, and possibilities, so once you've reviewed the possibilities, go for it.
- Remember to interact with people daily—don't become a slave to technology.
- Reward yourself—just like you got ice cream as a kid for finishing up your homework, take the gang out for coffee, beer, or even ice cream when you've completed a business project.
- Look at what you've learned from each mistake you make as your business grows.

CHAPTER 19

Managing Your Business

Y ou've launched the business, enjoyed the big party, and now it's on to making a success of it over the long haul. What can you do to successfully manage the business? No matter what your business, there are many fundamental elements that you can, or must, keep tabs on in order to remain successful.

Staying the Course

Just because investors took favorably to your business plan and gave you the startup money that you needed, that doesn't mean you can file the business plan away in a drawer, never to be seen again. You need to follow your plan now more than ever, to show your investors, your clients, your employees, and yourself that you're on track, working to achieve the goals you outlined.

Keep in mind that as you follow your business plan and reach each milestone, you can attract new investors based on your track record. Also keep in mind that, over time, you may want to become more self-reliant, using profits to grow the business and not the money of additional investors. The path to a profitable business was what you outlined in the business plan. If it wasn't feasible you would have stopped before starting. With each appropriate and inevitable adjustment that you will need to make along the way, you should remain faithful to your business plan.

Monitoring Cash Flow

Cash flow is a major area of concern for growing (and ongoing) businesses. You need cash on hand to operate, but you don't always have it. For that reason, you need to monitor your cash flow very carefully. If employees aren't getting paid, they're no longer enthusiastic, hard-working employees. Not being able to pay your vendors won't endear them to you either. Extending lines of credit can be a way of building relationships, but don't let such relationships abuse your trust. You need to maintain available cash at all times.

How can you do that? Try to turn all sales into cash as quickly as possible. Offer incentives for cash payments or for paying off a line of credit quickly. You can also make some of your own purchases of equipment or goods on credit. If you combine the two ideas by offering a discount if a customer pays in thirty days and then buying on credit that is due in forty-five days, you give yourself a two-week gap to collect payments and then make payments.

Establish a solid line of credit: If you're in good shape financially, it's recommended that you take out bank loans and pay them back quickly, thus establishing an excellent credit rating. This will help you for those times when you need a loan to get out of a cash flow crunch. You'll get the loan quickly and without difficulty.

It's also important to monitor your expenditures and keep them in line with your cash flow. When it looks like a cash flow problem is on the horizon, limit any unnecessary expenses and buy on credit. When cash flow is favorable, spend cash and don't run up your credit.

Here are some ways to eliminate unnecessary spending:

- Don't believe the hype that you need new software, hardware, a new car, and all sorts of other new equipment every year—make the most of what you already have.
- Limit expense accounts or even eliminate them—an expense account is often a license to spend needlessly.
- Watch entertainment and travel expenses closely—they're two areas where employees may try to take advantage.
- Set strict policies and guidelines regarding expenses.
- Buy what you'll need for business purposes, not what you think you might need down the road.
- Shop around for a good long-distance service provider.
- Look for barter deals where applicable.
- Don't waste money on high utility bills—conserve energy.
- Do marketing research before spending money on advertising and promotional campaigns that won't work.
- Don't hire full-timers for part-time jobs.
- As a last resort, implement a wage freeze to help you lower your expenses.

FACTS

If you maintain a smaller inventory, you will be able to manage your inventory more effectively and be able to shift gears when the trends suddenly change. You'll also be able to limit your technological needs for inventory management and control.

Being a Good Listener and Communicator

Managing successfully means being flexible and listening to the needs of your customers and to the suggestions of your employees. Flexibility means adapting to change, taking in what you hear, and using it constructively. Listen objectively: Don't make assumptions as to the meaning behind the message or the reason why someone is saying something. Just because a customer or employee has a suggestion to improve upon something doesn't mean your method is incorrect. It simply means there is another viewpoint, for better or for worse. If you keep your eyes and ears open, you'll also help plug into the changing trends within your industry and the business community.

Does everyone know what's expected of them? Does change take place in a well-thought-out, carefully planned manner, or are changes thrust upon employees? How you communicate with your personnel, customers, investors, vendors, suppliers, the media, and the community at large is vital to your business success. If you can communicate in a clear, respectful manner and establish strong relationships with everyone involved in the operations of your business, you'll be in an advantageous position.

SSENTIALS One of the premiere tools of a successful business, as noted by numerous top CEOs, is communications. Study communications techniques and pass on your expertise to your colleagues and your staff. Before you make changes that will involve your customers, let your staff know all your planning decisions. Seek their feedback. Get their responses.

Communication also includes timing. You need to know when to communicate your message and in what medium. A combination of e-mail, telephone calls, snail mail, and personal visits will all come into play while making your communications decisions. The mode of communication will depend on the nature of the message you wish to communicate and to whom you're communicating. For example, you don't send an e-mail telling someone they've been let go. Conversely, you need not travel for hours to give someone a simple message. While managing your business, you need to monitor and constantly review your listening and communications skills. Many business owners get lazy and don't pay attention to their manner of communications.

Gathering Information

Do ongoing research on your demographic base, changes in your industry, and changes in the market. Keep track of government policies and regulations, local business news, and environmental concerns that could effect your business. It's vital that you know your consumers. If their needs are changing, you have to be aware of those changes. There is no substitute for knowledge. You'll also need to be knowledgeable about your competition. Short of sending in a spy (and it's often done), you can gather as much data as possible on what your leading competitors are up to now and in the near future. Continue to do your homework. Then analyze the data you've gathered to determine how it affects or does not affect your business.

Information gathering includes ongoing market research. It's important to focus in on any potential new consumer group or niche that may be ripe for your products or services. It's also imperative that you uncover and evaluate any new means of communicating with your target market. Some businesses identified and utilized the Internet effectively in its breakthrough years. Others sat on the fence and only utilized the Internet after the initial excitement had lessened. Their message was therefore not as well received.

Ongoing research also includes retesting and even repackaging "tried and true" products and services. Just because something has been successful for twenty years, doesn't mean it can't be changed if the public no longer embraces the idea. On the other hand, as evidenced when Coca-Cola changed its formula, sometimes tried and true continues to be what the people want.

The knee-jerk reaction to the lowering of prices by your competition is to lower your prices. However, before you make any move, you should study the potential effects on your business. Don't just react without planning your next move carefully. Remember, you're playing a chess game.

Measuring Productivity

If you have a system in place for measuring productivity, you can identify problem areas and make appropriate changes to improve your production. It's important that you measure all the tangible elements that go into your business, including manpower, resources, equipment used, and anything else expended to create, develop, or provide what you're selling, making, or marketing. Measuring productivity starts with keeping track of whatever it takes to do business—from hours spent by your workers to gas expended by your trucks. You then look at the end results of time and money it takes to create, buy, or produce your product or service and compare it to your profitability.

Some products can be streamlined and manufactured on an assembly line, while others are handcrafted. Remember, not all productivity can be streamlined. Faster doesn't mean better when you're talking about a hand-crafted item.

Sometimes productivity is a matter of technology. For example, look at how many businesses have improved their checkout services through price scanners and cash registers that display how much change is owed. The new check out stations speed up customer activity while drastically cutting down on errors. Unfortunately many employees in various areas of business use technology to cover up for the inadequacies of the education system. Why not just let the calculators or computers figure out the answers?

Keeping Up-to-Date Files

Good managers can look into their files and pull up the latest information on anyone working for the company or any technology being used. Furthermore, all vendor information, invoices, and purchase orders need to be up to date. Make sure everything from personnel data to the serial number of the latest laptop is updated and filed accordingly. Hire competent help to properly maintain all electronic and paper files.

Collecting Money

Besides having an aggressive person handling your accounts payable, or doing the job yourself in an aggressive manner, it's imperative that you make sure all of your bills include all the vital information for payment purposes. Include the name of the project or list of the products or services, the purchase order contract number, and your company name, address, and phone number. Too many people work hard to make money, only to let others neglect to pay what they owe. Make specific payment terms—whether it's ten, thirty, or sixty days. If you offer a discount for people paying their bills sooner rather than later, make sure it's clearly stated on your statement.

SSENTIALS

When you're owed money beyond the terms of payment noted on the invoice, send a duplicate invoice or have someone whose position it is to handle collections. Send letters, keep on top of it and finally go to a collection agency or start legal action.

Knowing Your Business

When you start out, you're owner, manager, salesperson, technology manager, advertising director, office manager, marketing manager, bookkeeper, and janitor. It's you, you, and you doing it all. As the company grows, you delegate more and more responsibility to your employees. Over time, technology has changed and new methods of selling, advanced technology, cutting-edge advertisements, online bookkeeping, and unionized janitors have come along. In short, the business changes as it grows. Could you still sit down and do any or all of these jobs? Can you wear many hats in your own business or are you, the owner, becoming obsolete? No matter how big your business, you should have a firm understanding of the job being done. No, you don't need to be an expert in all areas, but when it comes to your own business, you should be able to step in and handle any role if necessary.

You can make sound decisions based on your knowledge of all aspects of your business. You'll also gain respect from your employees if you can discuss their tasks and work in an intelligent manner.

Staying Competitive

To maintain your market position and improve upon it, you must not only keep tabs on your direct competition, but evaluate where you stand. Compare the data you gather on your competitors with your own company facts and figures. At what price are they selling goods and services? Are you able to match their prices, beat them, or provide something that justifies your price being higher?

You'll occasionally make moves that are part of your own strategy (offense) and moves that are based on that which your opponent does (defense). Unlike chess, however, you'll also need to react to outside factors including the environment, trends, and economic factors. If you can foresee an external change before your competition, you'll have a leg up.

Staying competitive doesn't mean you have to do battle. Price wars can run you into financial trouble. You can run yourself into a situation whereby you're giving products or services away if you get into a price war. Find creative ways to attract customers, establish a relationship, and hold onto steady customers. If necessary, find a niche.

Knowing Whether to Be Proactive or Reactive

There are two approaches to remaining competitive in business. One approach is to monitor trends as they occur and adjust to the changes in business and the environment. This is a reactive approach, whereby you're reacting to what's going on in the business world. The other approach is to use data, market reports, and predictions by industry forecasters to be proactive and start the new trends or be on the cutting edge. Taking chances can be risky, but if you see the changes on the horizon, you can beat the competition to the punch. This approach means being very confident in your predictions and basing your strategy on solid research and analysis—not on hunches.

Whether you act in a proactive or reactive manner, you'll need to be able to act quickly and make changes in a short time span. The modern business community, because of the latest advances in communication and the Internet, can move fast and introduce customers to new products very quickly. Trends, prices, and economic factors can change very quickly in a new shrinking global marketplace. It's much harder to maintain customer loyalty with so many choices and attractive offers marketed at your customers. If you're out of stock or not carrying the latest models you could be out of business in a hurry. Keeping pace, or having the flexibility to make changes quickly, is essential.

One of the first shifts made by major companies as they tightened their belts during the economic slowdown of late 2000 and 2001, was cutting back on unnecessary travel expenses. Fancy suites and first-class plane tickets are not necessities. Watch the travel budget closely!

Understanding the Team Concept

Managing a business, unless you're on your own, means developing and maintaining a team of competent employees who will work together for the good of the business. This means you need to:

- Be accessible.
- Foster team spirit.
- Reward good work.
- Have occasional brainstorming meetings.
- Use constructive criticism of ideas, but don't criticize people.
- Listen to suggestions.
- Mediate and resolve conflicts.
- Encourage everyone to feel involved in the company.
- Be responsible for the actions of your team, and don't blame people.

If you can maintain a team of individuals who are encouraged and excited about working for your company, you'll have a winning team and a far better opportunity to run a successful business.

Scheduling Flexibly

Managing a business also means maintaining a schedule that's flexible yet includes all key tasks. If you can delegate a task or a project to someone you can trust, then do so. If it's something you must be involved in or you want to handle yourself, make sure you schedule the proper amount of time and allow for preparation. Manage your own schedule to allow yourself as much time as possible to manage the goings-on within the business. Maximizing your time also means including the little details. Sometimes being there for a birthday party for a long-time staff member is just as important as any meeting you'll have in the course of the day.

 **SSENTIALS**

> A good manager has a firm grasp of the needs of the customers, the employees, the vendors, and everyone else involved in the business. As a manager, you need to be sure to juggle successfully and not shortchange any one side.

A good business manager manages his own time well and prioritizes based on all areas of the business, including customer and employee needs. Conversely, a bad manager puts sales above the staff and above customer relations and looks only at the immediate profit regardless of the long-term ramifications. If you work to make a sale at the cost of a really satisfied customer or at the expense of a staff member, you may very likely lose out in the end. Likewise, if you don't take time to establish relationships with vendors or wholesalers, you may lose them and your competition will benefit. Your schedule needs to be flexible so that you can make adjustments. Business continues to grow and change, and so must you.

Combining Forces

If you're selling hair products and you're doing a good, but not fabulous, business, and if the store across the street sells makeup and cosmetics and is doing a good, but not fabulous business, did you ever think of teaming up? While you may not be looking to merge, the bottom line is that your two stores may compliment one another and your products could sell very nicely in a package deal. Similar products or services and corresponding products provide businesses with excellent opportunities to join forces.

Cooperative advertising can stretch your marketing dollar farther and reach more people. In addition, the steady clientele of the other business can also become your steady clientele and visa versa.

Managing a business doesn't mean you're an island unto yourself, unless of course your business is to literally run an island unto itself (and even then you'll need to cooperate with the nearby boating service). Keeping yourself abreast of businesses with which you might team up is an excellent way to grow your customer base.

If you do team up with other businesses in any manner, get everything you agree upon in writing. Make sure you establish a good working relationships before putting pen to paper. Although working together can be beneficial, it can also be a nightmare if you and your partner don't see eye to eye.

Growing and Expanding

Expansion can be a great thing. However, it also means more space, more bills to pay, more employees to hire, and numerous other expenditures. For this reason, expansion takes careful planning. It requires that you balance the equation every step of the way. For every dollar of projected income, you'll have some amount of forthcoming expenditures and you'll need to be confident that the scale tips in your favor. Therefore, you need to start slowly. Before adding a new sales team, add a sales person or two. Before launching your second Web site, add inventory to your first site. It's important not to commit great amounts of money and resources to expansion until you've tested the waters. Survey new territories and explore potential new markets. The bottom line is that you want to be able to manage and control your expansion. Many businesses have tried to expand too fast only to take a successful small business and grow it into an unsuccessful large-scale business.

Planning your company's growth or expansion means utilizing new ideas, and such ideas won't just come out of thin air. You need to make a list of ideas from the start of your business—ideas that may require more resources, manpower, or customers than you currently have to execute. Furthermore, you need to collect and consider the suggestions of employees and customers. From these ideas and your initial business plan, you can build an expansion plan.

FACTS

To maintain a successful business, or to expand, you will need to reinvent yourself periodically. This means pulling back, making changes, and starting out fresh. New marketing campaigns, new products, and a new image have reinvigorated companies that had been resting on their laurels.

Not unlike starting a business, you'll need financing to expand your business. However, if you're in a position to expand, it's likely that you're successful. If you've proven your worth, you should have established a solid line of credit, making loans easier to get. Your financial plan should be attractive to potential investors. Even if your business isn't landing you write-ups in *Entrepreneur* magazine, you can show that you're maintaining a positive cash flow, have a strong customer base, and have a solid marketing campaign in place.

CHAPTER 20

Words of Wisdom from Those Who've Done It

I n this chapter, we look at the stories of entrepreneurs. These are people just like you who started their own businesses. The types of businesses vary, as do the background and skills of the entrepreneurs who started them, but the one thing they have in common is the desire to succeed.

Trudi Bresner

Trudi Bresner started her own one-person business back in 1979 from her home in Westchester, New York. She took the skills she had honed working at the advertising giant Young & Rubicom in the training and consulting area and moved to a smaller company before deciding it was time to go off on her own. "I wanted the freedom and independence" says Trudi, now CEO and President of the Manhattan-based T. Bresner Associates. "At that time I was raising my four children and wanted to be able to develop a business on my own. I made an office at home and managed to find a balance between my family and my business."

Through a marketing campaign that consisted of only networking and word of mouth advertising, Trudi was fortunate to hook up with some major clients during her first year, including NBC and American Express. "I asked people to tell their friends who were CEOs or sat on the boards of major companies about the business," adds Trudi. For the next ten years, she focused on teaching people media skills, presentation skills, and leadership skills. Over the following ten years, the business would expand to include areas such as branding strategies, messaging work, and developing corporate identities. Trudi did nearly all the work herself, with some help from her husband in the training areas. She also outsourced the graphic work.

Having a master's degree in counseling, Trudi used her people skills to build relationships. "The skills that I learned are critical to why we are where we are now," she notes. "Business is very relationship driven, especially a service business."

Her relationship skills helped Trudi to maintain open lines of communication with her clients. It was those clients that wanted Trudi to expand and hire her own graphic designers for print and electronic media. "They felt I wasn't involved enough in those aspects of the business. I, too, wanted greater control by having my own people on staff rather than outsourcing work. So, after twenty years of being predominantly a one-person show, Trudi bit the bullet and invested $400,000 of her savings into building the business. Less than two years later, she has an office in a high-rise on Broadway, a staff of twelve highly skilled individuals on board, and an attractive Web site.

T. Bresner Associates became a full-fledged company, focusing on integrated marketing communications. Today the company does Web site design; develops CD-ROMs, sales kits, brochures, logos, and interactive presentations; develops branding strategies; and trains people to be first-rate speakers and presenters.

For Trudi, the biggest change was becoming responsible for the twelve other people on board. "I'm growing as manager of a company. I make mistakes and I learn from them," says Trudi. "I'm growing personally as well, which is why I think I wanted to expand and run an organization. I did all of this at the age of fifty-eight, which is late in life to grow a business. I began the business early on, but it's very different running a one-person shop from a twelve-person shop and I'm experiencing those growth pains and learning my own strengths and weaknesses as we go."

Among her philosophies, Trudi believes it's important not to try to be everything for everyone. After a brief foray into public relations, she decided that it would not be in the best interest of the company, since it was not an area in which they had the expertise. "Stick with what you do well," says Trudi. She also believes in calling in people to handle areas you're not as comfortable handling, such as bookkeeping, billing of clients, and making billing follow-up calls. Having not had a business plan in the past, she is working on one now, as well as a three-year plan for the company. She's looking to see which avenues have the strongest potential streams of revenue. "I also believe in starting small and growing," she adds, although noting with a smile that you may decide to grow sooner than twenty years.

T. Bresner Associates, 1776 Broadway, Suite 1206, New York, NY 10019; phone: 212-974-7400; Web site: *www.tbresner.com*

Karen Anderson

For more than thirty years, Karen Anderson taught grade one and grade two students in Ontario, Canada. Always a writer at heart, Karen had written romance novels but had never been published. Instead, she decided to write books to use as a guide for her own classes, utilizing her educational skills and knowledge of the Canadian school curriculum.

Upon retiring from teaching, Karen continued to develop her lessons and computerized a beginning reading program. She admits to making the mistake that many businesses make when starting out. "I went too big too fast," she says, referring to her initial printing of 1,000 copies of her first book. "I spent a lot of money too quickly and needed to begin making some back." That was how her business began, in part out of necessity.

Karen turned the upstairs of her large Victorian home into a business office. She wrote three more books and hooked up with a former student who helped her design a Web site where she could promote her books and add new titles as she completed them. Her former student acted as an unofficial business manager and recommended that she start a direct mailing campaign to the schools. Her teaching background and understanding of the workings of the Ontario school system also helped her to target her mailing accordingly. She then set up a database. "My strategy was to market my book directly to the schools, to grade one teachers. I knew if I just sent a letter to schools it would get thrown out . . . so I addressed it to the teachers."

For Karen Anderson, quality was very important, and she didn't want to compromise that quality to mass-produce books. For this reason, she did her own printing to maintain greater control over the final product. She progressed through stages in conjunction with the growth of the business, moving from a laser printer to more advanced printing technology. Over time, the technological needs of the business had grown to where she could now print in greater volume and more quickly without sacrificing the quality of the work.

Likewise, the mailings increased as the business grew. "I started mailing 300 fliers per month, then went to 500, and then to 1,000. I used to get one order per 100; now I get four or five, and the average book order is $200 to $300." From taking in just $500 her first year, Karen is now looking at $50,000 worth of business and has moved into the black in the three years since publishing her first book.

Her books now cover a complete curriculum for grades one and two and are used in 20 percent of the Ontario school system. She is looking to expand that to 50 percent. She has also been approached by companies in Florida and Canada about marketing her phonics book in a similar manner to the popular Hooked on Phonics. She's reluctant at present, not wanting to grow too quickly and also because the books (a full set is eleven titles) intermingle with one another and she doesn't want to become reliant on just one product for the bulk of her business.

Karen sees herself writing and publishing another four or five books in the next few years. She recommends that entrepreneurs remain in control as much as possible. She is also a believer in keeping a close eye on cash. "I buy everything with cash, no credit," she explains, "and I watch the cash flow very carefully."

KA Enterprises is growing steadily as Karen Anderson builds the business based on writing, publishing, and marketing top-quality (reproducible) books for teachers. She writes them in the manner in which children learn and includes worksheets within the books. Her marketing strategy now includes a customer database, which she uses to send out notices of new products, along with the databank of schools in the province, where she sends new mailings four times a year. She has hired one associate thus far and might need to add more if the business continues to grow at the rate it has over just three years.

KA Enterprises, P.O. Box 2216, Sturgeon Falls, Ontario, Canada POH 2GO; phone: 705-753-0227; Web site: *www.primary-ed.com*

Michael Russello

For Michael Russello, the founder and owner of Scottsdale Pension Systems, starting and building a business was a matter of meeting a need in a growing market. "Many small to mid-size companies now offer 401(k) plans to their employees. Many of these companies, however do not have available personnel to take the time to handle such plans.

Therefore, we provide third-party administration for 401(k) plans for smaller companies."

The market was perfect for such a business. "Phoenix doubled in size since we've been there and many small business of less than 100 employees opened up. We were fortunate, there was a growing market right here," he adds.

But before embarking on the business endeavor, he worked long and hard on a business plan. "It's very important to have a plan when you start out," notes Michael. "You need to refer to it as you go." He has since looked back at the business to find that the company has stuck very closely to the initial blueprint.

Within three to four years, the company had 700 clients and eleven employees. Referrals were coming from accountants, brokers, and financial advisors. Maintaining steady clients, however, was achieved through strong customer service. "People don't get customer service very often anymore," notes Michael. "It's important to treat your customers well and return their phone calls promptly."

Michael also points out the importance of being able to say no in business. "You don't want to say no, but if you say yes all the time, you end up doing things you weren't looking to do. Then you find yourself branching off and moving too far away from your original plan. You can't be everything to everyone. It's important to know what you're good at and stick to it. You should read your business plan after about six months. If it was a good idea then, it should still be a good idea now. Don't lose your focus."

Scottsdale Pension Systems, Inc., 7500 East Butherus Drive, Suite D, Scottsdale, AZ 85260; phone: 480-922-0363

Bob Stone

After graduating from Queens College in 1976, with a degree in science, Bob Stone decided to seek a more defined career and attended optician school at New York Tech College in Brooklyn.

Bob began working at Raymond Leahy Opticians in the late 1970s and by the mid-eighties had learned the business thoroughly and was ready to embark as an entrepreneur. Rather than starting from scratch and trying to establish his own clientele, Stone learned about an optician who was retiring and decided to buy the business. "I borrowed money from my uncle, and Mr. Danesi, the owner at that time, held a note for a portion of the business. This way I didn't need to borrow from the bank," explains Stone, who stepped into a business that had referrals from local ophthalmologists and a steady clientele.

"It wasn't hard to adjust to running the business," explains Stone, who had gained a lot of practical experience and had a great deal of responsibility working at the Raymond Leahy store. "Other than signing the checks and paying the bills, most of the job was not very different. The transition into owning my own business went pretty smoothly." In fact, Bob even decided to keep the store name of the previous owner to maintain the regular flow of steady customers. "Maintaining the name was a key decision," explains Bob. "The store had been established for some time and I wanted to take advantage of the name recognition and goodwill in the neighborhood that Mr. Danesi had established."

The late 1980s into the mid-nineties saw the business grow steadily. However, since 1995, business began to slow down. "The last several years have seen more people covered by insurance plans that drive them to using specific locations. In addition, there has been less support from ophthalmologists, some of whom have opened their own shops," adds Bob. To keep pace, Stone looked into joining several of the insurance plans and was accepted into some of them. He also looked to expand.

Then, in 1997, Bob's former boss, with whom he'd remained in contact, Raymond Leahy, decided he was ready to retire. His corner shop in Southampton was a good location and Bob was familiar with the shop and the area, having worked there for several years. Meanwhile, Bob's wife Laurie, had gone to school and also became an optician. Having two opticians in the family to run both shops, Bob was able to expand to a two-store operation. Once again, the store was purchased in the same manner, using some money from an inheritance for the down payment and having a note held by the retiring owner. This time, not only did the name remain the same, but Mr. Leahy even came in to work every Tuesday. "Customers still come in specifically asking for him," adds Bob.

Today, the two businesses include five full-time employees and an expanding stock that includes contact lenses, sunglasses, magnifying glasses, swim goggles, and even artificial eyes. Marketing is simple, with local advertising, word of mouth, referrals, and Yellow Page ads drawing customers. The summer season is particularly busy for the Southampton store, as crowds flock to the area beaches. Stone prepares by ordering sunglasses in the spring and kicks off the season with a sale.

As for that competitive edge? Bob has just patented his own invention called nitebrite *(www.nitebrite.com)*, which are clip on glasses that will help people see better at night. The new invention will be found exclusively at Danesi Optical and Raymond D. Leahy Opticians, owned by Bob Stone.

> Danesi Optical, 2350 Middle Country Road, Centereach, NY 11720; phone: 631-585-9634. Raymond D. Leahy Opticians, 145 Main Street, Southampton, NY 11968; phone: 631-283-4244

Fran and Larry Heit

The two stores owned by Fran and Larry Heit are popular locations in St. Helena, California, for casual and fashionable clothing. The successful venues, however, are the result of years of learning the retail business.

It was back in the seventies when Fran and Larry rented their first store. "Larry was a clerk in a store, and I was working for about $2 an hour when we found out about a 400-square-foot store that was for rent. It was going to be a stretch to afford the rent—we didn't even have a telephone—but we borrowed some money from a relative and rented the space," explains Fran. "We sold sun baskets, plants, gift items, and stuff like that. We also watched every penny carefully and Larry worked nights as a waiter to help keep us going."

From those humble beginnings, the small store, called Pentacle, in Mendocino, California, grew and gained a local following. By the eighties,

Fran and Larry were in a position to rent a second location. This time they started a home accessories store selling glassware, mugs, silk flowers, plastics, and other popular trendy items of the time.

Meanwhile, the first store was beginning to stock some clothing items such as scarves and flannel shirts. Customers responded favorably to the clothing and wanted more. "We fell into clothing," says Fran, who stresses that keeping abreast of what the customers want is crucial to business. "We always listen to our customers," she explains. "We also stay on top of the trends. Your inventory is your lifeline, so you need to have what your customers want in a retail business."

The trials and eventual success of the early stores taught Fran and Larry valuable lessons in all aspects of retail. They also learned the clothing business as they carried more items and lines such as Crazy Horse. Soon, they found themselves in a position to open two clothing stores in nearby St. Helena, California. "Location, location, location," says Fran. "We learned that, too. We rented stores on the main, heavily traveled highway." The high visibility of the two stores allowed business to grow without much need for marketing and advertising. Word of mouth and walk-in business led to a steady clientele.

But why two clothing stores? Fran points out the difference: One store features more sophisticated styles and the other has a more casual bent. Both, however, fit nicely in the area. "When we started in St. Helena, we saw that we needed to carry different lines of clothing than we had carried at our other locations. The customer base was different and so was the money base." Their inventory needed to reflect that customer base and they carefully determined the styles and fashions that would sell in those two locations. In fact, Fran and Larry for a short time expanded to three locations, but they realized that the third store was simply too much for them to handle.

While Fran and Larry never had a "formal" business plan, nor are they steeped in computer technology or responsible to outside investors, they have no need to be. Their stores run smoothly based on their depth of knowledge and understanding of their inventory and their customers. They rent the locations and have taken an occasional loan when necessary to do remodeling or add air-conditioning. Today, Fran talks about styles, fabrics, colors, hemlines, and price points, and is keeping in step with exactly what is going on in the ever-changing world of fashion. Together Fran and Larry travel to trade shows looking to maintain an inventory that meets the needs of their customers.

Reeds, 1302 Main Street, St. Helena, CA 94574; phone: 707-963-0500. Cricket, 1226 Main Street, St. Helena, CA 94574; phone: 707-963-8400

Tony Maniscalco

You see them all throughout the country, the small mom-and-pop eateries that are part of the American landscape in cities and small towns. For Tony Maniscalco, opening up a pizza restaurant was more than just a business venture, it was a chance to work together with family.

Tony had owned an Italian deli in New York City in the 1970s. He and his family, however, decided to leave the big city and join other family members in Hanover, Pennsylvania, a growing community of nearly 40,000 people. Borrowing some money from relatives, Tony purchased a small pizza shop in 1986. "We changed the name, made some menu changes, added different types of pizzas, brought in video games for the kids, and created a family-friendly atmosphere," adds Tony, who familiarized himself with the local food suppliers and the history of the previous business. "I knew what the business was doing when we bought it and, being in a residential neighborhood, there was a steady customer base, so I made changes slowly, adding a few new items to the menu." In fifteen years Tony estimates that he's taken seven items off the menu and added about fifteen. "We play it by ear," says Tony, "It's a little hit or miss when trying to determine what foods people will want to try."

Tony also stresses the need for maintaining quality. "If a ballplayer is hitting .500 using one stance, and he changes his stance and his average goes down, then he should have kept the old stance. The same is true with business, you find something that has quality and works and you stay with it, making some changes from there. You never want to just make changes that will sacrifice the quality of what you offer."

As Hanover grows, more competition has popped up, with various restaurants opening up nearby. Tony continues to do local advertising, along with Yellow Pages advertising and being included in the coupon books distributed by a local radio station.

He has tried to keep prices down but notes that the rising cost of cheese has forced him to raise his prices slightly. "We're still not too expensive," adds Tony, "but as expenses go up we need to cover them." Tony prefers to raise prices and not sacrifice the quality or quantity of the food offered.

The business has been run almost exclusively by family. Tony and his wife each put in some seventy hours a week. "It takes a lot of time and work to keep this kind of business going. Both husband and wife have to be very strong-willed, able to handle the pitfalls, and be supportive to maintain a business together. You won't become millionaires doing this, but you can make a living as long as you work hard." Despite the long hours, after fifteen years, Tony still finds it rewarding, especially when people come back asking for a specific dish that they've had at Rose's before.

Rose's Pizza and Restaurant, Route 116, Hanover, PA; phone: 717-632-2466

What This Means to You

Whether it's the Manhattan-based service business of T. Bresner Associates or the mom-and-pop small community pizzeria/restaurant, Rose's, entrepreneurs work hard to build their businesses. Quality, customer service, a need to know your customer base and your product and/or inventory, as well as knowing what you can't do (or when to say no) are all common elements of business. Location, name recognition, expansion (when possible), and experience in the field are all part and parcel to these businesses as well, whether it's Karen Anderson's knowledge of the Ontario school curriculum or Fran Heit's knack for knowing the fashion trends of the upcoming season.

ESSENTIALS

In the end, all six of these examples illustrate two truths. Anyone can open and run a successful business if they work hard at it. And it takes time, patience, an awareness of the market, and a competitive edge to succeed in your own business.

It's also worth noting that some of these businesses ran well without the formal business plans that are usually suggested, while it was a blueprint for success for Scottsdale Pension Systems. Others, such as Fran and Larry's stores worked from abbreviated plans. The key is that you're comfortable knowing your goals and the direction in which you want to take your business. Technology also varies with several of the above examples, such as Bob Stone's two optical stores, or Tony Maniscalsco having little need for advanced computer programs while Mike Russello, Trudi Bresner, and Karen Anderson depend heavily on them.

APPENDIX A

Sample Business Plan

I n this appendix, you'll find the elements of an abbreviated sample business plan designed to provide a general idea of each of the key elements necessary. Business plans differ considerably in tone and titles. However, they all include the same primary elements. (The plan in this appendix is merely a sample based on a fictitious company, and any likeness to a company by the same name is coincidental.)

Play-Break:
"A Place to Play While the Grown-Ups Shop"

Business Plan

A division of Athletics, Inc.
Denver, Colorado
E-Mail: Play-Break@ibc.com
Phone: 714-555-1212

Table of Contents

Executive Summary

Play-Break is designed to be a place where children can take a break from a day of shopping at the mall to play fun, athletic, supervised activities in a warm, friendly, and safe environment.

Many youngsters accompany their parents through busy shopping days at the local mall, only to get fidgety or bored. Parents often find themselves unable to select the products and merchandise they have come to buy, because they are paying attention to children who are touching items in the store or simply becoming cranky. Parents often find themselves at a toy store or buying food to simply appease a disgruntled youngster. In some malls, video arcades exist where children can spend money playing often-violent onscreen games that provide little actual activity. Parents are obligated to watch their young children in these environments, which are open to the public and frequented by teenagers.

Play-Break will offer a solution to this problem by providing fully staffed, on-premises child activity centers at shopping malls. The activities will be run by a highly trained staff of counselors who will lead youngsters in games such as volleyball, basketball, and Simon Says. Activities such as jump rope and arts and crafts will also be provided along with beverages and a relaxation room where young children can nap or listen to a story read by a Play-Break counselor. The non-technological environment will encourage children to run and play while emphasizing good sportsmanship.

Children at Play-Break will be divided into supervised age groups of 3–4, 5–6, 7–8, and 9–10 years of age. Parents will be able to sign their children up for a maximum of three hours on a first-come, first-served basis. The cost will be $9 per hour per child, which will include a beverage. Parents or guardians will be given beepers to be notified in case they need to be reached.

The unique aspect of Play-Break is that it offers children a fun, day-camp style activity center while parents are afforded the time they need to shop.

Play-Break can enhance the day at the mall or shopping center for both children and parents. In addition, Play-Break will provide jobs to teenagers fifteen and up, who will be trained to work as counselors.

The key to the success of Play-Break will be the ability to provide safe, child-friendly activities and a very well trained, knowledgeable staff to run such activities in a fun manner.

The necessary startup costs will be designed to open up two locations at the Pittsfield Mall and the Mile High Mall, both in the Denver area. Funding will be used primarily for interior design, athletic equipment, insurance, rent, beverages, and hiring a staff of managers and counselors. The projected revenue at a conservative estimated average of twenty children per seven hours of daily operation, six days a week, would total revenues of $32,500 per month or $390,000 for the year from one Play-Break location, or a net profit after expenses of $80,000 after the first year.

Industry Analysis

From 1995 through 2000, the number of shoppers at malls in the United States increased by 27 percent, while the number of children ages 3 through 10 increased by 23 percent in the overall population according to XYZ Source. This indicates that there is an increase of parents shopping with young children.

Several play facilities in major cities have shown to be very popular, as have daytime activity programs and athletics sponsored by schools and local associations. The childcare and play facility has emerged as a multi-million dollar industry in 2000, with projections of increasing in 2001. In addition, the number of children attending summer camp programs has increased by 42 percent in the past five years, indicating that despite video and computer games, children still respond well to physical activities with their peers.

While children would clearly prefer to play rather than shop, there are few, if any in-mall locations that offer supervised activities for youngsters. Play-Break will fill a void and become the first child activity center of its kind in Denver. The variety of activities will appeal to the various interests of children while freeing up the parents or guardians to shop.

Business Overview

Play-Break plans to open two locations in the Denver area. Within three years, the goal is to open fifteen locations at malls throughout the Northern and Midwestern United States. In five years, the goal is to become nationally recognized and open additional locations nationwide. The company will be structured as a corporation, but it will not become a public company for at least three years. The newly formed Athletics Incorporated will own and run the first fifteen locations, after which additional locations will be franchised. The corporation will set up specific guidelines for franchisees and assist in seeking funding and financing.

Each location will be designed in a similar manner, featuring the same interior design and activities. The space will be uncluttered, with activities set up in specific sections for each age group to participate without infringing on each other. Counselors will encourage each child to participate at his or her own level and to emphasize sportsmanship and fun over competition and winning. Counselors will also be trained in basic conflict-resolution skills to handle and prevent arguments between children. The upbeat and colorful atmosphere of Play-Break will encourage children and parents to stop in for a visit.

Startup expenses for each location will include interior design, rental or ownership of the storefront, equipment, insurance, training of staff members, and beverages. The overhead for maintaining a Play-Break location will be relatively low, as there will be no products or inventory other than beverages and an ongoing need to update equipment and items for arts and crafts and play activities.

There will be a minimum of six staff members on hand at all times, including a manager to oversee all activities and operations, a safety/security coordinator to assist the manager and to oversee that the environment is safe for children and belongings are watched closely, and four counselors, one for each of the four age groups. There will be a limit of ten children in any one group at any time. If additional counselors are needed and the size of the space allows for it, there will be additional groups added for any overflow in a particular age group. The business will run seven hours daily in conjunction with the operating hours of the mall or shopping center.

The need for activities for children who are not interested in shopping will spell success for Play-Break locations.

Products and Services

Play-Break will provide children ages 3–10 with various activities. A large gym area will include three half-court basketball courts with baskets at different height levels, with an additional fourth space for volleyball or other activities such as jump rope or other games. A separate room will be colorfully designed and include arts-and-crafts activities including drawing, cutting and pasting, clay, and similar activities. Sinks and towels will be set up for washing up afterwards. In addition, two smaller spaces will be set up, one with mats for napping or story-telling (from several children's books on hand) and one area with orange or apple juice, which will be distributed by the counselors. A front entrance area will provide limited access into and out of the actual play areas so that children cannot leave the premises unescorted. Parents will drop off and pick up children in the front area. They will be notified when their one, two, or three hours is up by being beeped on a portable beeper distributed by Play-Break. Handouts will be provided for parents to read all about policies and rules regarding Play-Break, and they will be required to sign that they have read all materials. Children will only be released to the person with whom they arrived.

Along with providing activities, Play-Break will provide qualified and knowledgeable managers and counselors to make sure the needs of each child are met so that the parents can be assured their children are in a most suitable environment.

Marketing Plan

Play-Break plans to market their mall and shopping center play facilities through ads in local shopping guides, signage throughout the mall or shopping center, and other advertising space within each shopping location. In addition, Play-Break can run promotional tie-ins with various stores to encourage parents to shop at the stores. This can also include cooperative advertising with stores running local print ads. Colorful fliers and handouts will also be distributed throughout the mall or shopping center to families.

Play-Break has already negotiated with the two initial mall locations to be included in all mall advertising and literature as an additional feature to attract families to the mall rather than to local competitors that do not offer any activities for children. Special family activities might also be included for parents and children to participate in when dropping off or picking up children, such as hula-hoop contest or foul-shooting contests where teams of parents and children compete for small prizes.

The colors and open space of Play-Break will stand out to passersby in contrast to the many products lining the windows of the neighboring stores. This, coupled with word of mouth from children and their parents, will encourage more families to stop by and check out the Play-Break experience. A Play-Break Web site will post locations and operating hours for each Play-Break facility.

Each area location will be determined by the size and scope of the mall, availability of adequate space, and the number of families in the area.

NOTE: This is where you can add demographic numbers if you have them, such as 100,000 families are living in the Denver area with children between the ages of 3 and 10 years of age. Depending on what your budget allows, this is also the place to talk about any TV or radio advertising plans, billboards, or any other manner in which you anticipate spreading the word of your new business.

Competitive Analysis

The only existing play-oriented facilities in the Denver area are X, Y, and Z. They offer a variety of activities focusing primarily on video and electronic games. There is no specific activity schedule and parents are generally encouraged to remain on the premises since the staff does not include trained counselors.

Five malls in the area include video arcades and one includes several rides such as a merry-go-round. These also require that parents be on hand as they are not supervised by counselors.

Otherwise, there is no viable competition at present for Play-Break in area malls. The hope is that Play-Break can establish a solid reputation for safety and fun activities run in a structured manner and gain a foothold in the area. This will then allow for further growth in the outlying regions and expansion into other markets based on the success of the initial facilities.

NOTE: Since there is little competition for Play-Break, this is a brief section. If you are opening a restaurant and there are others nearby, this is a place where you can provide further details on how you will beat the competition. Perhaps you will provide two for one specials, offer large square shaped pizzas, add new fillings or toppings, create the first double or triple decker pizza—whatever you are doing that the competition isn't, this is the place to point it out.

Operations Plan

Play-Break will open for employees thirty minutes before opening for customers. This will allow the staff to make sure that all equipment is in the proper place, the floors are clean, and there are no safety hazards.

Once the facility is opened for business, the manager will remain at the front entranceway, which will include a counter area where money will be collected as parents sign their children up for one, two, or three hours. The manager will collect all money and provide written and verbal information on the policies and rules of Play-Break.

Once the parent or guardian has signed a child up, the child and parent will meet the counselor for that age group. Activities will begin on the hour and children will be able to join in at fifteen-minute intervals as the day goes on, allowing for continuity in games. If, for example, an activity begins at 10:00 A.M. with six children, and two more children show up at 10:05, they will wait with their parents until the 10:15 break, at which point children can be added to the group. More children will be added at 10:30 and at 10:45 until the maximum is reached in an age group. Only if additional counselors are added and space allows will there be a second group formed.

At the conclusion of the day the staff will be responsible for putting away all equipment and cleaning the facility. A brief meeting will take place to determine any problems or new ideas based on the day's activities.

In addition, the manager will review all equipment on a weekly basis to determine when new balls and art supplies will need to be ordered. He or she will be responsible for the daily delivery of beverages. The security/safety coordinator will be responsible for reviewing mats, safety features, window guards, and all other such concerns on a daily basis.

All fliers and brochures will be supplied by Athletics, Inc., the main office for the two locations, which will be staffed by the management team of Play-Break on a regular basis and located in Smithville, near Denver.

Management Team

Robert G. Folson is the founder and creator of Athletics, Inc., a sports facility company designed to bring athletic and play locations to malls and shopping centers. Play-Break is the first venture of the new company, which will also look to open sports facilities for adults in the next ten years, including indoor basketball courts and driving ranges. Mr. Folson is the former CEO of Artimus Workout Centers, a gym and fitness center with nine locations in south Florida.

NOTE: Two paragraphs on the background of each of your key players are sufficient. Also make note of positions to be added, such as a Financial Officer. Don't forget to include your financial pages at the end. Projected income statements, balance sheets, and startup costs are essential.

Conclusion

The sample in this appendix is a brief overview/guide to a simple business plan. Your business plan only needs to be as elaborate or as complex as the business you are running. IT and business-to-business (B2B) plans have more technical terminology and explain in greater detail what their businesses are designed to accomplish. The more straightforward the business, the shorter the business plan. Most investors are looking for the meat and potatoes of what your business will entail, not superlatives as to why yours is the greatest business ever—they will need to make that determination for themselves. The business plan also needs to be a clear guide for you to follow. You know it's a great idea and therefore need not keep reminding yourself throughout the plan. Keep in mind for whom you are writing the business plan; potential investors, yourself, or both.

The newer and more innovative the business, the shorter the competitive analysis. Conversely, if you're opening a familiar type of business in a crowded market, you'll need more time to define what makes your business different from those around you.

Studies show that business plans with charts and graphs are generally more highly received than those without. Therefore you should add a couple of colorful charts and graphs showing projected sales growth or your piece of the competitive pie. Don't overdo it—two or three may be quite sufficient.

APPENDIX: B

Resources

There are numerous organizations, Web sites, and associations that can help you research and gather information and locate answers to questions regarding any aspect of business. Make a list of key phone numbers and save key Web sites so you will be able to access the resources you need. Business magazines are also very valuable as well as trade publications in your industry.

Associations and Organizations

U.S. Department of Commerce
14th Street and Constitution Avenue NW
Room 5055
Washington, DC 20210
Phone: 202-482-5061
Web site: *www.mbda.gov*

U.S. Department of Labor
200 Constitution Avenue NW
Washington, DC 20210
Web site: *www.dol.gov*

Federal Trade Commission
600 Pennsylvania Avenue NW
Washington, DC 20580
General information: 202-326-2222
Anti-trust and competition issues: 202-326-3300
Web site: *www.ftc.gov*

U.S. Small Business Administration (SBA)
403 3rd Street SW
Washington, DC 20416
Phone: 202-205-7701
Web site: *www.sba.gov*

SBA Regional Offices:
- Region 1, Boston: 617-565-8415
- Region 2, New York: 212-264-1450
- Region 3, King of Prussia, PA:
  215-962-3700
- Region 4, Atlanta: 404-347-4995
- Region 5, Chicago: 310-353-5000
- Region 6, Ft. Worth, TX: 817-885-6581

- Region 7, Kansas City, MO: 816-374-6380
- Region 8, Denver: 303-844-0500
- Region 9, San Francisco: 415-744-2118
- Region 10, Seattle: 206-553-7310

Internal Revenue Service
Washington, DC 20224
Phone: 800-829-1040
Web site: *www.irs.ustres.gov*
The IRS has an expansive Web site where you can find a great deal of tax help and a state-by-state guide for locating state tax information. There are also numerous tax publications (all numbered) including:

- Tax Guide for Small Business, Publication #334
- Self-Employment Tax, Publication #533
- Business Expenses, Publication #535

For tax forms go to *www.irs.ustres.gov/forms.*

International Franchise Association
1350 New York Avenue NW
Suite 900
Washington, DC 20005-4709
Phone: 202-628-8000

American Association of Franchises and Dealers
P.O. Box 81887
San Diego, CA 92138-1887
Phone: 800-733-9858
Web site: *www.aafd.org*

National Association of Women Business Owners
1411 K Street NW
Suite 1300
Washington, DC 20005
Phone: 202-347-8686
Fax: 202-347-4130
Information service line: 800-556-2926
Web site: *www.nawbo.org*

The National Association for the Self-Employed
1023 15 Street NW
Suite 1200
Washington, DC 20005-2600
Phone: 202-466-2100
Web site: *www.nase.com*
The NASE works to help the self-employed make their businesses successful and provides numerous benefits and services. It was formed over twenty years ago by small business owners.

Occupational Safety and Health Administration (OSHA)
200 Constitution Avenue NW
Washington, DC 20210
Web site: *www.osha-slc.gov*

Institute For Occupational Safety and Health
Phone: 800-35-NIOSH or 513-533-8328
Web site: *www.cdc.gov/niosh*

Dun & Bradstreet
Austin, Texas 78731
Phone: 800-234-3867
Web site: *www.dnb.com*

For over 160 years, D&B has been providing companies with information and assistance in making key business decisions.

American Entrepreneurs for Economic Growth
1655 North Fort Myer Drive
Suite 850
Arlington, VA 22209
Phone: 703-524-3743
Web site: *www.aeeg.org*

National Association of Home-Based Businesses
10451 Mill Run Circle
Suite 400
Owings Mills, MD 21117
Phone: 410-363-3698
Web site: *www.usahomebusiness.com*

U.S. Census Bureau
Washington DC 20233
Phone: 301-457-4608
Web site: *www.census.gov*

U.S. Patent and Trademark Office
General Information Services Division
Crystal Plaza 3, Room 2CO2
Washington, DC 20231
Phone: 800-786-9199 or 703-308-4357
Web site: *www.uspto.gov*

U.S. Securities & Exchange Commission
450 Fifth Street NW
Washington, DC 20549
Office of Investor Education and Assistance:
202-942-7040
Web site: *www.sec.gov*

Web Sites

www.allbusiness.com—A comprehensive site with resources for small and medium sized businesses.

www.bizweb.com—A guide to some 47,000 companies.

www.bplan.com—Numerous sample business plans for various industries.

www.bspage.com—The Business Start page includes a short course on starting a business, tips, and reviews of top business books.

www.business.gov—The U.S. Business Advisor is a one-stop shop for working with the many government agencies that impact upon business.

www.businessfinance.com—A major online source for finding potential investors.

www.businessnation.com—Business news, a library, discussions, opportunities, and resources.

www.businesstown.com—Information and articles from starting to selling your business.

www.catalogconsultancy.com—Information and guidance for catalog and direct mail businesses.

www.chamber-of-commerce.com—Links to local chamber of commerce Web sites, and e-mail addresses.

www.financenet.com—Sponsored by the U.S. Chief Financial Officers Council, FinanceNet has a wealth of information and resources available specializing in public financial management.

www.globalbizdirectory.com—Massive directory of retail, agricultural, mining, and numerous other business-related organizations and associations. Includes a state-by-state and international listing database.

www.gomez.com—Gomez offers business news and detailed report cards and consumer responses on e-commerce Web sites in various sectors.

www.homebusiness.com—Detailed information and business solutions for the home based business.

www.hoovers.com—Provides detailed business and company information, industry reports, links, professional help, business news, and more.

www.ideacafe.com—A good place for news, tips, expert advice, ideas, and schmoozing with other small business owners.

www.inc.com—A wealth of articles and advice about starting and growing your business from the folks at *Inc. Magazine*.

www.marketingsource.com/associations—Find any association in any industry at this valuable resource site.

www.morebusiness.com—Articles, tips, sample business and marketing plans, legal forms, contracts, a newsletter, and more offered for entrepreneurs.

www.nasbic.org—The National Association of Small Business Investment Companies promotes growth in the business sector through numerous programs.

www.pueblo.gsa.gov—The Federal
Communications Information Center has a
small business information section with
facts about getting started and more.

www.thecapitalnetwork.com—An online network
linking entrepreneurs and investors.

www.thomaspublishing.com—Publishers of
numerous industry trade directories, which
include listings of manufacturers and
distributors.

Magazines

*Entrepreneur Magazine, Business Start-Ups
Magazine,* and *Entrepreneur's Home Office*
Entrepreneur Media, Inc.
2392 Morse Avenue
Irvine, CA 92614
Phone: 714-261-2325
Web site: *www.entrepreneurmag.com*

Forbes
60 Fifth Avenue
New York, NY 10011
Phone: 212-620-2200
Web site: *www.forbes.com*

Inc. Magazine
38 Commercial Wharf
Boston, MA 02110
Phone: 617-248-8000 or 800-234-0999
Web site: *www.inc.com*

My Business Magazine
Hammock Publishing, Inc.
3322 West End Avenue
Suite 700
Nashville, TN 37203
Phone: 615-385-9745

Consumer Goods Manufacturer
Edgell Communications
10 West Hanover Avenue
Suite 107
Randolph, NJ 07869

Minority Business Entrepreneur
3528 Torrance Boulevard
Suite 101
Torrance, CA 90503
Phone: 310-540-9398
Web site: *www.mbemag.com*

Workforce
ACC Communications
245 Fischer Avenue
Suite B-2
Costa Mesa, CA 92626
Phone: 714-751-4106
Web site: *www.workforceonline.com*

Index

We Have EVERYTHING!

Everything® **After College Book**
$12.95, 1-55850-847-3

Everything® **American History Book**
$12.95, 1-58062-531-2

Everything® **Angels Book**
$12.95, 1-58062-398-0

Everything® **Anti-Aging Book**
$12.95, 1-58062-565-7

Everything® **Astrology Book**
$12.95, 1-58062-062-0

Everything® **Baby Names Book**
$12.95, 1-55850-655-1

Everything® **Baby Shower Book**
$12.95, 1-58062-305-0

Everything® **Baby's First Food Book**
$12.95, 1-58062-512-6

Everything® **Baby's First Year Book**
$12.95, 1-58062-581-9

Everything® **Barbeque Cookbook**
$12.95, 1-58062-316-6

Everything® **Bartender's Book**
$9.95, 1-55850-536-9

Everything® **Bedtime Story Book**
$12.95, 1-58062-147-3

Everything® **Bicycle Book**
$12.00, 1-55850-706-X

Everything® **Breastfeeding Book**
$12.95, 1-58062-582-7

Everything® **Build Your Own Home Page**
$12.95, 1-58062-339-5

Everything® **Business Planning Book**
$12.95, 1-58062-491-X

Everything® **Candlemaking Book**
$12.95, 1-58062-623-8

Everything® **Casino Gambling Book**
$12.95, 1-55850-762-0

Everything® **Cat Book**
$12.95, 1-55850-710-8

Everything® **Chocolate Cookbook**
$12.95, 1-58062-405-7

Everything® **Christmas Book**
$15.00, 1-55850-697-7

Everything® **Civil War Book**
$12.95, 1-58062-366-2

Everything® **Classical Mythology Book**
$12.95, 1-58062-653-X

Everything® **Collectibles Book**
$12.95, 1-58062-645-9

Everything® **College Survival Book**
$12.95, 1-55850-720-5

Everything® **Computer Book**
$12.95, 1-58062-401-4

Everything® **Cookbook**
$14.95, 1-58062-400-6

Everything® **Cover Letter Book**
$12.95, 1-58062-312-3

Everything® **Creative Writing Book**
$12.95, 1-58062-647-5

Everything® **Crossword and Puzzle Book**
$12.95, 1-55850-764-7

Everything® **Dating Book**
$12.95, 1-58062-185-6

Everything® **Dessert Book**
$12.95, 1-55850-717-5

Everything® **Digital Photography Book**
$12.95, 1-58062-574-6

Everything® **Dog Book**
$12.95, 1-58062-144-9

Everything® **Dreams Book**
$12.95, 1-55850-806-6

Everything® **Etiquette Book**
$12.95, 1-55850-807-4

Everything® **Fairy Tales Book**
$12.95, 1-58062-546-0

Everything® **Family Tree Book**
$12.95, 1-55850-763-9

Everything® **Feng Shui Book**
$12.95, 1-58062-587-8

Everything® **Fly-Fishing Book**
$12.95, 1-58062-148-1

Everything® **Games Book**
$12.95, 1-55850-643-8

Everything® **Get-A-Job Book**
$12.95, 1-58062-223-2

Everything® **Get Out of Debt Book**
$12.95, 1-58062-588-6

Everything® **Get Published Book**
$12.95, 1-58062-315-8

Everything® **Get Ready for Baby Book**
$12.95, 1-55850-844-9

Everything® **Get Rich Book**
$12.95, 1-58062-670-X

Everything® **Ghost Book**
$12.95, 1-58062-533-9

Everything® **Golf Book**
$12.95, 1-55850-814-7

Everything® **Grammar and Style Book**
$12.95, 1-58062-573-8

Everything® **Guide to Las Vegas**
$12.95, 1-58062-438-3

Everything® **Guide to New England**
$12.95, 1-58062-589-4

Everything® **Guide to New York City**
$12.95, 1-58062-314-X

Everything® **Guide to Walt Disney World®, Universal Studios®, and Greater Orlando, 2nd Edition**
$12.95, 1-58062-404-9

Everything® **Guide to Washington D.C.**
$12.95, 1-58062-313-1

Everything® **Guitar Book**
$12.95, 1-58062-555-X

Everything® **Herbal Remedies Book**
$12.95, 1-58062-331-X

Everything® **Home-Based Business Book**
$12.95, 1-58062-364-6

Everything® **Homebuying Book**
$12.95, 1-58062-074-4

Everything® **Homeselling Book**
$12.95, 1-58062-304-2

Everything® **Horse Book**
$12.95, 1-58062-564-9

Everything® **Hot Careers Book**
$12.95, 1-58062-486-3

Everything® **Internet Book**
$12.95, 1-58062-073-6

Everything® **Investing Book**
$12.95, 1-58062-149-X

Everything® **Jewish Wedding Book**
$12.95, 1-55850-801-5

Everything® **Job Interview Book**
$12.95, 1-58062-493-6

Everything® **Lawn Care Book**
$12.95, 1-58062-487-1

Everything® **Leadership Book**
$12.95, 1-58062-513-4

Everything® **Learning French Book**
$12.95, 1-58062-649-1

Everything® **Learning Spanish Book**
$12.95, 1-58062-575-4

Everything® **Low-Fat High-Flavor Cookbook**
$12.95, 1-55850-802-3

Everything® **Magic Book**
$12.95, 1-58062-418-9

Everything® **Managing People Book**
$12.95, 1-58062-577-0

Everything® **Microsoft® Word 2000 Book**
$12.95, 1-58062-306-9

Everything® **Money Book**
$12.95, 1-58062-145-7

Everything® **Mother Goose Book**
$12.95, 1-58062-490-1

Everything® **Motorcycle Book**
$12.95, 1-58062-554-1

Everything® **Mutual Funds Book**
$12.95, 1-58062-419-7

Everything® **One-Pot Cookbook**
$12.95, 1-58062-186-4

Everything® **Online Business Book**
$12.95, 1-58062-320-4

Everything® **Online Genealogy Book**
$12.95, 1-58062-402-2

Everything® **Online Investing Book**
$12.95, 1-58062-338-7

Everything® **Online Job Search Book**
$12.95, 1-58062-365-4

Everything® **Organize Your Home Book**
$12.95, 1-58062-617-3

Everything® **Pasta Book**
$12.95, 1-55850-719-1

Everything® **Philosophy Book**
$12.95, 1-58062-644-0

Everything® **Playing Piano and Keyboards Book**
$12.95, 1-58062-651-3

Everything® **Pregnancy Book**
$12.95, 1-58062-146-5

Everything® **Pregnancy Organizer**
$15.00, 1-58062-336-0

Everything® **Project Management Book**
$12.95, 1-58062-583-5

Everything® **Puppy Book**
$12.95, 1-58062-576-2

Everything® **Quick Meals Cookbook**
$12.95, 1-58062-488-X

Everything® **Resume Book**
$12.95, 1-58062-311-5

Everything® **Romance Book**
$12.95, 1-58062-566-5

Everything® **Running Book**
$12.95, 1-58062-618-1

Everything® **Sailing Book, 2nd Edition**
$12.95, 1-58062-671-8

Everything® **Saints Book**
$12.95, 1-58062-534-7

Everything® **Selling Book**
$12.95, 1-58062-319-0

Everything® **Shakespeare Book**
$12.95, 1-58062-591-6

Everything® **Spells and Charms Book**
$12.95, 1-58062-532-0

Everything® **Start Your Own Business Book**
$12.95, 1-58062-650-5

Everything® **Stress Management Book**
$12.95, 1-58062-578-9

Everything® **Study Book**
$12.95, 1-55850-615-2

Everything® **Tai Chi and QiGong Book**
$12.95, 1-58062-646-7

Everything® **Tall Tales, Legends, and Outrageous Lies Book**
$12.95, 1-58062-514-2

Everything® **Tarot Book**
$12.95, 1-58062-191-0

Everything® **Time Management Book**
$12.95, 1-58062-492-8

Everything® **Toasts Book**
$12.95, 1-58062-189-9

Everything® **Toddler Book**
$12.95, 1-58062-592-4

Everything® **Total Fitness Book**
$12.95, 1-58062-318-2

Everything® **Trivia Book**
$12.95, 1-58062-143-0

Everything® **Tropical Fish Book**
$12.95, 1-58062-343-3

Everything® **Vegetarian Cookbook**
$12.95, 1-58062-640-8

Everything® **Vitamins, Minerals, and Nutritional Supplements Book**
$12.95, 1-58062-496-0

Everything® **Wedding Book, 2nd Edition**
$12.95, 1-58062-190-2

Everything® **Wedding Checklist**
$7.95, 1-58062-456-1

Everything® **Wedding Etiquette Book**
$7.95, 1-58062-454-5

Everything® **Wedding Organizer**
$15.00, 1-55850-828-7

Everything® **Wedding Shower Book**
$7.95, 1-58062-188-0

Everything® **Wedding Vows Book**
$7.95, 1-58062-455-3

Everything® **Weight Training Book**
$12.95, 1-58062-593-2

Everything® **Wine Book**
$12.95, 1-55850-808-2

Everything® **World War II Book**
$12.95, 1-58062-572-X

Everything® **World's Religions Book**
$12.95, 1-58062-648-3

Everything® **Yoga Book**
$12.95, 1-58062-594-0

Visit us at everything.com

Everything® is a registered trademark of Adams Media Corporation.